THOMAS CHATTERTON

THOMAS CHATTERTON

by

JOHN CRANSTOUN NEVILL

KENNIKAT PRESS
Port Washington, N. Y./London

THOMAS CHATTERTON

First published in 1948
Reissued in 1970 by Kennikat Press
Library of Congress Catalog Card No: 71-103208
SBN 8046-0845-8

Manufactured by Taylor Publishing Company   Dallas. Texas

CONTENTS

TO THE MEMORY OF
BARRETT PRESTON
killed by enemy action on the
night of 24th–25th Sept. 1940
Aged 32

THOMAS CHATTERTON

"This is the most extraordinary young man that has encountered my knowledge. It is wonderful how the whelp has written such things."

DOCTOR SAMUEL JOHNSON

" *I thought of Chatterton, the marvellous Boy.*
The sleepless Soul that perished in his pride."

WILLIAM WORDSWORTH

" *To Chatterton, the Muse's Matchless boy,*
With every grace of ancient wisdom blest,
All untaught genius breathing from his breast."

THOMAS DERMODY (1775–1802)
(Written at the age of twelve.)

"*But Chatterton, methinks I hear thy name,*
For cold my fancy grows, and dead each Hope of Fame."

SAMUEL TAYLOR COLERIDGE

"*Chatterton,*
Rose pale, his solemn agony had not
Yet faded from him."

PERCY BYSSHE SHELLEY

"*Where we may soft humanity put on,*
And sit, and rhyme, and think on Chatterton."

JOHN KEATS

" With Shakespeare's manhood at a boy's wild heart—
Through Hamlet's doubt to Shakespeare near allied,
And kin to Milton through his Satan's pride,—
At Death's sole door he stooped, and craved a dart;
And to the dear new bower of England's art,—
Even to that shrine Time else had deified,
The unuttered heart that soared against his side,—
Drove the fell point, and smote life's seals apart.

" Thy nested home-loves, noble Chatterton;
The angel-trodden stair thy soul could trace
Up Redcliffe's spire; and in the world's armed space
Thy gallant sword-play :—these to many an one
Are sweet for ever; as thy grave unknown
And love-dream of thy unrecorded face."

DANTE GABRIEL ROSSETTI

ACKNOWLEDGMENT

My grateful acknowledgments are due to
Messrs. G. Bell and Sons, Ltd., for their
kindness in allowing me to quote from
Professor Skeat's modernized version of
The Rowley Poems, and also to make use
of his explanatory notes.

J. C. N.

CHAPTER I

BIRTH, PARENTAGE, AND EARLY YEARS

(1752–1760)

WHEN darkness fell on the night of 20th November 1752, strange things were happening in the heavens. Indeed, if any measure of reliance may be placed on the findings of Ebenezer Sibly, a contemporary astrologer, and the author of a work entitled *A New and Complete Illustration of the Celestial Science of Astrology*, seldom can there have been a more adverse configuration of the planets.

"Upon the ascendant," writes Mr. Sibly, "we find the sign Gemini, and Mercury lord thereof, which lays the foundation of a sharp wit and an acute understanding. But then Mercury, his principal significator, is posited in the sixth house, in his detriment, and in combustion of the Sun; an infallible argument of a wretched life and a fatal end."

Nor did this complete the tale of prospective disasters. Other complications abounded. The Moon was posited in the twelfth house—the house of imprisonment and affliction—receding from a sextile with Jupiter, and forming an opposition with the Sun; that is, departing from the early good and prolific temperature, to increase the virulence of the other malific rays. Moreover, Saturn was posited in a sign out of all his dignities, in the most noxious that could have happened, and where he usually prenotes the fatal commission of suicide, without so much as one friendly ray to oppose his influence, or to render the shocking attempt partial, or less destructive than a cause that will certainly touch life.

Altogether, even taking into consideration that Mr. Sibly, since his book on the Celestial Science was not published until the year 1787, was quite conceivably being wise a long time after the event, a most inopportune moment to have chosen for making one's first appearance in the world. Yet on this date, in the city of Bristol, between six and seven o'clock of a Monday evening, Thomas Chatterton was born.

*   *   *

The wretched life ordained for him by the stars began with the first breath he drew. Poverty, and all its attendant anxieties and hardships, had been his mother's portion throughout the few short years of her married life, and latterly the difficulties of a position, which could never at any period have been an easy one, were greatly augmented by the death of her husband, during the previous August, three months before the birth of this, her latest child. Even the roof over her head in the Free School in Pile Street, where Thomas Chatterton, senior, had been schoolmaster, was hers only by the courtesy and consideration of his successor, Mr. Chard, who being unmarried and requiring the accommodation provided by the schoolhouse less than she, had consented to her remaining there undisturbed until she could make plans towards meeting a future that offered little that was stable or reassuring from whatever angle she regarded it.

Unfortunately, the obscurity which enveloped the young poet until long after his death—for his fame, like his birth, was posthumous—leaves Mrs. Chatterton a dim, rather negligible figure. One is conscious of her in the background, struggling against adverse circumstances, doing her best to provide for her family and to keep her home together, never quite sure of herself where outsiders were concerned, an easy prey to those sharp-witted gentlemen, who beguiled her into handing over all such letters and manuscripts of her son as remained in her possession after his final tragedy; still, somehow, she never entirely "comes alive."

Of her actual origin little is known, save that her maiden name was Sarah Young, that she was born at Stapleton, in the year 1731, of humble country-folk, and that she married her schoolmaster husband, when he was thirty-five and she seventeen, at Chipping Sodbury, in Gloucestershire, a few miles out of Bristol, on 25th April 1748. In one's mind's eye one pictures her as a quiet, submissive, domestically efficient young woman who, while by no means illiterate, stood considerably in awe of her erratic and far more accomplished lord and master.

His loss, at a time when she most needed his protection, could not have been other than a cruel blow, yet it may be doubted whether the marriage had ever been an unqualified success. From all accounts, Thomas Chatterton, the elder, must have been a difficult problem for so young and inexperienced a wife to handle. He was a man of exuberant personality, quick temper, gregarious habits, and widely diversified pursuits. His roughness and boisterous conviviality have probably been much exaggerated by the poet's earlier biographers, and therefore one is reluctantly obliged to discredit the assertion that his mouth was so big that he could put his clenched fist into it, or that he would return home blind drunk with his boon companions and sit up half the night roaring out the choruses of bawdy pot-house songs at the top of his voice. A zest for life and good-fellowship he certainly had, but to the easy sociability of his character was allied a keen intelligence and a cultivated mind, and everything points to the fact that his abilities were greatly in advance of the humble position he occupied in the scholastic world. He had, for example, a practical knowledge of music, and in

1746 was appointed a "sub-chaunter" in the choir of the Cathedral. Furthermore, he composed a *Catch for Three Voices*, apostrophising the joys of a local tavern called the "Pine Apple." For this composition he provided both words and music, its one verse running as follows:

Since we are met, and resolved to be jolly,
And drink our good Liquor to drown Melancholy,
Then pass it about, my brave Boys, never fear ;
There's Meat, Drink, and Clothes, in Good Ale and strong Beer.
While Zealots and Fools with their Factions do grapplè,
They taste not those joys that are at the Pine Apple.

His energies, however, were far from being wholly confined to his duties in the Cathedral and at the Free School. In his leisure he read extensively, acquired books of his own and borrowed those of other people, made an interesting and valuable collection of old Roman coins, numbering upwards of several hundreds, which he discovered in the neighbourhood of his native city, and even had leanings towards magic and the black arts, which he studied from the writings of Cornelius Agrippa, a copy of whose works was subsequently found among the belongings that his son left behind him at the office of John Lambert —an attorney to whom the boy was apprenticed—when he set out to seek his fortune in London.

Within the space of four and a half years, Sarah Chatterton had produced three children—Mary, Giles Malpas, and Thomas. Mary, the eldest, had been born in 1749, after her parents had moved into the new schoolhouse, which had recently been built for the use of the schoolmaster by a Mr. Giles Malpas, at a cost of £120. Thus, when a son was born to the Chattertons the following year, they called him, out of compliment to their patron, Giles Malpas. But little Giles Malpas was a sickly

infant and lived only for a few months, though he survived
long enough to be christened in the church of St. Mary
Redcliff, on New Year's Day, 1751. In due course, also
on New Year's Day, exactly two years later, Thomas
Chatterton was christened in the same church, the Rev.
Mr. Giles officiating, and so he formed his first association
with that magnificent Gothic building—that "Wonder of
Mansions," as he afterwards described it—which was
destined to exercise so deep and lasting an influence over
his early life and work.

*   *   *

The school-house in Pile Street was a pleasant little
eighteenth century house, with a red-tiled roof, a paved
courtyard, and a small garden. It had flat white window-
frames, set almost flush with the outer walls, a simple
plaster pediment with scrolls at either side, and a fan-light
over the front door. On the ground floor were two rooms,
one a kitchen, the other a living-room, and two bedrooms
on the storey above. It was light, airy, and compact, and,
despite the desperate shifts she must often have been put to
in her husband's lifetime—for it is safe to surmise that
most of the money the schoolmaster earned had gone to
buy books, or else into the pockets of Mr. Golden, who kept
the "Pine Apple"—the young widow must have been
exceedingly loath to turn out and seek a home elsewhere,
for herself, her mother-in-law, and her two small children,
all of whom were now wholly dependent upon her.

Yet turn out she did, removing to a dark old house on
Redcliff Hill, where she opened a sewing-school for
children, took in what needlework she could get and, still
more enterprisingly, invented needlework designs, which
she drew in coloured inks on muslin, for the ladies of the
neighbourhood to work to in their own homes. It was a
slow uphill task, for she was without even the narrowest of

financial resources to fall back upon, without influential friends, and she had lived too long under the dominion of her masterful husband to have much confidence in herself; but with youth, tolerable health, and a quiet, unassuming belief in Providence, she fought her way onwards, managed to keep her head above water, and found time to devote more care and intelligence to the upbringing of her family than was customary in those days.

The dark old house on Redcliff Hill was nearly opposite to the main entrance of St. Mary Redcliff, and one wonders whether Mrs. Chatterton was drawn to establish herself almost within its precincts by accident, or by deliberate intention. For the church had been a good friend to her husband's forbears, providing them with a means of livelihood in the capacity of sextons "time out of mind." Throughout more than a century the office had passed in direct succession from father to son, the last Chatterton to hold it being John, the poet's great-uncle, who died in the same year that his great-nephew was born. Nothing is known of John Chatterton beyond the bare facts of the services he rendered to St. Mary's, as set forth in his epitaph:

> Near this place
> In a cold Bed of an other's making
> Lies JOHN CHATTERTON:
> Who was Death's Chamberlaine here
> For Twenty Years;
> And after having provided Lodgings
> For various passing Travellers,
> Lay down himself
> A.D. 1752 Of his sojourning 48.

> *When living, John, pursuant to his Trade,*
> *Many good Beds for weary Pilgrims made,*
> *May the same kindness now their Host receive,*
> *Dead John will lie among them—By their Leave.*

To each of the male Chattertons the church had given something. To Thomas Chatterton, senior, though he was less intimately connected with it than many others of his name, it gave the chance discovery of some forgotten parchments left strewn about the floor of the muniment room over the North Porch. Strange to relate of one who might have been expected to take the liveliest interest in such things, for the documents were obviously genuine, yellowed by age, covered with archaic writings, and intriguingly sealed and beribboned, the schoolmaster treated his treasure-trove as so much useless lumber. Calling in his pupils to help him, he collected as many of the papers as would fill a large-sized basket, afterwards using them to protect the backs of twenty new Bibles which had just been presented to the school. What were left over he took home to his wife to be put to such base domestic purposes as thread-papers and the like.

But the parchments, disregarded though they might be for the moment, were to assume a tremendous importance later on, when his son was old enough to grasp their value and significance, and to see in them a sure means of furthering certain dark projects of his own devising. By that time many of them were torn, illegible, or lost entirely; but there still remained a sufficiency upon which to hang an enigma that was to set half the literary bigwigs in the kingdom by the ears, and to rouse such a storm of controversy that the resultant hullaballoo resembled nothing so much as a free fight in a barnyard, with learned dons, and at least one very reverend dean, flapping their wings and clucking hysterically, each from his own intellectual dunghill, and so fierce a plucking of erudite feathers ensued that the eighteenth century had passed into the nineteenth, and a new generation had been born and grown to manhood, before the warring birds were finally at rest.

The parchments and the church of St. Mary Redcliff were the salient landmarks in young Chatterton's life. But neither troubled him as yet. Such of the parchments as had silk or thread wound round them were safely hidden in his mother's work-box, and if he saw them at all, it was only to stare at them with wide-open, childish eyes.

As for St. Mary's; it was nothing but a tall shadow that sometimes darkened the windows—or a peal of deep, reverberating bells.

*   *   *

"He had a face as round as an apple, rosy dimpled cheeks, flaxen hair, and blue eyes. And he had a little bag under his petticoat in front to carry nuts and fruit in."

This—a description said to have been given by a Mrs. Stephens, herself no literary lady drawing on a lush imagination, but a near relation of the Chattertons—is the first authentic portrait we have of the poet, and almost the only happy one. In after years the flaxen hair was to darken to chestnut brown, the brow and cheeks to acquire a warm yet melancholy pallor, and the eyes to turn from blue to grey. But always his eyes remained his most remarkable feature. The older men of Bristol, who were his friends, recalled them long after their other memories of him had faded. George Catcott said the boy had "a kind of hawk's eye—you could see his soul through it." William Barrett, who, being an anatomist, should surely have known, declared that he had never seen such eyes: "Fire rolling at the bottom of them." And he confessed that he had often purposely provoked disagreements between himself and Chatterton "to see how wonderfully his eyes would strike fire, kindle, and blaze up. . . ."

In infancy the fires were dormant, and for a while he was contented with his little bag, his store of nuts and fruit and such diversions and companionship as Redcliff Hill and the adjacent houses could provide, lording it over his small playmates, according to his sister, as though he were master and they his "hired servants." For one who was to show such astounding precocity and advancement from the age of ten upwards, his mental development was unusually slow. At five, being sent to his father's old school in Pile Street, he was promptly returned by its master, Mr. Love, who had succeeded Mr. Chard, as a dull-witted child, incapable of improvement.

Then one day, when Mrs. Chatterton, who seems to have had no more respect for the printed or written word than her late husband, was tearing up an old French folio music-book which had belonged to him, the boy looked up suddenly and caught sight of the large brightly illuminated capitals placed at the head of each verse, and at once, to use his mother's expressive phrase, "he fell in love with them." After that the rest was easy, and he began to memorize the alphabet as a matter of course.

But when it came to reading there was still a minor obstacle to be overcome. He displayed the most active dislike for what he called "small" books, and no amount of persuasion could induce him to open one. Nothing under a quarto volume appeared to him to be worthy of serious consideration. Size, not content, was his earliest maxim. And so his first lessons were derived from a big black-letter Bible, whose mediæval characters resolved themselves into yet another portent of events which were still to come.

As soon as he had mastered the meanings of single words, and could link whole sentences together, glimpsing the thought and purport that lay behind them, the difficulty was to get him to stop. Poor Mrs. Chatterton, her hasty strictures on his backwardness repented of at leisure, watched him with the maternal anxiety of a hen that has reared a duckling and sees it take to its natural element, the water. She could do nothing with him at all—he was impervious alike to her blandishments or her threats. The louder she called from the bank, the farther he swam out on to the shining receptive bosom of his new-found lake, indulging the while in aquatic extravagances of the most unnerving order.

He had dismissed his band of urchin followers—he had no use for them now—resolutely turning his back upon the meaner pleasures of the streets. There was an attic at the top of the house, remote from noise, reasonably secure from domestic irruptions, and admirably suited to his needs; he took possession of it, locked himself in, and read ravenously from morning till night. All this intensive study was bound to be prejudicial to his health and, to make matters worse, he became tiresome and not a little sententious over his food, refusing to appear at table, assuring his mother, in a manner ill-befitting his years, that he only wanted bread and water, and that he had a work in hand, and must not make himself more stupid than God had made him.

And presently symptoms of a still more disquieting nature supervened. He grew morose and silent, sat for long periods at a time as though oblivious of everything, and passed from these fits of abstraction into storms of passionate weeping. Already, unsuspected by himself and those around him, he was experiencing growing-pains. The leaven of creative genius, as yet inarticulate, and at this stage communicable solely by emotions the trend of which neither he nor they could understand, had started to ferment within him, and such scant peace of mind as he had ever known was slipping away. With the birth of spiritual consciousness—for him, as for all of us—his real troubles commenced.

He had turned seven, and better equipped than he had been before, he would soon be leaving home again to go

out to school.   Once, two years previously, a relative who
made delf ware had brought him a cup with a lion
rampant on it.   But he had objected to the lion.

"Paint me an angel with wings and a trumpet, to trumpet
my name over the world," he had cried grandiloquently.

He had been given his angel.   He had it still.   And now,
insensibly, he listened for the trumpet's first thin, silvery
note.

CHAPTER II

COLSTON'S

(1760–1767)

O N the 3rd of August 1760, a little more than three
months before his eighth birthday, Chatterton, on
the recommendation of the Rev. John Gardiner, Vicar of
Henbury, at the request of the Rev. Thomas Harris, master
of Redcliff Grammar School, was nominated to Colston's,
the Blue Coat School of Bristol, where his father had also
been educated.

The school had originally been founded by Edward
Colston, the descendant of a long line of merchant princes
who had flourished in Bristol since the days of Edward III.
Edward Colston was born in Bristol in 1636, but while he
was still a child, his father, William Colston, an ardent
Royalist, became embroiled in the political intrigues of the
Commonwealth era, and after the surrender of the city
by Prince Rupert, was deprived by order of Parliament of
his office of alderman, and forced to fly from his home
and to take refuge in London.

Edward was sent to Christ's Hospital, of which, in after
years, he was elected a governor. Though apparently
most of his life was spent in London—he certainly died at
Mortlake, unmarried, in 1721, in his eighty-fifth year—he
made frequent visits to, and still kept up his business
relations with Bristol, trading from there to the West
Indies, and his charitable activities in the city of his
birth were prodigious. He provided large sums for the restoration of local churches, founded almshouses on St.
Michael's Hill, enlarged the almshouses for poor sailors in

King Street, and also endowed Queen Elizabeth's Hospital, a school for boys, chiefly from lands in Somersetshire, strongly urging the city corporation, who were its governors to increase the number of scholars from forty-four to a hundred and twenty; a suggestion which was anything but enthusiastically received by certain members of the corporation, who declared that to do so would simply be turning the institution into "a nursery for beggars and sloths." Altogether—in London and Bristol—he is credited with having given away a fortune of over seventy thousand pounds.

When he first conceived his scheme for founding a school for the instruction and maintenance of a hundred Bristol boys, to be run on lines somewhat similar to those of Christ's Hospital, he wrote to the Society of Merchant Venturers, detailing his scheme, and proposing to put the establishment under their charge. The offer was gratefully received. Nor was there any difficulty in finding a suitable building. On St. Augustine's Back stood a fine old civic mansion, known as "The Great House." Elizabeth, on a progress through the West Country, had held court there; it had given shelter for a space to two later English queens, Anne of Denmark, the wife of James I, and Henrietta Maria, as well as having been the residence of Sir Ferdinando Gorges, whose surname did not escape the poet's notice, but was carefully stored away in his memory for future use. The Great House, then, was secured for £1,300, and opened as Colston's Hospital in the July of 1710.

*   *   *

Colston, though generous to a fault in most things, was singularly narrow in his religious outlook. It was said of him: "He had seen the Church in the beauty of holiness, purity, and peace. He had seen Dissent in the deformity of fanaticism, intolerance, and discord." Apparently this spectacle, or at least the latter part of it, had so unmanned him that he passed the rest of his life, supported by the moral influence of his great wealth, in waging a relentless blood-feud against "Whiggism" and Nonconformity.

To safeguard Colston's from any possible invasion by the two-headed serpent, the most elaborate precautions were taken. It was required that its master should be "of sound orthodoxy," and also that he should be approved by the major portion of the beneficed clergy of the city, and licensed by the ordinary. The pupils were to be instructed in the principles of religion as laid down by the church catechism, and should any boy allow himself to be persuaded by his parents and elders into entering a meeting-house, the penalty exacted for such experimental backslidings was instant expulsion. Even the trustees, the Society of Venturers, were not exempt from espionage, and special measures were provided to prevent the noxious doctrines of Nonconformity from gaining ground, or carrying weight, in their midst.

Mindful, maybe, of the slighting remarks upon pauperization made by the corporation, in regard to the proposed extension of Queen Elizabeth's Hospital, the daily regimen drawn up for the boarders at Colston's was calculated to brace rather than to enervate. The school hours, in the mornings, were from seven till twelve, and, in the afternoons, from one till five, during the summer; and from eight till twelve, and one till four during the winter. Before school, however, there were readings of the scriptures and singings of psalms on empty stomachs, which must have meant rising at least an hour in advance of the scheduled time for lessons; and it is exceedingly probable that further—and even longer—prayers, readings, and singings were insisted upon in the evenings. The boys sat down to meals in messes of eight, the food, though of the simplest kind, was reasonably plentiful, so that there was nothing of the "internal economy" of Dotheboys Hall about the establishment, and each mess was allowed a gallon of beer at breakfast, dinner, and supper. Bedtime was at eight o'clock all the year round, two of the bigger boys, or three of the smaller ones, sleeping in the same bed. Holidays were restricted to a half-day on Saturdays and Saints days. On Sundays no one was allowed out at all, the entire day being spent in religious exercises of the most exacting order, both in public at the cathedral and in the privacy of the school. Then, indeed, the High Church element came into its own, and the insidious encroachments of Lutherans, Calvinists, Methodists, and Wesleyans were held triumphantly at bay.

The resemblance between Colston's and Christ's Hospital went scarcely deeper than the school wardrobe. The boys wore the same kind of uniform: dark-blue gowns lined with yellow, yellow stockings, leather belts, blue bonnets, brass plaques—embossed with the founder's crest of a dolphin—on their breasts, and their heads were tonsured. But the curriculum of the Bristol school was restricted to the three bare essentials of knowledge—reading, writing, and arithmetic. Besides being taught, clothed, housed, and fed, each boy, on leaving school, was apprenticed for seven years to some useful trade, and a premium of ten pounds a head was paid out of a fund specially set apart for this purpose, when the indentures were signed. There were no scholarships or exhibitions by which a youth of exceptional gifts might raise himself above his fellows. A sober, workman-like standardization was the ideal aimed at—with its correlative implication that it was the duty of every scholar to be contented with his lot, and to acquit himself humbly and well n the situation into which it had pleased God and good Mr. Edward Colston to place him—a doctrine which was doubtless considered as serviceable as any to be engrafted on the minds and imaginations of the poor.

*   *   *

Blissfully unconscious of what was in store for him, Chatterton had been looking forward to his life at school. There were manifest disadvantages in being a lone male in a household that was rather overwhelmingly feminine. Women had a way of banding together, of moving in close formation, of impinging on one's personal liberties; and even at rising-seven he preferred to think and act for himself. Moreover, he had good reason to know that his intense preoccupation with books was not to the liking of his family, and that his almost daily ramblings in and about St. Mary's, which was even now beginning to cast a strange enchantment over him, were discussed behind his back with furtive hostility, grave shakings of the head, and uplifted brows. He knew that they suspected him of being odd and different from other boys—a fact he had long since discovered for himself. And then that business of being made to eat when he didn't want to. . . . It was time, perhaps, to think of making a change.

His subsequent disappointment was bitter and prolonged. On his first arrival at Colston's he had said: "Here I shall be able to get all the learning that I want." But soon he confessed to his mother that he had made more rapid progress when she had taken his education in hand than he was ever likely to make in class. He had counted on having the run of a library full of books, but the only books that turned out to be available, other than the few used by the master himself, were the *Bible* and the *Shorter Catechism* and those he already knew sufficiently well. At the Grammar School he would have been taught Latin, and the jealously guarded door of the classics would have

swung open for him; his, too, would have been the
opportunities afforded to one of his mental calibre by two
fellowships of thirty pounds a year to St. John's College,
Oxford, and sundry exhibitions. But this was the first of
the many misfortunes which befell him—he had been sent
to the wrong school.

He did not readily acclimatize himself to his new environment. He was not of a confiding disposition, and
although not actually unpopular, he made few friends.
The Sundays, with their incessant hymns, prayers,
catechizings, and *Bible* readings, their walks in all weathers
to and from the cathedral, must have been a decided
thorn in the flesh. Instead of qualifying him to become a
staunch son of the church, as was assuredly the founder's
intention, these arbitrary shepherdings merely aroused in
him a profound mistrust for machine-made religion, and
an equally violent contempt for its practitioners. Upon
spiritual matters, as upon most other subjects, he had
his own individual opinions, and his was not the sort
of intelligence that meekly submits to be forcibly
fed.

The process by which he was alienated from his childish
beliefs, though positive enough in its results, was a slow and
gradual one. His earliest creative work is tinged with a
naïf and rather touching piety. Nor, if we accept his
sister's testimony, was his attitude towards confirmation
in any degree adversely affected, for we are told: "He
made very sensible, serious remarks on the awfulness of
the occasion and his feelings and convictions during
it."

At Colston's it was the custom to make each of the boys
in rotation act for a week as doorkeepers at the main gate,
which was flanked on either side by tall pillars surmounted
by dolphins. Chatterton's turn came shortly after his
confirmation, and in the leisure and comparative solitude

thus ensured to him, he began to try his hand at making verses. His first attempt, *On the Last Epiphany; or, Christ Coming to Judgment*, pleased him so much on its completion that somehow or other, probably on his next Saturday's half-holiday, he managed to slip it into the letter-box at the offices of *Felix Farley's Journal*, in which it appeared on 8th January 1763, seven weeks after his tenth birthday. This was followed by *A Hymn for Christmas Day*—another artless and unpretentious affair, yet showing a remarkable facility and range of language for so young a boy.

Thereafter, for a while at least, he abandoned the sacred for the profane, and launched out into the wider fields of satire.

His earliest essays in this new genre, which later he was to use with such devastating fluency and sureness of technique, were *Sly Dick*, *The Churchwarden and the Apparition*, and *Apostate Will*. And while it would be idle to pretend that these pieces possess any outstanding literary value, they are interesting because of the light they throw upon their author's psychology.

Sly Dick, the first in order of production, is a gay little unfinished narrative poem about a thief who is tempted by "a dark infernal sprite" to plunder a well-stored garret lying unsuspected overhead, and is chiefly remarkable from the fact that in it, twice over, Chatterton introduces an old English dialect word—"reeve"—to wrinkle—thus foreshadowing the extensive and ingeniously contrived "antique" vocabulary on which all his major works were to be built.

Next comes *The Churchwarden and the Apparition*, setting forth the misdoings of one, Joseph Thomas, a churchwarden of St. Mary Redcliff, who, without due authority, caused the graves round the church to be levelled, and carted the clay and rubble to his place of business, where, being a builder by trade, it was alleged that he converted the material into bricks. A further charge of vandalism was preferred against him in that he had ordered a beautiful old cross to be removed from the churchyard, and altogether he had succeeded in making himself extremely disliked by the neighbourhood.

The theme, of course, was a purely topical one, and its treatment anything but inspired. Yet the mere performance of it serves to indicate that the boy visionary, who stole off unperceived whenever he could to spend lonely hours in St. Mary's, conscious of a curious affinity between himself and the church's history, was none the less sharply observant of small contemporary happenings in the outside world.

But *Apostate Will*, dealing with a mealy-mouthed Nonconformist parson, who utilized his religion for his personal advancement, dated 14th April 1764, when the poet was eleven years and five months old, is by far the most self-revealing of the three. Herein are unmistakable evidences of a precocious cynicism that is, to say the least, disquieting, and that unwittingly supplies a sure token of the extremes to which the sledge-hammer religious training, always working at top pressure at Colston's, was driving him. One has only to set such verses from *Apostate Will* as:

> He then his circumstance declared,
> How hardly matters with him fared,
> Begged him next morning for to make
> A small collection for his sake.
> The preacher said, "Do not repine,
> The whole collection shall be thine."

and again:

> He was a preacher and what not,
> As long as money could be got;

> *He'd oft profess, with holy fire;*
> *" The labourer's worthy of his hire."*

beside:

> *My soul, exert thy powers, adore ;*
> *Upon devotion's plumage soar*
> *   To celebrate the day :*
> *The God from whom creation sprung*
> *Shall animate my grateful tongue ;*
> *   From Him I'll catch the lay !——*

taken from *A Hymn for Christmas Day*, to form a more or less accurate estimation of how far he had travelled along the road to disillusionment and loss of faith, in the space of a little over a year.

*   *   *

When his dissatisfactions at the poor chances offered for the acquirement of knowledge and the improvement of his mind at Colston's had somewhat abated, instead of uselessly repining, he very characteristically set himself to see what could be done in the way of rectifying these deficiencies and educating himself. Latin and Greek were out of the question, naturally—he would never be able to learn them now. But the classics, if one wished to study them, were to be had in translations, and meanwhile there was much which might privately be added to the arithmetic (wherein he made rapid progress), the writing, and the morning, evening, and all-day-Sunday spiritual jerks. Accordingly soon after he was ten years old, with the little pocket-money his mother was in a position to allow him, he joined a circulating library—there were several in the city—and thenceforward, in play-time, and whenever a suitable opportunity occurred, he read more assiduously than ever. To such good purpose did he withdraw himself from the sports and recreations of the other boys, which never held any great attractions for him, that between the ages of eleven and twelve he made a list of over seventy books he had read, most of them concerned with history and divinity.

In his historical researches—devoted principally, it may be surmised, to the reigns of the Plantagenet Kings—he was helped and encouraged by an usher, or assistant-master, Thomas Phillips. Phillips was young, intelligent, and eager-minded, and had the interests of the school much at heart. He even tried, through the medium of a kind of poetry-circle organized among the more promising of his pupils—for he dabbled in verse-making himself—to infuse some small, but badly needed, element of variety into Colston's cut-and-dried routine. Tradition affirms— on the slenderest of premises—that a romantic friendship existed between Phillips and Chatterton. Phillips died in early manhood, at the beginning of November 1769, and Chatterton wrote an *Elegy* in commemoration of his untimely death. The *Elegy*, however, can scarcely claim to be a *cri de cœur*. Nor is it one of the poet's most inspired compositions. The continual evocation, after the artificial manner of the time, of the deceased subject by his surname strikes disconcertingly on the modern ear and, even allow-ing for this, there is something flat and halting about the whole poem, while to hail the usher, none of whose writings has survived, as "Great Master of the boundless lyre" was surely a little excessive. Indeed, Chatterton himself, for once in a way, appears to have doubted the quality of his lines, for at the end of the poem he adds, as an *apologia*:

To the Reader

Observe, in favour of a hobbling strain,
Neat as exported from the parent brain,
Are each and every couplet I have penned,
But little laboured, and I never mend.

Still more destructive of the romantic friendship legend is Chatterton's behaviour at school. Far from rushing forward, as he might easily have done, eclipsing all other competitors, and thereby exalting himself in the eyes of his hero, he refused to have any truck with the poetry circle, affected a complete indifference in regard to its activities, and remained significantly silent and secretive with respect to his own achievements.

The incident—the gentle, kindly Phillips, the admiring, receptive boy—has been given much sentimental prominence by most of the poet's biographers, yet it is difficult to determine from what sources it arose. Chatterton's, from the very outset, was a virile, self-reliant, curiously adult personality. Being a romanticist at heart, and, one might say, in spite of his head, some practicable means of escape from the drab, homespun texture of everyday existence was essential to his well-being. But he had found the outlet he was looking for in the church of St. Mary Redcliff long before his meeting with Phillips. His own interior life was not lived in the Bristol of the eighteenth century, but in a Bristol, half real, half imagined, of mediæval days, whose narrow, twisting streets were thronged with priests and monks, with ladies wearing wimples or high steepled head-dresses, and with knights, fully caparisoned, riding into the lists. It was as if his native scepticism, eternally at war with the rest of him, had warned him that it was safer to put one's trust in those things that were already lightly powdered with the golden dust of immortality, than in brief personal relationships, blown to the winds by the first breath of malignant circumstance, for ever fluttering out of reach, for ever letting one down. And so he kept his counsel, stood securely on his feet, and gave absolutely nothing of himself away.

*   *   *

During the seven years he remained at Colston's Hospital, Chatterton's poetical output appears to have been limited to those pieces already enumerated, namely, *On the Last Epiphany; or, Christ Coming to Judgment, A Hymn for Christmas Day, Sly Dick, The Churchwarden and the Apparition,* and *Apostate Will.* Mention is also made by his sister of his having paraphrased the ninth chapter of Job and some chapters of Isaiah. He was continually scribbling in small marble-backed notebooks however, and much of his experimental work no doubt shared the usual fate of such *juvenilia,* and was either torn up—he developed a positive mania for tearing up as he grew older—or got scattered abroad and lost.

Yet there is one richly suggestive gleam of enlightenment which calls for attention at this stage of his career, almost midway between his entering Colston's and leaving it to become a scrivener's apprentice.

It chanced that Phillips had a young friend called James Thistlethwaite, to whom eventually he introduced Chatterton. At the time of their first encounter—towards the end of 1763—Thistlethwaite was twelve years old, Chatterton eleven. Each had literary aspirations, and owned to kindred interests in other directions, but although they met frequently during Chatterton's schooldays, and again—after an interval of separation—when they were both apprentices, the acquaintanceship, probably held in check by the younger boy, seems always to have been a somewhat superficial one. Yet this did not prevent Thistlethwaite from forcing his way into the limelight, seventeen years later, when the question of the authenticity of the Rowley Poems was being hotly debated on every side, and when he hoped he might be able to deflect a certain amount of publicity to himself by posing as a self-appointed authority on all the facts and details of the poet's early life. But the story, in so far as it affects the present situation, is best told in Thistlethwaite's own words:

"Going down Horse Street, near the School, one day, during the summer of 1764," he writes to Dean Milles, in a letter dated 4th April 1781, "I accidentally met with Chatterton. Entering into conversation with him, the subject of which I do not now recollect, he informed me that he was in possession of certain old MSS. which had been found deposited in a chest in Redcliffe Church and that he had lent some or one of them to Phillips. Within a day or two after this, I saw Phillips and repeated to him the information I had received from Chatterton. Phillips produced a MS. on parchment, or vellum, which I am confident was 'Elenoure and Juga,' a kind of pastoral eclogue, afterwards published in *The Town and Country* for May 1769. The parchment appeared to have been closely pared round the margin, for what purpose, or by what accident, I know not, but the words were evidently entire and unmutilated.

"As the writing was yellow and pale, manifestly, as I conceive, by age, and consequently difficult to decipher, Phillips had with his pen traced and gone over several of the lines (which, so far as my recollection serves me, were written in the manner of prose, and without any regard to punctuation) and by that means laboured to attain the object of his pursuit, an investigation of their meaning. I endeavoured to assist him, but from an almost total ignorance of the characters, manners, language, and orthography of the age in which the lines were written all our efforts were unprofitably exerted, and although we arrived at an explanation, and corrected many of the words, still the sense was notoriously deficient.

"For my own part, having little or no taste for such studies, I repined not at the disappointment. Phillips, on the contrary, was to all appearances mortified. . . . Indeed, much more so at the time than I thought the object deserved, expressing his sorrow at his want of success, and repeatedly declaring his intention of resuming the attempt at a future period."

Such, then, was the tale that James Thistlethwaite told long after Phillips and Chatterton, the only two people

who might have contradicted him, were both conveniently
dead. Could what he wrote to Dean Milles be accepted
unconditionally, the information contained in the letter
would be invaluable. But, unhappily, Thistlethwaite,
after his own long-winded, self-seeking, coldly superior
fashion, was a thorough-paced rascal. Furthermore, he
was and had always been desperately jealous of
Chatterton's incomparably finer poetical gifts, and was
out to discredit and betray him by whatever means came
readiest to hand. That he was disposed to stick at nothing
in the pursuit of his own ends is sufficiently demonstrated
by the fact that in a satire, written by him some time in
the middle seventeen-seventies, entitled *The Consultation,*
he made highly incriminating statements about Henry
Burgum, a local pewterer—of whom much will be heard
hereafter—who, rightly or wrongly, was supposed to have
robbed his business associates of three thousand pounds,
but offered to suppress publication should Burgum make
it worth his while.

   When the Rowley Controversy was at its height, and the
poems were at one moment attributed to Chatterton, and
at the next to Thomas Rowley, the mythical fifteenth
century priest, according to whichever party happened to
be in the ascendant, it was Thistlethwaite's undeviating
purpose to prove that they were merely transcriptions, and
not the original work of his friend. This noising abroad of
Chatterton's name—the angel at last having appeared with
his trumpet—was gall and wormwood to Thistlethwaite,
who had never, in spite of all his devious strivings, succeeded in raising himself above the dead-level of free-
lance journalistic mediocrity. Therefore, if, by a little
artful juggling with dates, he might contrive to bring the
first of the Rowley Poems in advance of its actual time,
and at a period when Chatterton, by reason of his extreme
youth, inexperience, and lack of education might be

B

deemed incapable of having written it, here was at least one point to be gained.

On the other hand, there are gleams of truth now and then among the reminiscences. And although it is generally believed that Chatterton knew nothing about the parchments his father had found in the muniment-room of St. Mary Redcliff until after he had become a full-fledged apprentice in his lawyer's office, it appears incredible that if the remains of the parchments were used every day by his mother as thread-papers, he should not have been aware of their existence, lying scattered about the house, as they certainly would be, long before then.

And so rapid and exotic was the growth of his genius, leaping into sudden flame-like maturity, as though conscious of the brief space allotted for its blossoming and the imminence of its ultimate decay, that it is not outside the bounds of possibility that before he said good-bye to Colston's the first stone of the Rowley Saga, which was to constitute itself his life work, was well and truly laid.

CHAPTER III

THE SCRIVENER'S APPRENTICE

(1767–1768)

THE Bristol into which Chatterton was born still retained most of its mediæval characteristics, and might have served as a fitting background for the Rowley Poems.

The streets, paved with roughly hewn blocks of stone, many of them with open and unsavoury sewers running down the middle, were narrow, dark, and tortuous, and lined on either side by tall timbered buildings, whose upper portions projected outwards, often within a few feet of the heads of passing pedestrians, leaving visible above only a thin strip of sky. Few of the shop-windows were glazed, the majority being entirely open, as are those of the fishmongers and poulterers of the present day. If any kind of protection for the goods inside was attempted this usually took the form of loose curtains of hessian, or lattices of woven osier branches. And everywhere the wayfarer went he was assailed by a bewildering assortment of sounds and smells: the hammerings of smiths, coopers, joiners, and braziers; the fumes of the tallow-chandler, the soap-boiler, the tanner, and the dyer. Moreover, since few of the populace, especially the country people who came into market from the adjoining villages, could read, and also because, owing to the open condition of the shops themselves, it was most likely considered imprudent to display too much merchandise in full public view, lest the light fingers of the passers-by should be tempted as well as their eyes, each tradesman had his own individual emblem, slung on an iron bracket, and resembling the signboard of an inn, by which his occupation could be distinguished at a glance from that of his neighbour: a "Turkish Bashaw," for a mercer; a "Golden Boy," for a jeweller; a "Tye-Wig and Griffin," for a barber; a "Half-Moon and Wheatsheaf," for a draper; and a "Sword and Crown," for a cutler; so that on stormy days, when gales blew up from the broad estuary of the Severn, there was a mighty creaking of rusty hinges, a fluttering of shadows on the roadways, and a continual blinking of dim yellow lamplight after darkness had set in.

*   *   *

Chatterton was now to have a closer acquaintance with the city, exchanging the quiet, well-to-do, residential neighbourhood in which the school was situated for closed-in thoroughfares, thronged with traffic, and re-sounding to the hurried footsteps of busy merchants and burgesses, given over body and soul to a commercialism that he detested, and enriched by their extensive tradings with Africa, the West Indies, and the American Colonies. For he left Colston's on 1st July 1767, and the same day was taken into the office of Mr. John Lambert, scrivener.

The preliminary negotiations, and the payment of the usual premium of ten pounds were, of course, undertaken by the school authorities under the terms of the Colston Trust, Chatterton himself being, to all intents and pur-poses, a passive agent in the matter. He was bound for seven years, during which time he was to receive no salary, and the indentures were very explicit as to what was looked for and required from him in the way of moral deportment, since they stipulated that: "Taverns he shall not frequent, at Dice he shall not play, Fornication he shall not commit, Matrimony he shall not contract, or damage to his said Master within the said Term he shall not do; but well and faithfully shall he behave himself in all things, as well in

Words as in Deeds, as a good and faithful Apprentice, according to the Use and Custom of Bristol. . . ." And in return for all this Mr. Lambert, in addition to instructing him in his business, pledged himself to find him "Good and sufficient Meat, Drink, Linen, Woollen, Lodging and all other Necessaries, Washing and Mending excepted, during the said Term;" and, at the end of his time to "pay the said Apprentice Four Shillings and Sixpence towards his Freedom of Bristol with Two suits of Apparel, one for Holydays and the other in lieu of his Salary."

There was also appended to the contract a rather ambiguous secondary clause, to the effect that: "It is agreed that the Friends or Relatives of the Within Apprentice shall at their own Expense find and provide for him Washing and Mending during the within Term anything within contained or Custom of Bristol to the contrary notwithstanding."

Chatterton signed the first agreement, his mother the second, and their signatures were witnessed by the Mayor and Sheriffs of the city.

The office hours were from eight in the morning till eight in the evening, with an interval for a mid-day meal at Lambert's house, which was some distance away. Then, when the long day's work was over, Chatterton was free to do what he liked until ten o'clock, at which hour he was expected to be indoors and ready to go to bed.

At first sight, these conditions would seem to be little or no improvement on the Spartan regimen in force at Colston's; but at any rate, where he himself was concerned, there would be no more compulsory attendances at the cathedral, no more kneelings on hard and draughty class-room floors, while Mr. Haynes, the master, prayed interminably and Phillips led the responses in high-pitched, gently authoritative tones, no mumblings and slurrings of the scriptures, no irksome memorizings of the Collect for the Day. The unspeakable dreariness and monotony of the school Sundays were over and done with for good and all. In future he would be able to dispose of the one day in the week on which he might almost be said to belong to himself exactly how he pleased—decide whether to rush back to his own small attic room, high among the chimney-pots, on Redcliff Hill, or make his way out beyond the streets and houses of the city into the soft green solitudes of the surrounding country.

But before he had time to savour any of the delights of his emancipation, a new and unexpected calamity befell him—he found, immediately upon entering Lambert's household, that he was obliged to take his meals in the kitchen with the servants. Worse still, he was made to sleep with the footboy. Nothing could have infuriated him more. In all probability the servants disliked his company quite as much as he did theirs. His was not the sort of nature that suffers in silence; and as the "sharp wit and acute understanding" foreshadowed by the conjunction of Gemini with Mercury at the time of his birth was already largely in evidence, it may be assumed that he became very vocal indeed on the subject of his real or imagined wrongs.

The discomforts he was compelled to undergo in the kitchen had their inevitable repercussions in the office. Lambert found his apprentice "sullen and of a gloomy temper, which particularly displayed itself among the servants"; and Chatterton, nervous, restive, and resentful —a racehorse harnessed to a brewer's dray—could hardly conceal the contempt he felt for his master.

Much has been written in dispraise of Lambert, and no one has been more eloquent in abusing him than a Mrs. Edkins, the wife of a Bristol painter and glazier, who represented herself as the life-long friend of the Chattertons, and a "second mother" to the poet himself.

The confidential outpourings of this lady are, however, notoriously suspect. Her identity has never yet been satisfactorily established. Neither Mrs. Chatterton nor her daughter makes any allusion to her, and in the letters which Chatterton wrote home from London, although he is most punctilious in wishing to be remembered to all his old friends, her name is never once mentioned. Yet according to Mrs. Edkins, whose information, given to George Cumberland, forms an appendix to John Dix's *Life of Chatterton*, published in 1837, Lambert was continually harassing Chatterton, making his life unbearable, seeking to thwart him by every possible means, and if he found any chance manuscripts lying about on the boy's desk, he snatched them up, tore them into pieces, and exclaimed: "There's your stuff!" Chatterton, we are told, was strictly prohibited from making fair copies of his verses on the office stationary, and Mrs. Edkins was consequently obliged to supply him with money to buy paper for his private use.

That there were constant clashes between Chatterton and his employer seems only too probable, but that there was any sustained attempt at tyrannization on the part of the elder man is most unlikely. Temperamentally, apart from his unshakable belief in his work, Chatterton was always at the mercy of a not uncommon type of inferiority complex which made him outwardly aggressive when he was inwardly least sure of himself, as well as rendering him hypersensitive to fancied slights and rebuffs. And Lambert, an ordinary, perhaps not over-intelligent young man of twenty-eight, self-centred, more interested in his own creature comforts than in anything else—for he possessed a considerable private fortune which made it immaterial whether he worked at his profession or neglected it, to say nothing of an indulgent mother who maybe looked after him too well at home—can scarcely be blamed for failing to appreciate the sulky, intractable Charity School boy at more than his surface value.

Though the kitchen rankled, and continued to rankle, the young poet might have gone farther and fared worse. He was tied down to the office for at least eleven hours a day, admittedly; but his duties, mainly the copying of precedents, were light enough and rarely occupied him for more than two hours at a stretch, after which, in Lambert's absence—and the attorney was more often absent than present—he could devote his time to reading, or to writing verse. In this respect he was fortunate, since no other calling could have afforded him so many opportunities for pursuing his lone, predestined course among the stars. Sometimes for days together he had the office entirely to himself, and only at odd moments would he look out of the window and find, to his great indignation, that one of the servants had been sent down from the house to spy upon him and to make sure that he had not deserted his post. But always he was there, bent over his desk, surrounded by piles of books and papers, and the servant, who doubtless would have given a good deal to have been able to catch him off his guard, would go back reluctantly with nothing detrimental to report.

* * *

Shortly after Chatterton entered Lambert's service, the office, which hitherto had been either in Small Street or below St. John's Steps, was removed to 37 Corn Street, opposite to the Bristol Exchange. Here the front shop was occupied by a bookseller, Becket by name, and the premises behind it by Anthony Henderson, a jeweller. Thus Chatterton, in his daily comings and goings, was brought into touch with other youths of about his own age, also working as apprentices in or near the building. Among these were three who bore the same Christian name

as himself—Thomas Capel, Thomas Palmer, and Thomas
Tipton, with whom he soon became on friendly terms.
Curiously enough, each was interested in books, and
dabbled in a sort of amateur journalism, and though
Chatterton made it clear that he did not care to be
disturbed in the daytime, even when Lambert was away,
the young men frequently dropped into the office in the
evenings to discuss their own and each other's work, and
draft out prospective articles for the local newspapers.
Most nights, however, during his two hours of freedom,
Chatterton went home to see his family, for in spite of his
adolescent hardness and egoism—and he needed to be an
egoist to carry out the gigantic task he had in view—he
was genuinely loyal and devoted to his mother and sister,
and long after these Bristol days were over, his sister wrote
of him: "We saw him most evenings before nine, and he
would in general stay to the limit of his time. He was
seldom two evenings together without seeing us."

Lambert rented two rooms in Corn Street, which
suggests that Chatterton must have had an office to himself, even when the attorney came down to business. And
now began that tremendous output of literary craftsmanship—mediæval poems, satires, burlettas, topical pieces,
political squibs, letters in the style of Junius—that gathered
momentum as it rushed along, never slackening its upward-
sweeping curve until the last few desolate weeks of his
existence.

The library at the office was small and consisted mainly
of legal works, but it did contain a copy of Camden's
Britannia, and *The Charters of Bristol*. By the aid of Speght's
Chaucer and Bailey's and Kersey's dictionaries, he compiled,
in between his customary copyings of precedents, a glossary
of antique and pseudo-antique words, and he still went on
borrowing from the circulating libraries anything that
might increase his knowledge of, and give him a deeper

B *

insight into, the life and conditions of the Middle Ages in England, and especially in his native West Country. A perfect frenzy for work had seized him, and often, finding the day was not long enough for the accomplishment of all he had in mind, he would sit up writing the whole night through in his bedroom at Lambert's, so that the footboy, unless he was a heavy sleeper, must have had every reason for complaint.

It was some time towards the end of that first winter at Lambert's that Thistlethwaite again appeared upon the scene. He was now apprenticed to a stationer, and had actually been sent to collect at Lambert's office some books that required binding. And later he had much to say—to Dean Milles, of course—about the "eccentricity" of the poet's mind, and "the versatility of his disposition":

> One day he might be found busily employed in the study of Heraldry and English antiquities, both of which are numbered amongst the most favourite of his pursuits; the next, discovered him deeply engaged, confounded and perplexed, amidst the subtleties of metaphysical disquisition or lost and bewildered in the abstruse labyrinth of mathematical researches; and these in an instant again neglected and thrown aside to make room for astronomy and music, of both of which sciences his knowledge was entirely confined to theory. Even physic was not without a charm to allure his imagination, and he would talk of Galen, Hippocrates, and Paracelsus, with all the confidence and familiarity of a modern empirick. . . .

Every line of which was obviously intended to present Chatterton in the light of a capricious *dilettante*, who paltered with one recondite subject after another, merely, when the first impulse of attraction had spent itself, to discard each in turn, as a spoilt child pushes away its toys; and incidentally, it goes without saying, to prove to the very reverend dean that Thistlethwaite himself was no mean student of psychology. The reunion at Lambert's was in all probability more enthusiastically welcomed by Thistlethwaite, who loved nothing so much as poking his nose into other people's affairs, than by Chatterton. But Chatterton had immense reserves of caution. Nothing was likely to be disclosed by him which he felt had best remain hidden. He could retire behind a cloud of vague taciturnity at any given moment, and knew very well how to take care of himself.

Then, early in March of the following year, comes the first reference made by the poet to one of his mediæval poems—*The Tournament*—and this occurs in a letter to a friend named Baker, who, on leaving school, had gone out to America and settled in Charlestown, South Carolina. The letter, written with an affectation of gay, wordly-wise cynicism, shows Chatterton, in mind, spirit, and outlook, a pure product of the eighteenth century, and, for all its undercurrent of unconscious *naïveté*, is a sufficiently startling production for a boy not yet sixteen and a half. It is dated 6th March 1768.

DEAR FRIEND,

I must now close my poetical labours, my master being returned from London. You write in a very entertaining stile; though I am afraid mine will be the contrary. Your celebrated Miss Rumsey is going to be married to Mr. Fowler, as he himself informs me. Pretty children! about to enter into the comfortable yoke of matrimony, to be at their own liberty: just apropos to the old law—but out of the frying-pan into the fire! For a lover, heavens mend him; but for a husband! O excellent! What a female Machiaval this Miss Rumsey is! a very good Mistress of Nature to discover a *demon* in the habit of a parson; to find a spirit so well adapted to the humour of an English wife, that is, one who takes off his hat to every person he chances to meet, to show his staring horns, and very politely stands at the door of his wife's chamber, whilst her gallant is entertaining her within. O mirabili! What will human nature degenerate into? Fowler aforesaid declares he makes a scruple of conscience of being too free with Miss Rumsey before marriage. There's a gallant for you! Why a girl with any thing of the woman would despise him for it. But no more of him. I am glad you approve of the ladies in Charles-Town; and am obliged to you for the compliment of including me in your happiness; my friendship is as firm as the white rock when the black waves roar round it, and the waters burst on its hoary top, when the driving wind ploughs the sable sea, and the rising waves aspire to the clouds, teeming with the rattling hail. So much for heroics. To speak plain English; I am, and ever will be, your unalterable friend. I did not give your love to Miss Rumsey, having not yet seen her in private, and in public she will not speak to me, because of her great love to Fowler; and on another occasion. I have been violently in love these three-and-twenty times since your departure; and not a few times came off victorious. I am obliged to you for your curiosity, and shall esteem it very much, not on account of itself, but as coming from you. The poems, etc., on Miss HOYLAND I wish better, for her sake and yours. The TOURNAMENT I have only one cento of, which I send herewith; the remainder is entirely lost. I am, with the greatest regret, going to subscribe myself, your faithful and constant Friend, "till death do us part."

THOMAS CHATTERTON.

Mr. Baker,
   Charles-Town,
    South Carolina.

Baker, it would seem, though sending affectionate messages to Miss Rumsey, had left at least a portion of his heart behind him in the keeping of Miss Eleanor Hoyland, and had entered into an agreement with Chatterton to keep him supplied with poems extolling her beauty, virtues, and accomplishments. Some half-dozen or more of these, including an acrostic on the fair one's name, were dispatched across the Atlantic, and afterwards duly returned to the lady in Bristol by her lover, as the fruits of his own pen. As poetry they have no intrinsic value whatsoever. Indeed, one of them, facetiously headed "Miss Hoyland is Coy," appears in an Anthology of Bad Verse—*The Stuffed Owl*—and its compilers, D. B. Wyndham Lewis and Charles Lee, remark that "Chatterton lacked, to some extent, a sense of humour." The chances are, however, that, knowing Baker and Miss Hoyland, and having his own private opinion as to the depth and sincerity of their mutual attachment, he composed his love lyrics with his tongue in his cheek.

In one way and another, Baker came in for a considerable amount of attention from the poet. The British Museum possesses, among its large and valuable collection of Chatterton's writings, a manuscript entitled *Journal Sixth*, in which, after invoking his friend and having disrespectfully criticized Whitfield's manner in the pulpit, he proceeds to discourse at some length, and with a rather dangerous facility, on sex-relationships; and as everything seems to indicate that the correspondence between himself and Baker must have been both voluminous and self-revealing, it is a thousand pities that all of it, with the single exception of the example already quoted, should have been irretrievably lost.

*   *   *

That allusion by its author to *The Tournament* brings up once more the question of the parchments, and whether one credits Thistlethwaite's story that Chatterton knew all about them while he was still a schoolboy, or inclines to the more generally accepted theory that they did not come to his knowledge, nor into his possession, until after he had been apprenticed to Lambert, it is manifest that by this time he was fully aware of their existence, for from now onwards he gave out that he was making transcriptions from them. Sir Daniel Wilson, in his *Thomas Chatterton*, published in 1869, says, in regard to the letter to Baker: "Chatterton, it must be remembered, is here writing to an intimate friend, and is forwarding specimens of his own work, not palming off spurious antiques." But—setting aside the Hoyland verses—was he doing anything of the kind? Without having access to the entire correspondence, or at any rate to a great deal more of it than the one letter which happens to be available, it is impossible to arrive at any very definite conclusion. But surely the sentence: "I have only one 'cento'—the remainder is entirely lost," is intended to convey an impression that the rest of the original manuscript from which it purported to be transscribed was missing. Otherwise Chatterton could have completed the poem himself.

And now it is essential that the whole history of the parchments should be given in full. Briefly their history is this; from the days of the Wars of the Roses there had lain, stored up in the muniment-room of St. Mary Redcliff, a number of old chests, seven in all, the largest of which was known as "Mr. Canynges' Cofre." A sum of money had been left for the preservation and annual opening of Mr. Canynges' Cofre, which was bound with iron bands and secured by six keys, two of the keys being traditionally handed over to the Vicar and Procurator of the church, two to the Mayor, and one to each of the churchwardens. But with the passing of centuries the ceremony of opening the chest each year had fallen into abeyance, and finally was discarded altogether. Then at some unspecified date in the early part of the eighteenth century—the actual year varies according to different authorities, but was undoubtedly sometime between 1720 and 1730—the Vestry wanted to have access to certain documents and, as all the keys were discovered to have been lost, the locks not only of the largest coffer, but of all the others as well, were forced open, and the papers within subjected to what would appear to have been a somewhat cursory examination. Such parchments as related to church lands and property were removed to a place of safety, but the remainder, which Sir Daniel Wilson—from the fact that one of the Rowley manuscripts in the British Museum is attached to a portion of a genuine fifteenth-century deed—assumes to have been "presentments, assessment rolls, records, and discharges of parochial disbursements, and inventories of vestments, church ornaments, etc.," were either stuffed back into the open chests or left lying where they had fallen, not the slightest precaution being taken to protect them from the ravages of dust and damp, or the predatory hands of any stray person who might chance to be wandering about the interior of the church.

That the poet's father was not the only despoiler is quite certain, for William Barrett, long before he met with young Chatterton, had bought a bundle of the parchments—large enough to fill a single volume—from a barber called Morgan, who, as a sort of side-line to his regular business, trafficked in antiques. We have already seen how Mrs. Chatterton converted such as came her way into thread-papers, and it is also stated that some of the papers were used by the church cleaners for polishing up the altar candlesticks.

By the time his own inherited share of the Redcliff parchments reached Chatterton, they must necessarily have dwindled and been fewer in number than was commonly supposed. Yet this did not lessen his delight in their discovery. He ransacked the house for all the papers it contained, exclaiming, his pale cheeks flushed with unwonted excitement, that "he had found a treasure, and was so glad, nothing could be like it."

Whereupon he took his treasure away with him, poring over it in secret, patiently trying to decipher its unfamiliar lettering, to translate its snatches of Latin and dog-Latin, to amplify its contemporary abbreviations; and, smoothing the creamy surface of the vellum sheets beneath the tips of his fingers, it may well have been that the writing with which they were covered changed—almost before his eyes —into the penmanship of Thomas Rowley, a secular priest of St. John's. Copying the oldest of the manuscripts, tracing over and over again their cramped and pointed characters—for the voices of those who were to cry out "Forger!" were as yet inaudible and infinitely remote— his own handwriting became gradually gothicized, and soon he found that he himself could write as Rowley must have done.

CHAPTER IV

THE OLD BRIDGE

(1768)

D URING Chatterton's childhood and early schooldays, the Avon at Bristol had been spanned by a stone bridge, built in the days of Henry II, and later reinforced and widened by additional flying arches. On one of these, supported by a massive pier in midstream, Edward III and his consort, Philippa of Hainault, had erected the Chapel of the Assumption of the Blessed Virgin Mary. Then gradually a row of tall timbered houses, with high pointed gables, small-paned windows, and stout oaken doors began to appear on either side, until very much after the fashion of old London Bridge, there was a complete thoroughfare of houses and shops from one bank to the other.

So well and so solidly had the bridge been designed and carried out that, even in the middle of the eighteenth century, it showed few signs of deterioration. But the approaches at both ends were narrow and precipitous, which made it difficult for the ever-increasing press of vehicular traffic to get across without the maximum amount of inconvenience and delay. The river itself, too, crowded at all seasons with barges, lighters, and small craft of every description, was hopelessly congested by the tremendous breadth and thickness of the central piers.

At length, in 1761, the civic authorities decided that the Old Bridge was now obsolete, and must forthwith be swept away and replaced by a new one of lighter yet more ample proportions. Therefore the Chapel of the Blessed Virgin

Mary and the houses and shops opposite and alongside it were pulled down; the original structure demolished; and work on the New Bridge was commenced. The building operations lasted seven years. But in September 1768 the bridge was opened for foot passengers, and two months later, in November, for carriages and other horse-drawn traffic.

It was one day during this same September that the editor of *Felix Farley's Journal* received the following covering note and manuscript—the latter describing, in archaic language and with a wealth of circumstantial detail how, six centuries earlier, the Mayor of Bristol had first crossed over the Old Bridge that was now no more.

Mr. Printer,
       The following Description of the Mayor's first Passing over the Old Bridge, taken from an old Manuscript, may not at this time be unacceptable to the Generality of your Readers.
                          Yours, etc.,
                                Dunhelmus Bristoliensis.

On Fridaie was the time fixed for the passing the newe Brydge: aboute the time of the tollynge the tenth clock, Master Greggorie Dalbenye mounted on a Fergreyne[1] Horse, enformed Master Maior all thyngs were prepared; when two Beadils want fyrst streyng fresh Stre, next came a Manne dressed up as follows:—Hose of Goatskyn, Crinepart[2] out-wards, Doublet and Waystcoat also, over which a white Robe without Sleeves, much like an Albe but not so longe, reeching but to his Lends;[3] a Girdle of Azure over his left Shoulder, rechde also to his Lends on the ryght, and doubled back to his Left, bucklyng with a Gouldin Buckel, dangled to his knee; thereby representing a Saxon Elderman.

In his Hande he bare a Shield, the maystrie[4] of Gille a Brogton, who paincted the same, representing Sainte Warburgh crossynge the Ford. Then a mickle strong Manne in Armour, carried a huge Anlace,[5] after whom came Six claryons and Six Minstrels who sang the song of Saincte Warburgh then came

---

[1] Iron grey.   [2] Hairy side.   [3] Loins.   [4] Masterpiece.   [5] Sword.

Master Maior, mounted on a white Horse, dight with sable trappyngs wrought about by the Nunnes of Saincte Kenna with Gould and Silver, his Hayr braded with Ribbons, and a Chaperon[1] with the auntient Armes of Brystowe fastende on his Forehead. Master Maior bare in his Hande a goulden Rodde, and a Congean[2] Squier bare in his Hande his Helmet, waulking by the Syde of the Horse; then came the Eldermen and Cittie Broders, mounted on Sable Horses dyght with white trappynges and Plumes and Scarlet Copes and Chapeous[3] having thereon Sable Plumes; after them the Preests and Freeres, Parysh, Mendicaunt and Seculor, some syngyng Saincte Warburghs Song, others soundyng Clarions thereto, and others some Citrialles.[4]

In thilk manner reechyng the Brydge, the Manne with the Anlace stode on the fyrst Top of a Mound yreered in the midst of the Bridge; then want up the Manne with the Sheelde, after him the Minstrels and clarions, And then the Preestes and Freeres, all in white Albs, makyng a most goodlie Shewe; The Maior and Eldermen standyng round, theie sang, with the sound of Clarions, the Songe of Saincte Baldwyn; which beyng done, the Manne on the Top threwe with great myght his Anlace into the See, and the Clarions sounded an auntiant Charge and Forloyn.[5]

Then theie sang againe the Songe of Saincte Warburgh and proceeded up Chrysts hill, to the Cross, when a Latin Sermon was preached by, Ralph de Blundeville. And with Sound of Clarion theie agayne went to the Brydge, and there dined, spendyng the rest of the daie in Sportes and Plaies, the Freers of Saincte Augustine doeyng the Plaie of the Knyghtes of Brystowe, makynge a greate Fire at night on Kynwulph Hyll.

*   *   *

New bridges were not built every day, and the opening of this one had been a local event of the first importance. Hence the appearance of the foregoing article in *Felix Farley's Journal*, on 1st October, while the topic was still fresh in every one's mind, excited widespread interest and discussion. Several amateur antiquaries were thrown into

---

[1] An escutcheon on the foreheads of horses.   [2] Dwarf.
[3] Chapeaux-hats.   [4] Cithern, or guitar.   [5] Retreat.

a state of highly pleasurable curiosity, and among them
much speculation was rife as to who might be the owner
of the "old manuscript" from which the Passing of the
Bridge had been taken, and whose the identity disguised
under the signature of Dunhelmus Bristoliensis. The editor
of the paper was approached, but he could throw very
little light upon the matter, until one of his staff remembered that the packet containing the letter and the article
had been left at the offices by a youth of fifteen or sixteen,
named Chatterton, who was believed to be apprenticed
to an attorney.

If Chatterton had planned his prose description of the
inauguration of the Old Bridge in a spirit of experimental-
ism, for the purpose of gauging what sort of reception his
mediæval poems were likely to receive from the public—
and in both instances the idiom employed was almost
identically the same—he must have been gratified by the
success of his device. But if he had expected to have his
cake and eat it, hoping that his impressive pseudonym
would enable him to take his bearings and, at the same
time, to remain socially invisible, he was notably out in
his reckoning. Success has its penalties—often in a direct
ratio to its rewards—and public curiosity is more readily
aroused than suppressed.

Before he knew what was happening, he found himself
dragged into the open, and confronted by a number of
persons who, though they had swallowed whole his
ingenious gallimaufry of the processional Middle Ages—
with its modern words sandwiched in between quasi-
antique ones, and its strange alternations of spelling—
were in nowise disposed to be equally indulgent where he
himself was concerned. But the select committee, gathered,
one naturally supposes, in the editor's office, made the
fatal mistake of adopting a bullying tone. No youth of
Chatterton's age and position, they very characteristically

felt, had any right to be in possession of knowledge that was apparently denied to themselves, or, if he were in the possession of such knowledge, it was a foregone conclusion he must have acquired it by illicit means. How had he come by the ancient manuscript? they demanded. What had he got to say for himself?

He had scarcely anything to say. No surer method could have been contrived for curbing his tongue or putting him on his guard. For while he resented their attitude towards him, he found, having much to conceal, that opposition and mistrust were not nearly so difficult to stand up against as sympathetic understanding might have been. All his innate rebelliousness leapt instantly into a posture of self-defence. He became, and with his looks it was a simple matter, coldly and unapproachably proud. He refused to answer a single question they asked. By now he was used to being in a minority of one.

Finding that high-handedness was not advancing their cause, the learned gentleman assumed a milder and more conciliating aspect. Then, and then only, he told them, grudgingly, and in as few words as possible, that he was in the habit of transcribing old manuscripts for a gentleman by whom he was also employed to write love poems (evidently with thoughts of Baker in his mind) and this but half convincing his audience, he added that the Bridge article had been copied from one of the parchments discovered by his father in the muniment-room, over the North Porch of St. Mary Redcliff. His explanation was accepted, no further questions were put to him, and this was the story he held to unwaveringly throughout the short remainder of his life.

Yet not altogether unwaveringly. He did, if report speaks truly, on two separate occasions, make a full and open confession of his misdoings; once to a fellow apprentice, one of those who often came round to Lambert's office of an evening, a boy named John Rudhall; and again, later on, to Barrett. But both admissions turned out to be abortive in their results. Rudhall remained passive and took no action at the time, and Barrett, having reasons of his own for doing so, ignored all that had been said and went on exactly as before.

The Rudhall confession happened directly after the printing of the description of the Old Bridge, and was obviously the effect of reaction. Chatterton began to be afraid that he would be forced to produce the original manuscript from which "The Account," as he called it, had been taken, and therefore, yielding to a sudden impulse, he confided to Rudhall that no such manuscript existed, and that he had concocted the article himself. He also, it is said, produced a new piece of parchment, about the size of half a sheet of foolscap paper, and demonstrated to Rudhall how it could be doctored to give it a genuine, mellowed antique appearance. And apparently not satisfied even then that he had convinced the other, he went to the length of writing on the parchment several words, if not lines, in what Rudhall afterwards defined as "characters totally unlike English," and which he himself did not understand. But still Rudhall kept his counsel, even after Chatterton, possibly repenting of his lapse into a too unguarded frankness, had quarrelled with and broken away from him.

It is quite conceivable that the incident actually occurred. The one doubtful factor is, however, that it should have been passed over for so long in silence. For nothing was heard of any confession until years after Chatterton's death, not until, in point of fact, that biographically fruitful period when a great many young men, who had known and been known by the poet, were eagerly importuned by Sir Herbert Croft, Dean Milles, and others, for any personal reminiscences and scraps of

information they might chance to possess relating to the
early Bristol days. And then most of the young men being
at least potential writers, and looking back and recalling
—as in the cases of Thistlethwaite and Rudhall—past
animosities and rivalries, the temptation to improve on
truth, to add a little here and deduct a little there, to give
it sundry twists and embellishments, must have been
almost too strong to resist. They remembered Chatterton,
as one of their circle—Thomas Capel—has described him,
with "a dreariness in his look, and a wildness, attended
by a visible contempt for others." And now at last they
had the field to themselves.

The Barrett affair goes deeper, rests on a firmer basis,
and is in every respect far more significant. At the time
of its happening, Chatterton was regularly supplying the
future historian of Bristol with material for his great work;
faked deeds and civic records; amplifications of existing
maps of the city; imaginary plans and drawings of the
demolished Norman castle; descriptions of churches and
religious institutions, some of them authentic enough,
others, as for instance, St. Baldwyn's Chapelle, in Baldwyn
Street, the Chapel of St. Mary Magdalen, in Earl Godwyn's
day, and Seyncte Austin's Chapelle—"with its aunciantrie
and nice carvellynge"—purely apocryphal, yet all alleged
to be the spoils of Mr. Canynges' treasure-chest.

In the ordinary course of things, Barrett was not much
interested in Chatterton's poetry, that is unless it were so
extravagantly garnished with archaic words as to be
practically unintelligible, and might thus be included in
his forthcoming book as a literary curiosity of bygone days.
But Chatterton did succeed in drawing his attention to the
Battle of Hastings, one of the longest and earliest of the
Rowley Poems, which, according to its title-page, was
"wrote by Turgot the Monk, a Saxon, in the Tenth
Century"—in spite of the somewhat disconcerting fact

that the battle was not fought until the latter half of the eleventh century—"and translated by Thomas Rowlie, a parish preeste of St. John's, in the City of Bristol, in the year 1465."

The poem comprised fifty-six ten line heroic stanzas, the lines alternately rhyming, closing with a couplet. A further unfinished stanza of four lines was added, with the endorsement: "The remainder of the poem I have not been happy enough to meet with."

A detailed account of *Battle of Hastings* will presently be given in the first part of the chapter devoted to the Rowley Poems. The one feature that Barrett noticed about it was that it was set down in Chatterton's hand-writing, and he instantly demanded to be shown the original manuscript from which it had been transcribed. Then, for the second time, Chatterton momentarily lost his mental balance. Either he was beginning to tire of the elaborate web of deception he had spun between Barrett and himself; for in *Battle of Hastings*, realizing that Rowley could not be expected to have an inside knowledge of an event that had taken place nearly four hundred years before his birth, the poet, with his usual ready adapt-ability, had invented the Saxon, Turgot, to act as a sort of connecting link between the two epochs, carrying dis-simulation to such a hitherto unequalled pitch of virtuosity that, in this instance, he was, in effect, presenting an imitation of an imitation; or he had reached a stage when he felt that the small and infrequent sums of money he received for his brilliant archæological improvisations were a very inadequate return for the labour entailed in writing them up and making them sound credible. But whatever his reasons, at this juncture, he made it perfectly plain to Barrett that *Battle of Hastings* was, from first to last, his own creation, adding—as he had done at the time of the Bridge affair—that he had written it for a friend.

Yet Barrett, by implication, by saying as little as he could, by letting the whole matter slide, refused to be persuaded. Manifestly it was not in his own interest to allow himself to be made the recipient of any embarrassing disclosures, which might shake his faith in Chatterton and necessitate the elimination of certain attractive ingredients in his *History*. Therefore, he affected what he probably intended to be a Machiavellian obtuseness, complacently bided his time, and then, after a safe interval had elapsed, pressed for the conclusion of the poem. By now, if not even before, Chatterton, always a shrewd judge of character, had measured to the fraction of an inch the moral stature of the man with whom he had to deal. Foreseeing that further protestation would be a waste of breath, and taking the line of least resistance, he eventually produced the poem in full—still with the same title-page—still purporting to be the work of Turgot, translated by Rowley in 1465. Barrett accepted the offering without comment, and the incident was closed.

Much gratuitous abuse has been heaped upon the poet —particularly by his biographers of the last century, a period when writers were only too eager to abandon their subjects and indulge in irrelevant exhibitions of self-righteousness—because now and then he stooped to take a few miserable shillings under false pretences, and he has been consistently represented as a creature devoid of all decent scruples, incapable of telling the same tale twice in the same manner, or of running a straight course for more than a yard at a time.

But, in this instance, were the pretences quite so false as they seemed? Or were they pretences at all? Barrett was a fully qualified surgeon, a man of some consequence in the city of Bristol, and, approximately, twenty years older than his young protégé. After what had been revealed to him in regard to *Battle of Hastings*, can it be seriously

contended that his credulity was anything more than a
mere equivocation, or that Chatterton's odd scraps of
pocket-money were not, in one sense at any rate, legiti-
mately earned?

*   *   *

One immediate effect of the publicity gained by the
article in *Felix Farley's Journal* was the broadening out
of Chatterton's social horizon. Formerly his circle of
acquaintance, which had grown rapidly while he had been
at Lambert's, had been—with the notable exception of a
young man named William Smith, the son of a well-to-do
brewer—confined to other youths of his own age and
position in life, all of them, like himself, apprentices.

But now, through the agency of Smith, who brought
him to the notice of George Symes Catcott, and the Rev.
Alexander Catcott, Vicar of Temple Church, the former
of whom introduced him to his partner, Henry Burgum,
and still more momentously to William Barrett, the whole
circumstances of his life underwent a radical and perma-
nent change.

George Catcott was a fussy, superficial, scatter-brained
little man, with a long upper-lip, a slight impediment in
his speech, and eyebrows that were perpetually arched
in an expression of rather plaintive surprise. He came to
be known as "Rowley's midwife," and he had a mind
that hopped about from one bright object to another, like
a jackdaw. He could not bear the idea of being left out of
anything. Whatever was happening in the city he always
desired to be at the centre of it—raised, if possible, a little
above the crowd. It was one of his boasts that his library
contained no book under a hundred years old, and he
professed a profound admiration for the reputed writings
of Charles I, asserting that he knew them—the *Icon
Basilike*, one supposes—off by heart. So insatiable was his

thirst for local notoriety that, a year before the New
Bridge was completed, he cheerfully paid five guineas for
the privilege of riding his horse over the loose planks
which had been temporarily laid down, in order that he
might claim to have been the first person to cross from one
side to the other. On another occasion he gave the same
sum for having himself hauled by ropes and pulleys up
the steeple of St. Nicholas's Church, so that he might lay
two pewter plates, engraved with his name—he was a
pewterer by trade—under the topmost stone. Neither of
these feats went unrecorded by Chatterton, who provides
a neat little character sketch of his own:

> Catcott is very fond of talk and fame—
> His wish, a perpetuity of name—,
> Which to procure, a pewter altar's made,
> To bear his name and signify his trade,
> In pomp burlesqued the rising spire to head,
> To tell futurity a pewterer's dead.
> Incomparable Catcott, still pursue
> The seeming happiness thou hast in view:
> Unfinished chimnies, gaping spires complete,
> Eternal fame on oval dishes beat;
> Ride four inch bridges, clouded turrets climb,
> And bravely die—to live in after-time.

But whatever might be his private opinion of Catcott's
eccentricities, this new connection of the brothers Catcott,
the Smiths, Barrett, and Burgum, seemed to him a very
influential one, and, ambitious, quite frankly an oppor-
tunist, and tremendously intent on securing a hearing for
the Rowley Poems, he worked it for all it was worth. He
was intelligent, he had manners infinitely superior to his
obscure origin, his voice was singularly charming and
ingratiating when he cared to make it so, he knew by

instinct the soft spots of his victims, and could flatter
as adroitly as he could flay alive, he was manly and
self-possessed beyond his years; and at first it looked
as if he had definitely found his feet, the Bristol
bigwigs being so beglamoured by his personality and
achievements that they were only too willing to accept
him at his own valuation and to eat tamely out of his
hand.

For a while all went well. Barrett had found an amanu-
ensis in a thousand; indeed, to him, it was doubtful
whether such another existed in the world. In his dusty,
pedantic, Molière-ish way, he scratched his bushy wig
with a long thin forefinger, and worked himself up into
solemn transports. The boy had been dropped from the
clouds by a beneficent Providence for no other purpose
than to assist him in his labours. Whenever he was at a
loss, whenever he got stuck in any portion of his book,
lo! his heaven-sent helper obligingly flew to his rescue,
furnishing, with the most exquisite and unfailing sense of
rightness, just those archæological tit-bits which alone
could release his congested faculties and cause them to roll
smoothly onwards as though on greased wheels.

No wonder that the historian considered himself as
singularly blessed, nor yet—for his mind worked slowly—
that, two years after Chatterton's death, and seven years
before his own ill-fated *History* issued from the Press, we
should find him writing to Dr. Ducarel: "No one ever
surely had such good fortune as myself in procuring MSS.
and ancient deeds to help me in investigating the history
and antiquities of this city."

Meanwhile, George Catcott, swerving a little from his
allegiance to the works of Charles the Martyr to those
of Thomas Rowley, the fifteenth-century priest—dates
meant a great deal to him, naturally, since he estimated
the value of books solely by their antiquity, and Rowley

could give King Charles nearly two hundred years; George Catcott, then, began to collect all the Rowley Poems on which he could lay his hands. That the poems might conceivably possess literary merits of their own never for an instant entered his head. He knew they were old. He believed them to be genuine. It was curiosities he was after, not inward graces of the mind.

In the early days of his association with Chatterton, the poet, mistakenly imagining that Catcott would help him to bring his work to the notice of the world, presented him with one composition after another, almost as soon as they came into being and were set down on paper; gave them freely and generously, and certainly without any thought of direct payment in return. But afterwards, realising that his hopes of practical assistance were not likely to be fulfilled, he became exceedingly averse to parting with anything, and when Catcott pestered him again and again for more "Rowleys," he put him off by saying that he had destroyed all the transcriptions that were left.

Catcott, however, did not fare badly in the end. He saved up carefully all the poems he had already received and, after the boy was dead, he was one of those people who shamefully exploited poor Mrs. Chatterton, persuading her out of her dire necessity to part with a further supply of manuscripts for the paltry sum of five pounds.[1] Thus having to all intents and purposes amassed a complete set of the Rowley Poems, he set up a "corner" in Rowley-Chatterton manuscripts in which, for the rest of his life, he drove a very profitable trade.

Contrasted with Catcott's reprehensible treatment of Chatterton and his work, there is an added irony in a bill, written in red ink, that the poet made out, but probably never presented, and which was assuredly never paid.

[1] *The True Chatterton*, by John H. Ingram, pp. 123–4.

Mr. G. Catcott.

			£	s.	d.
To the Executors of T. Rowley.		Dr.			
To the pleasure received in reading his historic works	. . . .		5	5	0
To the pleasure received in reading his poetic works	. . . .		5	5	0
			£10	10	0

For some inexplicable reason, a harsher and more in-discriminating light has always been shed on Chatterton's shortcomings than on those of the three men, Barrett, Catcott, and Burgum—none of them over forty years of age, despite the fact that they are so frequently referred to as the "Bristol Elders"—who exercised so strong and, in many respects, so baneful an influence over him during the latter days of his Bristol life. Chatterton received no salary at Lambert's, and was entirely dependent upon such trifling sums of pocket-money as his mother could provide, and the equally negligible tips that Barrett reluctantly doled out to him from time to time. The discomfort of going about among men of ample means, often without a penny in his pocket, especially to one of Chatterton's proud and self-reliant nature, need not be emphasised. He longed to earn money quickly for himself. Above all else, he longed to gain public recognition for his work— the one thing he believed in and for which he was willing to make any sacrifices. Never at any period, even when he was struggling single-handed against an adversity such as few of his age could ever have been called upon to encounter, did his faith either in himself or in his claim to immortality waver or die down. In his lonely London garret he died undefeated, convinced that though he found the world too ugly and too difficult a place to endure any longer, his work would live. In him the dreamer and the realist were not warring and disruptive forces, but complemental parts of the same entity, as light and darkness, though the antitheses of each other, may be the complemental portions of a single day. He could, whenever the impulse moved him, shut out actualities and withdraw himself completely into his secondary world of the Middle Ages. No one can read the Rowley Poems without being struck by their detachment, their inherent nobility, their insistence upon those ideals of chivalry and honour—*sans peur et sans reproche*—which were commonly held to have constituted themselves the prevailing creed of a bygone golden age. While he is engrossed by his knights and princely merchant benefactors, his Kings and priestly poets, he is curiously purified, exalted and remote; and it is only when he comes down from the heights into the petty frets and anxieties of a normal workaday existence that the mantle of light slips from his shoulders, and he becomes, inevitably, an astute, none too scrupulous youngster, struggling for a firm foothold on the slippery earth.

And always he worked with an almost maniacal intensity, for ever waging an instinctive battle against the encroachments of time, burning, with a wanton disregard for the future, the flame that leapt up within him, eating sparingly, sleeping hardly at all, consumed with impatience to set down the tumultuous thoughts and images that seethed to the surface of his brain. Underneath the professions of admiration made to him by Barrett and Catcott, he knew very well that there was more than a hint of patronage. They were incapable of appreciating what he did; they looked upon him as a clever, promising boy —nothing more than just that. For them he was a new sensation. He was useful, too. They were ready enough to believe in Rowley, but they could not be induced to believe in him.

And so, except in his moments of creative ecstasy, a

confirmed sceptic at the age of sixteen, corrupted maybe, consciously or unconsciously, by the get-on-or-get-out commercial spirit of the city in which he lived, with no one to help or direct him, he matched his wits against those of his antagonists and fought them gamely on their own ground.

But what can be said of the antagonists themselves? Surely little to their credit. They chafed under no serious social disabilities, were comfortably free from economic pressure, and each had found his own particular draught-proof niche in life. There was no shadow of excuse for the manner in which they treated the poet, inflating him with false promises, manipulating him now this way, now that, in any direction best suited to their own purposes, keeping their eyes closed to certain irregularities, and, even though it be frankly admitted that he had already embarked upon his dubious courses before he met them, Barrett, at any rate, was not slow in deciding that there should be no turnings back, no inconvenient recantations, but a steady pursuance of deception to the last stroke of the pen.

The manipulations, the aidings and abettings, the graspings and general greedinesses may not have endured for long—nor was Chatterton ever the sort of docile person to be led indefinitely by the nose. But when accusations of knavery are hurtling loosely through the air, let the elders also take their share. The honours—or dishonours—were fairly evenly distributed on either side.

*   *   *

Of this outwardly respectable, but inwardly shady, triumvirate, Burgum was by far the most worthy member. Save by association, it is perhaps unjust to include him in it at all. For he was less sophisticated than the others and, moreover, had no personal axe to grind. A native of Gloucester, and in very poor circumstances when he first arrived in Bristol, he seems, notwithstanding the deficiencies of his education, and a rough, though good-natured vulgarity, which not infrequently made him the butt of his more cultured companions, to have prospered in a material sense, and undoubtedly his was the controlling mind behind the successful pewtering business he ran in conjunction with Catcott at this time. His own tastes were musical rather than literary. He avowed a great partiality for Handel. And, as E. H. W. Meyerstein tells us, subscribed to quartets by Kotzwara and concertos by Thomas Norris of Oxford. His music-sheets were bound in impressive volumes of red morocco, with his full name, Henry Burgum, stamped in gold lettering on the covers, and he showed himself a generous and enthusiastic supporter of the city's musical activities. Like most self-made men he was exceedingly sensitive on the subject of his lowly birth and early beginnings, and lost no opportunity of asserting that there was nothing in the least equivocal about his origin. One day, therefore, Chatterton called upon him and, with an air of the most engaging innocence, told him that, though he might not be aware of it, he was related to several of the noblest families in England. From the Redcliff parchments, whose potentialities were evidently as inexhaustible as the magical virtues of Aladdin's lamp, and from other authoritative sources as well, the boy declared that he had carefully compiled Burgum's pedigree, and had it, all completed and in order, at that very moment at home.

That it was a truly remarkable coincidence that Mr. Canynges' Cofre should contain allusions to his own family of all others, and he not even primarily a Bristol man, does not seem to have occurred to the simple-minded pewterer. After all, he may have reflected that Fortune had always showered her choicest gifts upon him, and have come to the sensible conclusion that goddesses should be

c

propitiated rather than rudely cross-examined. He rose
to the bait almost before it had touched the water, expressed a desire to see the pedigree at once, and a few days
later Chatterton returned, bringing with him an ordinary
school exercise-book in which was written a long and
detailed account of the other's aristocratic lineage,
headed: "An account of the Family of De Bergham, from
the Norman Conquest to this time; collected from original
records, Tournament Rolls, and the Heralds of March
and Garter Records, by T. Chatterton."

Whatever Chatterton set his hand to he brought off
with tremendous *éclat*. Heraldry, so far as the actual
business of draughtsmanship went, he never entirely
succeeded in mastering, though he is said to have studied
it under the tuition of Thomas Palmer, who, it will be
remembered, worked at the jeweller's in the same building
as Lambert's office, and whose occupation it was to
engrave coats of arms and heraldic devices on silver-ware;
but in the letterpress he was insolently sure of his medium,
and the document, with its Latin epitaphs and antique
French mottoes (these latter translated by Barrett who,
unless they were handed to him separately and wholly
detached from their context, could hardly have helped
realising that he was giving his sanction to a hoax upon his
friend), its plausible references and copious marginal
notes, was a miracle of misdirected ingenuity, and might
easily have convinced a wiser man than Burgum.

Burgum was enraptured. The one fly in the ointment
of his happiness had been removed. Henceforward, when
he had reason to believe that veiled innuendos were being
levelled at his ancestry and breeding, he could quite
conclusively prove that he was descended from Simon de
Seyncte Lys, *alias* Senliz, who had come over to England
with William the Conqueror, and married Matilda,
daughter of Waltheof, Earl of Northumberland,

Northampton, and Huntingdom, of Burgham Castle, Northumberland. Words could not express the exultation he felt, and out of the fulness of his gratitude, he rewarded the author of his ennoblement with what John Dix aptly calls "the plebian remuneration of five shillings."

At the same time, it may be doubted whether Chatterton, knowing his man, had expected to receive so much. Five shillings might appear a small return for all his pains and industry, but to him it was a real godsend. And now he began to speculate as to the advisability of tapping the mine a little farther. The original pedigree had belied its title, inasmuch as it did *not* extend to the present day. So, after about a fortnight had elapsed, he reappeared with another exercise-book, tracing the De Burghams down to the reign of James II—beyond which, he most likely felt, it would be inexpedient to probe. In this second instalment he included one of the Rowley Poems, *The Romaunte of the Cnyghte*, claiming that it had been written by John De Burgham, "the greatest ornament of his age," adding by way of an introductory note: "To give you an idea of the poetry of the age, take the following piece, wrote about 1320."

The poem, beginning

> *The Sunne ento Vyrgyne was gotten,*
> *The floureys al arounde onspryngede,*

he judged, not unnaturally, to be above the pewterer's somewhat primitive understanding, and thus he thoughtfully provided a longer and more modernised version, in order that none of the finer shades of the fourteenth century poet's achievement should be missed by his less gifted descendant.

Once more Burgum reacted according to plan, and a supplementary five shillings was brought forth. And there

the matter rested until Burgum, at some future date, be-
thought himself that it might be as well to submit his
pedigree to the College of Heralds, not because he was
under any apprehension as to its genuineness, but simply
to have its contents officially ratified. To his lasting and
bitter mortification, he was told that the whole thing—
Latin epitaphs, French mottoes, Norman knights notwithstanding—was a fabrication from beginning to end. What
happened then we have no means of knowing, but perhaps
by that time the culprit had escaped to Shoreditch, to
Holborn, or even farther afield to a region where the
wrath or the indifference of men were alike powerless to
touch him, and where his ardent, much-vexed spirit had at
length found rest.

Genealogy was, of course, a bye-product of Rowleyism,
which accounts for the ascendancy it had gained over his
mind. His mythical researches did not stop short at
Burgum. In the July of the ensuing year we find him
writing to his relative, Mr. Stephens of Salisbury: "When
you quarter your Arms, in the Mullet, say, Or a Fess Vert
by the name of Chatterton," (an exhortation that must
sorely have perplexed the good man, who was a breeches-
maker), "I trace your Family from Fitz-Stephen Son of
Stephen, Earl of Aumerle in 1095 Son of Odo Earl of
Bloys & Lord of Holderness."

And yet again, there is the heraldic joke he played upon
Miss Martha Catcott. Miss Catcott, an elderly spinster,
familiarly known to the horde of Smiths and Catcotts as
"Aunt Martha," was at first greatly attracted to young
Chatterton, whom she saw constantly at her brothers'
house, for George and the Rev. Alexander lived together,
and it is very probable that Aunt Martha kept house for
them. But on one occasion, feeling herself obliged to
reprimand the poet for some misdoing or other, her well-
intentioned interference offended him and, by way of

retaliation, he wrote her a "scolding letter," wherein was enclosed her coat of arms, surrounded by a garter, and surmounted by a "queer-looking" flower, tinted ·gules, above which was a scroll upon which was inscribed "The Rose of Virginity."

After this passage of arms the old lady's affection perceptibly declined, and whenever his name was mentioned in her presence, she shook her head, pursed her lips, and remarked that he was "a sad wag of a boy."

*   *   *

Taking them all in all, those months of October and November, in the year 1768, were full and eventful ones. New interests had sprung up about him; he had now two distinct circles of friends—the Barrett, Catcott, Burgum *coterie*—and the "Juvenile Club" composed of eager, questing youths, whose tastes and enthusiasms were the same as his own, and amidst whom he aspired to move, as he had done in the days of his childhood among the small boys of Redcliff Hill, as an acknowledged leader. He still had his recurrent spells of black and incommunicable depression, of cynicism, of disbelief—never disbelief in himself, but in the external world around him. But Rowley was making rapid and heartening progress, he had habituated himself to life in Lambert's kitchen; and, all things considered, he was not too unhappy.

To quote his sister:

His ambition increased daily. His spirits were rather uneven, sometimes so gloom'd that for many days he would say but little, and that by constraint. When in spirits he would enjoy his rising fame; confident of his advancement, he would promise my mother and me should be partakers in his success.

CHAPTER V

IN SEARCH OF A PUBLISHER

(1768–1769)

UNTIL close on the Christmas of 1768, he drifted with the tide of events, working tirelessly as ever, but taking no active measures to secure the publication of his mediæval poems. His older friends he watched speculatively, out of the corner of his eye, debating within himself whether or no any practical aid or encouragement might haply be looked for from them; but, for the most part, he sat all day in the office, received his youthful colleagues there in the evenings, wrote whenever his master's back was turned and spent his Sundays out in the open air, roving the countryside, taking with him a sketch-block and a pencil, so that he might make drawings of any church, ruined building, or ancient landmark that happened to attract his attention. Now and then William Smith went with him, and although Chatterton was wont to be reserved concerning his Rowley compositions, there were times when he would throw secrecy to the winds and talk openly and enthusiastically to his companion.

"He was always very fond of walking in the fields," Smith wrote to Jacob Bryant, in after years, "particularly in Redcliffe meadows; and of talking about these manuscripts and reading them there. *Come*, he would say, *you and I will take a walk in the meadow. I have got the cleverest thing for you, that ever was. It is worth half a crown merely to have a sight of it; and to hear me read it to you.* When we were arrived at the place proposed, he would produce his parchment; shew it, and read it to me. There was one spot in particular, full in view of the church, in which he always seemed to take a peculiar delight. He

70

would frequently lay himself down, fix his eyes upon the church; and seem as if he were in a kind of extasy or trance. Then, on a sudden and abruptly, he would tell me, *that steeple was burnt down by lightning; that was the place where they formerly acted plays:* (meaning, if I remember right, what is now called the Parade). I recollect very assuredly that he had a parchment in his hand at the very time, when he gave me this description: but whether he read this history out of that parchment, I am not certain."

Once more, as at school, life had fined itself down into a level, monotonous routine.

By the middle of December, if not before, his "tragycal enterlude" of *Ælla* was completed; a major work of the first importance, in which he scaled imaginative heights he was never quite to reach again, except perhaps, within a smaller compass, in the consummate beauty and simplicity of his swan song, *An Excelente Balade of Charitie*, produced after months of clever ephemeral hack work—at a time of great agony of mind—to form a fitting apex to the whole Rowley edifice.

But with the completion of *Ælla*, and his own consciousness of its transcendent qualities, the black dog of spiritual impatience which haunted him intermittently throughout his childhood, boyhood, and adolescence, until finally it hounded him out of existence altogether, once more started growling and snapping at his heels. Now that the fever of creativeness had left him, he stood shivering on the brink of actuality again, and things reverted, stripped of the factitious curves and softnesses that had lately transfigured them, into their normal angular, three-dimensional shapes.

And suddenly he saw his life stretched out before him as bleak and cheerless as the winter's landscape. Nothing could be hoped for from Barrett, Catcott, or Burgum; of that he was absolutely sure. Barrett lent him books, such as Thomas Benson's *Vocabularium Anglo-Saxonicum*, and

Stephen Skinner's *Etymologicon Linguae Anglicannae*, books he needed badly, which might otherwise have been difficult to come by; Catcott and Burgum could always be counted upon to give him loads of platitudinous advice; and all three set themselves out to exploit him in their various ways.

Now he despised himself for having been even temporarily misled by their attitude towards him—or not altogether that, for he had seen through their pretences of friendship and approbation from the very outset of his relations with them—but for seeming to truckle under, for appearing to accept their compliments as delivered in all sincerity, for actually allowing himself to feel a certain complacent satisfaction in being lifted on to social eminences that were, admittedly, higher than those to which his poverty and humble parentage might be said to have entitled him.

Yielding to their flatteries he had come near to losing the only personal possessions he held in any esteem; his proper pride, his freedom of action, his independence of mind. What, after all, could Barrett, Catcott, or Burgum do for him that was worth the sacrifice of these? Barrett was an absurdly credulous, muddle-headed, would-be pedant; the other two just empty prating windbags—with nothing solid, nothing real, behind them—always excepting, of course, their wealth.

Not from them, but from within himself, must advancement come. One can see the workings of his mind in *Ælla* when the Saxon warrior, called into battle on his wedding-morn, steels himself against his bride's entreaties that he will forswear his duty and his vocation and remain with her. "Yet I will be myself." "Yet I must be myself"—the cry is reiterated with increasing vehemence throughout the swift unfolding of the parting scene.

And here was *Ælla*, a hostage to fortune, a weapon that might be used to carve the way to fame and recognition, lying, all brave and shining, like an untried lance ready to be carried into the lists. He decided that he would submit the play, and some of the shorter Rowley pieces, to James Dodsley, of Pall Mall, one of the most fashionable and distinguished publishers of the day; and on 21st December he wrote and dispatched his letter.

> BRISTOL. *December* 21, 1768.
>
> SIR,
>   I take this method to acquaint you that I can procure copies of several ancient Poems; and an Interlude, perhaps the oldest dramatic piece extant; wrote by one Rowley, a Priest in Bristol, who lived in the reigns of Henry VIth and Edward IVth.—If these Pieces will be of service to you, at your command, copies shall be sent to you, by
>
> > Your most obedient Servant,
> >
> > > D. B.
>
> Please to direct for D. B. to be left with Mr. Thomas Chatterton, Redclift Hill, Bristol.
> For Mr. J. Dodsley, Bookseller, Pall Mall, London.

It is not authentically known whether any reply was received from the publisher. Since no trace of an answer can be found, most biographers have assumed that the offer was disregarded and passed over in silence. John H. Ingram, however—inclined on occasion to be a somewhat didactic writer—in his book *The True Chatterton*, remarks:

> ... the biographers not having a reply before them, surmise that none was ever sent. This is most improbable. In a letter of Chatterton to his relation, Stephens, of Salisbury, quoted later he says, "My next correspondent of note is Dodsley, whose collection of modern and antique poems are in every library."

He does say so. But that was ever the poet's way. For him the fact that *he* had written to Dodsley would be all-sufficing. When things were hanging fire, or going badly for him, he was always at the greatest pains to create a

c *

surface-atmosphere of bustle, achievement, and success, as
a proof of which nothing can be more poignant to the
reader, who knows both sides of the story, than the light-
ness, the gaiety, the boundless self-confidence of the letters
written home to his mother and sister from London, while
all the time he was engaged in a life or death struggle
against incalculable odds, thwarted and checkmated at
every turn, and playing most gallantly a losing game.
Besides, when writing to Mr. Stephens, as may easily be
discerned between the lines, particularly in regard to that
gentleman's *soi-disant* Norman lineage, his sole object is,
quite unmistakably, to impress. Moreover, if Dodsley had
received his advances favourably, it is scarcely feasible
that he should have waited over seven weeks, as he
certainly did, before taking the matter up; nor would he
have felt compelled to repeat his offer a second time,
enlarging upon it, and tricking it out in still more attractive
guise. For, on 15th February, he wrote to Dodsley again.

BRISTOL. *Feb.* 15, 1769.

SIR,
        Having intelligence that the Tragedy of Ælla was in
being, after a long and laborious search, I was so happy as to
attain a sight of it. Struck with the beauties of it, I endeavoured
to obtain a copy to send you; but the present possessor absolutely denies to give me one, unless I give him a Guinea for a
consideration. As I am unable to procure such a sum, I made
search for another copy, but unsuccessfully.—Unwilling such a
beauteous Piece should be lost, I have made bold to apply to
you: several Gentlemen of learning who have seen it, join
with me in praising it.—I am far from having any mercenary
views for myself in this affair, and, was I able, would print it
on my own risque. It is a perfect Tragedy, the plot clear, the
language spirited, and the Songs (interspersed in it) are flow-
ing, poetical, and elegantly simple. The similes judiciously
applied, and though wrote in the reign of Henry VIth, not
inferior to many of the present age. If I can procure a copy,
with or without the gratification, it shall immediately be sent

to you. The motive that actuates me to do this, is, to convince
the world that the Monks (of whom some have so despicable
an opinion) were not such blockheads, as generally thought, and
that good poetry might be wrote in the dark days of super-
stition, as well as in these more enlightened ages. An immediate
answer will oblige me. I shall not receive your favour as for
myself, but as your agent.

I am, Sir,

Your most obedient Servant,

T. CHATTERTON,

P.S.—My reason for concealing my name, was, lest my
Master (who is now out of Town) should see my letters and
think I neglected his business.

Direct for me on Redclift Hill.

Enclosed in the letter was part of the speech of *Ælla* to
his Saxon soldiers, exhorting them to courage and endurance on the battle-field, beginning:

"Ye Christians, do as worthy of the name, These spoilers of
our holy houses slea,"

to which was added a further explanatory note:

"The whole contains about 1,000 lines. If it should not
suit you, I should be obliged to you if you would calculate
the expenses of printing it, as I will endeavour to publish it
by subscription on my own account.

For *Mr. James Dodsley*,
    Bookseller,
      Pall Mall,
        London.

These two letters, subsequently recovered on the
clearing out of Dodsley's counting-house, were first
published in 1813, in John Britton's *History of Redcliffe
Church*. They tell their own story. Tactics of so clumsy
and transparent a nature were bound to end in failure.
It has been contended that the maturity of Chatterton's
poetry gives him the right to be regarded as a man already
in the possession of the plenitude of his intellectual

powers, rather than as a raw schoolboy who had still a great deal to learn about life. Any such assertion is manifestly unfair. For the precocious mind, especially when tinged by genius, is a strangely variable instrument, full of seemingly unaccountable inconsistencies and reversions to type, and resembling a newly broken male voice, in that it will steadily keep to the lower register for the greater part of the time, only to leap upwards into a shrill, childish treble, just when one least expects it to do so, and always with the most disconcerting results. In his dealings with Dodsley, Chatterton showed himself to be even younger than his accredited sixteen years. The mystery piled on mystery, the obvious concealments and circumlocutions, the crafty yet ingenuous demand for a preliminary guinea—notwithstanding that this latter may merely have been designed to safeguard himself against the possible loss of his manuscript which had, of course, all been carefully written out by hand—were likely to weigh heavily in his disfavour in the eyes of an experienced man of the world; whereas even if the flimsy fabric he had built up had been capable of remaining upright for an instant, the final crass stupidity of that utterly damning postscript must have brought the entire contraption fluttering to the ground.

In the fatal postscript there are evidences of an uneasy conscience, of an urge towards self-vindication, not so much on moral grounds perhaps, as on those of common expediency; but by this time he had become so involved in a fine-drawn system of false trails, blind-alleys, and fantastic feats of legerdemain in regard to Rowley and himself, that had he been a hundred times more astute than he was, it would have been almost impossible for him to extricate himself. His one chance now was to stick to the road he had chosen, push his way stubbornly onwards, and hope for the best.

The best did not happen. Nothing happened. Once more he was up against a dead-end. Expectation slowly faded, merging into that gnawing sense of helplessness and frustration which, of all the trials that continually beset him, he found the hardest to endure. Dodsley would have been an ideal publisher for the Rowley Poems; he had brought out Percy's *Reliques* and made a success of them; he was a man of discernment and some pretension to scholarship—though never so potent a personality as his brother Robert, the poet, dramatist, and intimate friend of Doctor Johnson, who had been in partnership with James and was the original founder of the business—and, even making allowances for the very questionable manner in which Chatterton's work had been placed before him, it is extraordinary that he should have read the excerpt from *Ælla*—if, indeed, it was ever read at all—and have remained indifferent to its burning intensity, its virile, clear-cut romanticism, and its almost perfect stage craftsmanship.

Yet so it was. During the last two weeks of February and well into March, Chatterton waited for some reassuring response, until, eventually, he was compelled to acknowledge that his efforts had miscarried. He was disappointed, discomfited, sharply at loggerheads with life again, but he did not utterly despair. Baulked in one direction, his inexhaustible energy sought an outlet elsewhere. He cast exploratory glances into the future, and presently a new, and even more ambitious scheme presented itself to his mind.

CHAPTER VI

IN SEARCH OF A PATRON

(1769)

HAVING failed to arouse Dodsley's interest in his work, Chatterton now decided that the surest method of establishing himself was to seek the patronage of some rich and influential man of letters. His choice immediately fell upon Horace Walpole, and there were several excellent reasons why this name should have come uppermost in his thoughts. For Walpole had converted his villa of Strawberry Hill into a miniature Gothic castle—"lean windows fattened with rich saints"; as a matter of fact, the process of conversion was still in progress; the Grand Parlour, the Library, the Picture Gallery, and the Cloister were already in being, but the Great North Bedchamber was not added until 1770.

With Walpole the word Gothic possessed almost talismanic properties; he lived and breathed in an atmosphere of stucco-mediævalism, seasoned by moth-like dartings and curvetings into the brighter light of the social world. His castle was clogged with the flotsam and jetsam of the Middle Ages; pieces of ancient armour, missals, illuminated manuscripts, rare prints, black letter volumes, medals, coins, and the famous Domenichinos, not to mention a large and heterogeneous assortment of china, snuff-boxes, miniatures, and enamels of his own time. Therefore, over such a rabid collector, the Rowley Poems might have been quite confidently expected to exercise an irresistible appeal.

Also there was a certain topographical link between the

poet and his prospective Mæcenas, Walpole having, in 1762, published in his *Anecdotes of Painting*, a copy of an old manuscript relating to an Easter Sepulchre—"well gilt with golde and a civer thereto"—which had been presented to the church of St. Mary Redcliff by William Canynges in the year 1470. The document was full of those quaintnesses and oddities that Walpole adored, as, for example:

Item, An image of God Almighty rising out of the same sepulchre, with all the ordinance that 'longeth thereto.
Item, Thereto 'longeth Heaven, made of timber and stained clothes.
Item, Hell made of timber, and ironwork thereto, with Divels to the number of 13.
Item, 4 Knights armed, keeping the sepulchre, with their weapons in their hands.
Item, 4 payr of Angels' wings for 4 Angels, made of timber and well painted.
Item, The Fadre, the Crowns and Visage, the Ball with a Cross upon it, well gilt with find Gould.
Item, The Holy Ghosht coming out of Heaven into the sepulchre.
Item, 'Longeth to the 4 Angels 4 Chevelers.

As this same Easter Sepulchre record was used by Barrett in his *History of Bristol*, it is not improbable that it was he who first drew Chatterton's attention to Walpole's work, but however he came by it, the book certainly passed through his hands. The subject was very much his own line of country, and it is a simple matter to perceive how deep an impression the introduction of William Canynges and St. Mary Redcliff was bound to produce upon his mind, and how, by a natural sequence of ideas, he might be beguiled into drawing parallels concerning the relationship he had invented between Canynges and Rowley and that which he hoped to set up between Walpole and himself.

Nor was this all. A still more subtle and inescapable

bond of union existed, and one that touched even more closely on the Rowley preserves. Five years earlier Walpole had been instrumental in bringing before the public a "Gothic Romance," entitled *The Castle of Otranto*, described on its title-page as "translated by William Marshall, Gent., from the original Italian of Onuphrio Muralto, canon of the church of St. Nicholas at Otranto," and an introduction gave a learned and sufficiently plausible account of the ancient black letter edition, published at Naples in the year 1520, from which the modernized adaptation had been made.

To-day *The Castle of Otranto* reads as if it had been flung off by David Wyndham Lewis in an access of wildly exuberant spirits. The chief purpose of the story is to inspire terror, to chill the blood, to cause the flesh to creep and the hair to stand on end. All the ingredients of horror are poured forth in a lush profusion; an isolated mediæval castle, set in the midst of a sinister landscape; dark winding passages, underground cellars, heavy doors that crash to without the agency of human hands; muffled groans, clanking chains, flitting supernatural figures dimly seen; a huge casque, sprouting funereal plumes, that slowly descends from nowhere and squats, like a monstrous bird of ill-omen, in the courtyard; and, as a last crowning touch of pure bathos, a statue that bleeds, not from the heart, or from any of the cardinal points of the stigmata, but from the nose!

How, in an epoch that was in many respects the most rational, discriminating, and highly civilized the European world has ever known, so crude a production—the forerunner of that cult for the eerie and mysterious which, thirty years later, was to be turned to such profitable account by Mrs. Radcliffe, in her *Romance of the Forest* and *Mysteries of Udolpho*—ever came to be taken seriously, it is difficult to conceive, unless the explanation lies in the fact that it presented an entirely new aspect of fiction. Maybe, a little wearied by too long an exposure to the glare of abstract reason, the reading public of the year 1764 were minded, by way of an antidote, to rush to the opposite extreme. Or again, *The Castle of Otranto* may just have conformed to that special standard of badness which never fails to secure for itself an enthusiastic reception in any age. But, whatever the initial causes, it achieved a very conspicuous success. The first edition was sold out shortly after publication, a second was called for, and then Walpole stepped blandly forward and confessed that William Marshall, Onuphrio Muralto, and the black letter original were merely so many theatrical properties requisitioned to heighten the general effectiveness of the scene, and that he, alone and unaided, had written the tale.

Thus, in Chatterton's eyes at any rate, the analogy between his own case and Walpole's was complete. What was sauce for the goose was sauce for the gander—or so he mistakenly supposed. Here, inevitably, was the right man for him; the one person on earth who should be capable of understanding and sympathizing with him, and to whom, had it been in his nature to be perfectly frank, he might have unburdened himself. But frankness, as it happened, was entirely outside the limits of his moral radius, and all he could hope for now was such uncertainly poised security as might ensue from an association with one who had erred in the same direction as himself, reinforced by the knowledge that, in the event of discovery and exposure overtaking him at any time, it was better to have a *tu quoque* to defend himself with than no other kind of weapon at all.

He therefore wrote to Walpole on the 25th of March:

SIR,
         Being versed a little in antiquitys, I have met with several Curious Manuscripts among which the following may

be of Service to you, in any future Edition of your truly entertaining *Anecdotes of Painting*—In correcting the Mistakes (if any) in the Notes, you will greatly oblige

Your most humble Servant,

THOMAS CHATTERTON.

Bristol, March 25th, Corn Street.
For *Horace Walpole, Esq.,*
   To be left with *Mr. Bathoe,*
               Bookseller,
                  near Exeter Change,
                  London.

Enclosed in this admirably brief and business-like communication was what might fitly be called a companion-piece to the *Mayor's Passing over the Old Bridge*, headed *The Ryse of Peyncteynge yn Englande, wroten by T. Rowleie, 1469, for Mastre Canynge*, and tricked out in the usual Rowleian dialect, wherein it was affirmed that painting had flourished in England from the earliest times, when "the Brytonnes dyd depycte themselves yn sondrie wyse, of the fourmes of the Sonne and Moone wythe the hearbe Woade," and tracing the gradual development of painting, carving, the "couneynge mystery of steineynge glasse," textile fabrics, embroideries, and heraldic devices. Nor was poetry forgotten, for a sample of the verse of the Abbott John, of St. Augustine's Minster, was also included, the Abbot himself being referred to as the first English painter in oils, and the Greatest Poet of the Age in which he lived. The whole concluded with an account of the frescoes on the walls of Mastre Canynge's house, which had been painted by one, Henrie a Thornton, "a geason depeyctor of countenances," who was held to have contrived "a most daintie and feetyve performaunce nowe ycrasede beeynge donne ynne M.CC.I."

Once again he had carried out a notable piece of work, full of minute subsidiary detail, richly suggestive of scholarship and patient research and, for all its frequent lapses into modernity and latent spuriousness, oddly impressive and attractive to read. Yet some of the "Notes," which he asks Walpole to correct, knowing quite well beforehand that, since he had fabricated all the material himself, any such correction was impossible, are even more illuminating; and the most rigid moralist could scarcely refrain from smiling at the ingenious manner in which they are designed less to elucidate Rowley than to cast a helpful beam on the poet's own ambitions and requirements.

In one of the Notes he explains that:

T. Rowlie was a Seculor Priest of St. John's in this City: his Merit as a Biographer, Historiographer is great, as a Poet still greater: some of his Pieces would do honour to Pope; and the Person under whose Patronage they may appear to the World will lay the Englishman, the Antiquary, and the Poet, under an eternal obligation.

In another he describes Canynges as:

the Founder of that noble Gothic Pile, St. Mary Redclift Church in this City; the Mæcenas of his time: one who could happily blend the Poet, the Painter, the Priest, and the Christian—perfect in each; a friend to all in distress, an honour to Bristol, and a Glory to the Church.

And finally he remarks:

I have the lives of several ancient Carvers, Painters, &c., of Antiquity, but as they all relate to Bristol, may not be of Service in a General Historie; if they may be acceptable to you, they are at your Service.

The lines attributed to the Abbot John, of St. Augustine's Minster, were:

On King Richard I

Harte of Lyone ! Shake thie Sworde,
Bare thie mortheynge steinede honde:
Quace whol Armies to the Queede,
Worke thie Wylle yn burlie bronde.

Barons here on bankers-browded,
Fyght yn Furres gaynste the Cale ;
Whilest thou ynne thonderynge Armes,
Warriketh whole Cyttyes bale.
Harte of Lyon! Sound the Beme!
Sounde ytte ynto inner Londes,
Feare flies sportinge ynne the Cleembe,
Inne thie Banner Terror Stondes.—

Walpole subsequently made two different modernized
versions of this poem; the following is taken from Volume
IV of *The Works of Horatio Walpole*, in which it appears on
page 235.

Heart of lion, shake thy sword;
Bare thy slaughter-stained hand:
Chase whole armies with thy word,
Work thy will in holy land.

Barons here, with coursers prancing,
Boldly breast the pagan host:
See, thy thund'ring arms advancing
See, they quail! Their city's lost!

Heart of lion, sound the trumpet!
Sound the charge to farmost lands!
Fear flies sporting o'er the combat;
In thy banner terror stands.

*   *   *

The letter, with its enclosures, found Walpole, not at
Strawberry Hill, which would have occasioned some
extra delay, but at his town house in Arlington Street,
and one may judge of his delight in being made the
recipient of so much gratuitous Gothic information by the
velvety complacency of his reply, sent off, it would
appear, by return of post.

ARLINGTON STREET. *March* 28, 1769.

S<small>R</small>,

    I cannot but think myself singularly obliged by a Gentleman with whom I have not the pleasure of being acquainted, when I read your very curious & kind letter, which I have this minute received. I give you a thousand thanks for it, & for the very obliging offer you make me of communicating your MSS. to me. What you have already sent me is valuable, & full of Information; but, instead of correcting you, Sr; you are far more able to correct me. I have not the happiness of understanding the Saxon language, & without your learned notes, shoud not have been able to comprehend Rowley's text.

As a second Edition of my Anecdotes was published but last year, I must not flatter myself that a third will be wanted soon; but I shall be happy to lay up any notices you will be so good as to extract for me, & send me at your leisure; for as it is uncertain when I may use them, I woud by no means borrow & detain your MSS.

Give me leave to ask you where Rowley's poems are to be found. I shoud not be sorry to print them, or at least a specimen of them, if they have never been printed.

The Abbot John's verses, that you have given me, are wonderfull for their harmony & spirit; tho there are some words I do not understand. You do not point out exactly the time when he lived, which I wish to know, as I suppose it was long before John ab Eyck's discovery of oil-painting. If so, it confirms what I had guessed, & have hinted in my Anecdotes, that oil-painting was known here much earlier than that Discovery or revival.

I will not trouble you with more questions now, Sr; but flatter myself, from the humanity & politeness you have already shown me, that you will sometimes give me leave to consult you. I hope too you will forgive the simplicity of my Direction, as you have favoured me with no other.

I am, Sr,

Yr much obliged and obedient humble Sert

H<small>OR</small> W<small>ALPOLE</small>.

P.S.—Be so good as to direct to Mr. Walpole in Arlington Street.

This is, of course, the quintessential Walpole; easy, polished, compact of small literary airs and graces, and tinctured throughout by a deference intended not in the least to detract from the sense of his own importance, but to add, if possible, a further lustre to it. From the context of the letter, one visualizes the man and his surroundings; the sombre, low-toned library in Arlington Street, where the warmth of the fire draws out a vague pervasive perfume of cedar-wood and morocco leather bindings; the atmosphere of quiet, studious repose; the solitary seated figure of the writer, bending over his task; the pen skimming lightly, with smooth, unbroken movement from line to line; the little self-satisfied pauses; the quick egotistical flicks of the wrist; and on the pen races once more, to an accompaniment of soft feline purrings of gratified achievement. Mr. Walpole is taking his fill of æsthetic enjoyment, rolling life round on his tongue, and finding its savour wholly exquisite.

*   *   *

Any attempt to portray Chatterton's rapturous excitement at the manner in which his overtures had been received must needs fall wide of the actual truth. A short while ago he had been plunged into the profoundest gloom, there had been no friendly light, no glimmer of hope, only a crushing sense of thick invisible walls, rising on every side of him, cutting him off from the outside world; and now—miraculously—all was transformed. The infallibility of his own genius he had still left unquestioned, that was fixed and immutable as the tides, the seasons, and the stars in their courses; but the lesser part of him, the material, earthbound part, had been imprisoned in darkness, awaiting the hand of a deliverer. In Walpole he veritably believed he had found that deliverer, and his spirits, ever susceptible of violent alternations, bounded dizzily upwards at the first foreshadowings of release.

No doubt there were rejoicings on Redcliff Hill, and some pardonable swaggering and spreading of plumage before the Bristol Elders and the rival apprentices. And characteristically eager to embrace to their fullest extent his new-found opportunities, as well as failing to discern that note of polite dismissal-for-the-moment which Walpole had sounded towards the close of his letter, he wrote again to Arlington Street, forwarding another instalment of the *Historie of Peyncters yn England*, supplemented by verses said to have been written by two Saxon bishops of the Sixth Century, Ecca and Elmar (translated by Rowley), some additional stanzas of the Abbot John, and one of the Rowley Poems which, from Walpole's account of it later, can only have been *Elinoure and Juga*.

Along with the purely literary contents of this budget, Chatterton, perhaps with some idea of appealing to the more human side of a man who had hardly ever been known to do a kindly, disinterested action in his life, or else because he could scarcely have expected his needs to be ministered to unless he set forth specifically what those needs were, furnished a full account of his circumstances —with results that were even more shattering to his hopes than had been the ill-advised postscript to Dodsley.

From the moment that Walpole learned of the poet's distressed condition his whole attitude changed. Seemingly he had been misled by the urbanity and address of Chatterton's earlier letter, and had imagined the writer to be a gentleman of wide learning, ample means, and unrestricted leisure, with whom it might be pleasant and instructive to enter upon one of those voluminous correspondences in which he so happily combined the polished *littérateur* and the subacidly vivacious maiden aunt.

For all his much-vaunted republicanism—before Wilkes

gave a somewhat too full-blooded significance to democracy
—and despite his avowed approval, when the tyranny of
Kings became a menace to the commonweal, of regicide—
in support of which theory he slept at Strawberry Hill with
an engraved facsimile of the death warrant of Charles I
hung by the side of his bed—he remained invincibly an
aristocrat, within the narrowest, die-hard interpretation of
the word. Consequently the shock of finding himself
approached by a mere nobody, a beggarly apprentice—
and a hobbledehoy at that—must have caused him severe
disquietude of mind.

Of Chatterton's confession not a trace survives. His
letter has been cut across, either by Walpole, who may
have wished to retain the more personal passages until
such time as he could make inquiries into the truth of the
poet's story, or by Chatterton himself after the whole series
of letters was finally returned. All that is left of the original
are the following lines:

I offer you some further Anecdotes and Specimens of Poetry,
and am,
      Your very humble & obedient Servt,

                    THOMAS CHATTERTON.

March 30, 1769.
  37 *Corn Street,*
    Bristol.

Not only was this letter mutilated, the major portion of
its contents being thereby lost for ever, but there is every
reason to believe that Chatterton, in the first onrush of his
anger and disappointment, destroyed the letter of good
advice which Walpole declares he sent in answer to the
other's second attempt to gain his patronage; and since
Chatterton has left no record of this part of the proceedings, we are, in default of any less one-sided testimony,
thrown back on Walpole's account of what actually
occurred.

"I wrote," he states, in his *Letter to the Editor of The Miscellanies of Thomas Chatterton*, issued from the Strawberry Hill Press, in 1779, "according to the inclosed direction, for further particulars. Chatterton, in answer, informed me that he was the son of a poor widow, who supported him with great difficulty; that he was clerk or apprentice to an attorney, but had a taste and turn for more elegant studies; and hinted a wish that I would assist him with my interest in emerging out of so dull a profession, by procuring him some place, in which he could pursue his natural bent. He affirmed that great treasures of ancient poetry had been discovered in his native city, and were in the hands of a *person*, who had lent him those he had transmitted to me; for he now sent me others, amongst which was an absolute modern pastoral in dialogue, thinly sprinkled with old words. Pray observe that he affirmed having received the poems from another person; whereas it is ascertained that the gentleman at Bristol, who possesses the fund of Rowley's poems, received them from Chatterton."

Then Walpole goes on to recount how he wrote to a relation of his—"a noble lady of virtue and character"— to inquire into the situation and character of Chatterton, and how nothing was returned as to his character, but his story was admitted to be substantially true. Meanwhile, he had got into touch with Gray, a life-long friend, to whom he submitted the poems—a move that could not fail to be to Chatterton's detriment, since Gray must instantly have recognized in—

> *No more the miskynette shall wake the morn,*
> *The minstrel-dance, good cheer, and morris-play;*
> *No more the ambling palfrey and the horn*
> *Shall from the lessel rouse the fox away—*

something that, far from recalling the fifteenth century, came suspiciously near a paraphrase of his own *Elegy*. The opinion of Mason was also solicited, and both he and Gray pronounced the poems to be modern forgeries, strongly advising Walpole to have nothing whatever to do with them, but to return them to Bristol at once. Whereupon Walpole, according to the *Letter* of 1779, wrote to Chatterton with as much "kindness and tenderness" as if he had been the boy's guardian.

"I undeceived him," he writes, "about my being a person of any interest, and urged; that in duty and gratitude to his mother, who had straitened herself to breed him up to a profession, he ought to labour in it, that in her old age he might absolve his filial debt; and I told him, that when he should have made a fortune he might unbend himself with the studies consonant to his inclinations. I told him also, that I had communicated his transcripts to better judges, and that they were by no means satisfied with the authenticity of his supposed MSS."

*   *   *

This sudden *volte-face* on the part of Walpole hit Chatterton, figuratively speaking, straight between the eyes, and his pride, his future prospects, his wavering belief in mankind, all went reeling backwards under the impact. To have stood on the very threshold of the attainment of his most cherished desires, only to find the door incontinently slammed in his face, was an experience as embittering as it was unexpected.

Yet his spirit was unbroken. He had still immense reserves of righteous scorn. The grey eyes that could leap in a flash from brooding apathy to the highest pitch of emotional intensity were prodigal of their lightnings now, and Barrett, self-confessedly fascinated by their brilliant pyrotechnic displays, must have been in a position to indulge himself to his heart's content.

How deeply Barrett was implicated in the affair will never be rightly known. E. H. W. Meyerstein ingeniously suggests that, with an eye to obtaining, even though it were at second-hand, Walpole's suffrage for his *History of*

Bristol, he was, in effect, the scheme's chief instigator from the first. This is sound reasoning, and may well have been the case, but his hand is not apparent until Chatterton, as will presently be seen, felt compelled to write to Walpole in his own defence.

Among the later writers there is a marked tendency to hold the surgeon-antiquary responsible for most of the poet's misdeeds.

"Something in this compact between the boy and the man has never been revealed,"

writes C. E. Russell, in his *Thomas Chatterton,* hinting at sinister mysteries.

J. H. Ingram, in *The True Chatterton,* goes a step farther, and declares:

It would have been much better for Chatterton's happiness and reputation had he never known Barrett or his books. The conversation the already too precocious lad had to listen to and doubtless take part in at the surgeon's destroyed the last remnants of his boyish innocence and faith; the very super-ficial medical knowledge he obtained there not only vitiated the tone of his writings but eventually caused him to build his last hope upon turning that knowledge to account, whilst Barrett's refusal to help him to do so, perhaps from interested motives, precipitated, even if it did not cause, the final tragedy.

Thus does sentimentality wanton with common-sense. For, quite frankly, this presentment of Barrett in the guise of a middle-aged Mephistopheles and Chatterton as a genuinely youthful and submissive Faust will not do. Seduction is surely nothing more nor less than a matter of personal ascendancy, an imposing of the will and guiding principles—or lack of guiding principles—of one person on the weaker and more receptive mind of another, and the question of relative ages can hardly be said to enter into the matter at all. Chatterton had more intelligence in his little finger-nail than Barrett possessed in the whole of his body, and one has only to recall the manner in which the latter allowed himself to be played fast and loose with, and the resultant havoc his too-confiding nature wrought upon his *History of Bristol*, to determine at a glance which was the active and which the passive factor of the two. The solitary advantage Barrett could lay claim to was his money, and this he was too short-sighted or too close-fisted to use in redressing the balance.

*   *   *

Though ostensibly animated by the most benevolent feelings towards Chatterton, Walpole had none the less omitted to send back the poems. And so, nine days after the dispatch of the second letter to Arlington Street, we find the poet, with a resentful irony that escapes despite his obvious efforts to control it, writing to the same address:

Sir,
          I am not able to dispute with a person of your literary character. I have transcribed Rowley's poems, &c., &c., from a transcript in the possession of a gentleman who is assured of their authenticity. St. Austin's Minster was in Bristol. In speaking of painters in Bristol, I mean glass-stainers. The MSS. have long been in the hands of the present possessor, which is all I know of them.—Though I am but sixteen years of age, I have lived long enough to see that poverty attends literature. I am obliged to you, sir, for your advice, and will go a little beyond it, by destroying all my useless lumber of literature, and never using my pen again but in the law.
                    I am,
                              Your most humble servant,
                              THOMAS CHATTERTON.
Bristol, April 8, 1769.

To the above, which he afterwards described as "a rather peevish answer," Walpole did not deign to reply. Another six days went by, and then Chatterton, calling

Barrett to his assistance, made a first appeal for the return of his manuscripts. Evidently the drafting of this letter occasioned some difficulty to them both, for in the British Museum there are two alternative versions, in addition to the one that was eventually approved and sent.

The letter that was forwarded to Walpole ran as follows:

SIR,

Being fully convinced of the papers of Rowley being genuine, I should be obliged to you to return the copy I sent you, having no other. Mr. Barrett, a very able antiquary, who is now writing The History of Bristol, has desired it of me; and I should be sorry to deprive him, or the world indeed, of a valuable curiosity, which I know to be an authentic piece of antiquity.

Your very humble servant,

THOMAS CHATTERTON.

Bristol, Corn Street.
April 14, 1769.

P.S.—If you wish to publish them yourself, they are at your service.

Then there are the somewhat mangled remains, cut across in two places, of Chatterton's earlier attempt, which was longer and decidedly more disputatious:

SIR,

As I am now fully convinced that Rowley's Papers are genuine: should be obliged to you, if you'd send Copys of them to the Town & Country Magazine; or return them to me for that Purpose:—as it wd be the greatest Injustice, to deprive the World of so valuable a Curiosity—

I have seen the original from whence the Extracts first sent you were first Copyed—

The Harmony is not so extraordinary:—as Joseph Iscan is altogether as Harmonious—

The Stanza Rowley wrote in, instead of being introduc'd by Spencer was in use 300 Years before

(*Lower part of sheet cut away.*)

by Rowley—tho' I have seen some Poetry of that Age— exceeding Alliterations without Rhyme—

I shall not defend Rowley's Pastoral: its merit can stand its own defence—

Rowley was employ'd by Canynge to go to the Principal Monasterys in the Kingdom to Collect drawings, Paintings & all MSS relating to Architecture—is it then so very extraordinary he should meet with the few remains of Saxon Learning— 'Tis allow'd by evry Historian of Credit, that the Normans destroy'd all the Saxon MSS., Paintings, &c., that fell in their Way; endeavoring to suppress the very Language—the want of knowing what they were, is all the Foundation you can have for stiling them a barbarous Nation.

If you are not satisfied with these conspicuous Truths—
            (*Further excision.*)
the Honor to be of my opinion.

                    I am
                        S^r y^r very hble & ob^t Servt
                            T. CHATTERTON.
Bristol, Corn Street.   *April 14th 69.*

And, lastly, comes Barrett's variation on the same theme.

SIR,

Being fully convinc^d of the papers of Rowley being Genuine, I should be oblig^d to you to return ye Copy, I sent you having no other; Mr Barrett, who is now writing the History & Antiquities of ye City of Bristol, has desir^d it of me, & I should be sorry to deprive him or the World indeed of a Valuable Curiosity; wch I know to be an authentic piece of Antiquity. However Barbarous ye Saxons may be call^d by our Modern Virtuosos, it is certain we are indebted to to (*sic*) Alfred & other Saxon Kings for ye wisest of our Laws & in part for ye British Constitution—The Normans indeed destroy'd ye MSS., paintings, & of ye Saxons that fell in their way; but some might be & certainly were recover^d out of ye Monasteries &c., in wch they were preserv^d—Mr Vertue[1] could know nothing of ye Matter—'twas quite out of his Walk —I thought, Rowleys pastoral had a degree of merit, that would be its own Defence. *Abbot Johns* Verses were translated by Rowley out of the Greek; & there might be poetry of his Age something more than meer Alliterations, as he was so great a Scholar. The Stanza if I mistake not was us^d by

---

[1] Walpole's *Anecdotes of Painting* was largely compiled from Vertue's MS.

Ischan, Gower, Ladgate &c—long before Spencer. Glumm is us^d by John a Beverly, Gower & Ladgate in ye Same Sence as by Rowley, & ye Modern Gloomy seems but a refinement of ye Old Word—Glommung in Anglo Saxon is ye Twilight—

                    from Sr Y^r Very Hble Servt

                              T. CHATTERTON.

The sentence: "I thought Rowleys pastoral had a degree of merit, that would be its own Defence," carries so subtle a sting of rebuke in its tail that it is surprising that it should have found no place in the letter sent.

Not that its inclusion would materially have helped the situation, for Walpole was curiously lacking in taste and discrimination in regard to such matters, and was at all times disposed to look upon the writing of verse as an elegant accomplishment which should be confined to the leisured classes. As Macaulay has said of him:

His judgment of literature, of contemporary literature especially, was altogether perverted by his aristocratical feelings. No writer surely was ever guilty of so much false and absurd criticism. He almost invariably speaks with contempt of those books which are now universally allowed to be the best that appeared in his time; and, on the other hand, he speaks of writers of rank and fashion as if they were entitled to the same precedence in literature which would have been allowed to them in a drawing-room.

The imputation is not unjust. Gray passed muster because he was socially eligible, comfortable, provided with worldly goods, and had been educated at Eton and Cambridge. Upon Lady Temple also, the authoress of a slim volume of arch little drawing-room rhymes and fables, the freedom of the Strawberry Hill Press was conferred, a copy of the work in question being presented to the Princess Amelia, and graciously acknowledged by Her Royal Highness. But the pretensions of Miss Hannah More's *protégée*, Mrs. Yearsley, a Bristol milkwoman, whose poems won her a small and transitory vogue in and out of the city of her birth, were not so readily sanctioned by Walpole.

"Were I not persuaded by the samples you have sent me, Madam, that this woman has talents," he wrote to Miss More, on November 13th, 1784, "I should not advise her encouraging her propensity, lest it should divert her mind from the care of her family, and, after the novelty is over, leave her worse than she was."

And as a further confirmation of this point of view, we have his counsel to Chatterton, already quoted: "I told him when he should have made a fortune he might unbend himself with the studies consonant to his inclination." In fine, the gifts of the favoured few became, automatically, the propensities of the less fortunate many, and Chatterton was to take up poetry, as he might take up the collecting of old prints, or the breeding of race-horses, only when his circumstances might justify such an extravagance.

*   *   *

The joint attack of Barrett and Chatterton proved quite as unavailing as Chatterton's single-handed onslaughts had done, and the transcripts were still retained. Over three months elapsed, and then, on 24th July, now thoroughly incensed by Walpole's persistent neglect of him, and determined at any cost to force an issue, the poet wrote a final letter of remonstrance.

SIR,
        I cannot reconcile your behaviour to me with the notions I once entertained of you. I think myself injured, sir: and, did not you know my circumstances, you would not dare to treat me thus. I have sent twice for a copy of the MS.:—No answer from you. An explanation or excuse for your silence would oblige

                                        THOMAS CHATTERTON.
July 24th.

Walpole afterwards declared that when the Barrett-Chatterton letter reached him he was on the eve of starting out for Paris, but from his Correspondence for the year 1769, edited and chronologically arranged by Mrs. Paget Toynbee, no such journey is discoverable until the middle of August. It must, however, be borne in mind that he was making this statement ten years later, when he was sixty-two years of age, and his memory for dates and suchlike had always been notoriously inaccurate. Either, he says, he forgot the request of the poems or, not having time to have them copied, deferred complying until his return, which was to be in six weeks' time.

He then resumes:

Soon after my return from France, I received another letter from Chatterton (*i.e. the one quoted above*) the style of which was singularly impertinent. He demanded his poems roughly; and added, that I should not have dared to use him so ill, if he had not acquainted me with the narrowness of his circumstances.

My heart did not accuse me of insolence to him. I wrote an answer, expostulating with him on his injustice, and renewing good advice—but upon second thoughts, reflecting that so wrong-headed a young man, of whom I knew nothing, and whom I had never seen, might be absurd enough to print my letter, I flung it into the fire; and, wrapping up both his poems and letters, without taking a copy of either, for which I am now sorry, I returned all to him, and thought no more of him or them, till about a year and a half later, when

Dining at the royal academy, Dr. Goldsmith drew the attention of the company with an account of the marvellous treasure of ancient poems lately discovered at Bristol, and expressed enthusiastic belief in them; for which he was laughed at by Dr. Johnson, who was present. I soon found this was the trouvaille of my friend Chatterton, and I told Dr. Goldsmith that his novelty was none to me, who might, if I had pleased, have had the honour of ushering the great discovery to the learned world. You may imagine, sir, we did not at all agree in the measure of our faith; but though his credulity diverted me,

D

my mirth was soon dashed; for, on asking about Chatterton, he told me he had been in London, and had destroyed himself. I heartily wished then that I had been the dupe of all the poor young man had written; for who would not have his understanding imposed on to save a fellow-being from the utmost wretchedness, despair, and suicide!—and a poor young man not eighteen—and of such miraculous talents—for, dear sir, if I wanted credulity on the one hand, it is ample on the other. . . . In short, I do not believe that there ever existed so master a genius, except that of Psalmanaazar, who before twenty-two could create a language that all the learned of Europe, though they suspected, could not detect.

Brave words, yet with a lurking sense of crocodile tears behind them, and surely, from one who had been able to discern in *Elinoure and Juga* no native beauties of its own, a little excessive. Besides, in common fairness, it must be admitted, though many impassioned arguments have been advanced to the contrary, that there was every reason why Walpole should have fought shy of espousing Chatterton's cause. Possibly some vague vibration of conscience with respect to the first edition of *The Castle of Otranto*, may have suggested, once his eyes had been opened to the doubtful origin of the Rowley transcripts, that he was being approached in a birds-of-a-feather spirit, a thought that could not but be obnoxious to his self-esteem. Then, too, it is quite within the margin of probability that he might have recalled how in Paris, four years earlier, when he was well past the middle forties and certainly old enough to know better, he had concocted a letter alleged to have been written by Frederick the Great to Jean Jacques Rousseau, offering the much harassed and perpetually disgruntled philosopher sanctuary within his dominions. That bogus letter had been a none too creditable exploit, since it had made mischief even in this country between Hume and Rousseau, and Walpole had come safely out of it only by the skin of his teeth.

And if these considerations were not weighty enough in themselves to exercise a restraining influence, it must not be forgotten that he had been expressly warned by Gray and Mason that any alliance with the young adventurer of Bristol would assuredly end in trouble.

The greatest mistake he made, of course, was not to have sent back Chatterton's transcriptions at once, and forthwith dismissed the matter from his mind. Yet this was just what he could not bring himself to do. There was a sort of backstairs fascination about the whole thing that he was unable to resist. It was not, however, to the living Chatterton, but to the dead poet's memory, that he behaved so unpardonably. During Chatterton's lifetime he did contrive to maintain some semblance of passivity, which required no effort as they never came into actual contact with each other again; also there would have been no point in his making any public reference to Chatterton, for until the first publication of the Rowley Poems by Tyrwhitt, few people outside Bristol had heard of the boy's name. But no sooner did the poems begin to attract interest and discussion among the leading literary men of the day than Walpole entered upon a course of deliberate persecution, losing all sense of proportion, making the wildest and most unfounded accusations—as, for example, his declaration to Mason that Chatterton was "a consummate villain and had gone to enormous lengths before he destroyed himself"—when he had no means of knowing except from hearsay, what the poet's conduct had been. His suavity, his fastidiousness, his wonted good-breeding vanished in the twinkling of an eye. One might almost suppose that he had persuaded himself into believing that Chatterton had achieved a posthumous notoriety from no other motive than to spite him. To Mason, Hannah More, and his most frequent correspondent—his "oracle in any antique difficulties"—the Rev. William Cole, he harps to distraction upon the subject of his wrongs; Chatterton is "a liar," "a young rascal," "a complete rogue," "a lad who, they do not deny, forged the poems in the style of Ossian, and fifty other things."

By this wholesale defamation of Chatterton's moral character he doubtless hoped to divert attention from himself; but naturally, as he might have foreseen had he been less engrossed by his own imaginary grievances, a directly opposite result was produced. Gradually public opinion mounted up in his disfavour, and since, next to ridicule, he feared and hated hostile criticism more than anything else in the world, his position became an exceedingly uncomfortable one.

"Some jackanapes at Bristol (I know not who)," he writes to Mason, on July 24th, 1778, "has published Chatterton's works, and I suppose to provoke me to tell the story accuses me of treating that marvellous creature with contempt; which, having supposed, contrary to the truth, he invites his readers to feel indignation against me."

And again, on the same date, in a letter to Cole, he complains:

In a word, somebody has published Chatterton's works, and charged me heavily with having discountenanced him. He even calls for the indignation of the public against me. It is somewhat singular, that I am to be offered up as a victim at the altar of a notorious imposter! but as many saints have been imposters, so many innocent persons have been sacrificed to them.

But for a while, however discursive he may have been in private, he held his peace in public, gathered about him such shreds of dignity as still happened to be available, and retreated apprehensively within himself. Then the appearance of *The Miscellanies of Thomas Chatterton* ploughed up the ground from under his feet, and at last he was compelled to come forward and issue an authoritative statement in his own defence. This took the form of the *Letter to the Editor of the Miscellanies of Thomas Chatterton,* from which extracts have been given in the preceding pages. It told the story of Walpole's relations with Chatterton from the moment of their first encounter— needless to remark, from the Walpole standpoint. Yet notwithstanding that Walpole tried his hardest to be impartial, his private feelings occasionally ran away with him, especially when, in seeking to exonerate himself from the main charges of indifference and contempt, he observes:

I should have been blameable to his mother, and society, if I had seduced an apprentice from his master to marry him to the nine muses: and I should have encouraged a propensity to forgery, which is not the talent most wanting culture in the present age. All of the house of forgery are relations; and though it is just to Chatterton's memory to say that his poverty never made him claim kindred with the richest, or most enriching branches, yet his ingenuity in counterfeiting styles, and, I believe, hands, might easily have led him to those more facile imitations of prose, promissory notes.

Such a suggestion, coming from a man whose own financial position had always been unassailable was, it goes without saying, perfectly monstrous. Nor was it in any degree mitigated by—

Yet it does not appear to my knowledge that his honesty in that respect was ever perverted.—

which follows immediately afterwards by way of a tardy and mean-spirited *amende.*

*   *   *

Two hundred copies of the *Vindication* were printed at Strawberry Hill and circulated privately; but the troubled waters were not perceptibly smoothed. And by

1782, the year in which the Rowley Controversy reached its zenith, when Bryant, Milles, Tyrwhitt, Warton, and a score of others, were all bringing out books with long explanatory titles, and engaging the while in an intellectual scrimmage concerning the authenticity or non-authenticity of the poems, Walpole's situation, aggravated by unflattering commentaries in the Press, had grown so intolerable that, at his own request, the *Letter* was reprinted in four consecutive monthly parts—from April to July—in *The Gentleman's Magazine*.

After this gesture one might reasonably have expected him to remain silent. But no; in and out of season he was at it again; and seven years later, on the publication of Barrett's long-delayed *History of Bristol*, we hear of him protesting:

> Mr. Walpole gives all his friends full authority to say that he never before saw the letters published by Mr. Barrett, in his *History of Bristol*, as letters sent to him by Thomas Chatterton, and he wishes this to be generally known, lest after his death, some pretended answers to them should be produced as having been written by him.[1]

So the thing became a veritable obsession, vexing and worrying him almost to the end of his life.

Yet one other point calls insistently for examination. In Volume IV of his *Works*, the *Letter to the Editor of the Miscellanies of Thomas Chatterton* is given in its entirety, along with various *personalia* in connexion with the Chatterton affair, and then—most surprisingly—on pages 237–238, appears an unfinished draft of that very letter, designed to accompany the poems on their return, which, elsewhere in the same book, he explicitly states was thrown into the fire. Its text is as follows:

---

[1] Barrett had printed Chatterton's first two letters to Walpole, of March 25th and 30th, 1769, as well as *The Ryse of Peyncteynge* and *The Historie of Peyncters*, in his *History of Bristol*.

Mr. Walpole's Letter to Chatterton, on his redemanding his Manuscripts.

(Not sent.)

SIR,

I do not see, I must own, how these precious MSS. of which you have given me a few extracts, should be lost to the world by my detaining your letters. Do the originals not exist, from whence you say you copied your extracts, and from which you offered me more extracts? In truth, by your first letter, I understood that the originals themselves were in your possession by the free and voluntary offer you made me of them, and which you know I did not chuse to accept. If Mr. Barrett (who give me leave to say, cannot know much of antiquity if he believes in the authenticity of those papers) intends to make use of them, would he not do better to have recourse to the originals, than to the slight fragments you have sent me? You say, sir, you know them to be genuine: pray let me ask again, of what age are they? and how have they been transmitted? In what book of any age is there mention made of Rowley or of the poetical monk, his ancient predecessor in such pure poetry? poetry so resembling both Spenser and the moderns, and written in metre invented long since Rowley, and longer since the monk wrote. I doubt Mr. Barrett himself will find it difficult to solve these doubts.

For myself, I undoubtedly will never print those extracts as genuine, which I am far from believing they are. If you want them, sir, I will have them copied, and will send you the copy. But having a little suspicion that your letters may have been designed to laugh at me, if I had fallen into the snare, you will allow me to preserve your original letters, as an ingenious contrivance, however unsuccessful. This seems the more probable, as any man would understand by your first letter, that you either was possessed of the original MSS. or had taken copies of them; whereas you now talk as if you had no copy but these written at the bottom of the very letters I have received from you.

I own I should be better diverted, if it proved that you have chosen to entertain yourself at my expense, than if you really thought these pieces ancient. The former would show you had little opinion of my judgment; the latter, that you ought not to trust too much to your own. I should not at all take the former ill, as I am not vain of it; I should be sorry for the latter, as you say, sir, that you are very young, and it would be pity an ingenious young man should be too early prejudiced in his own favour.

N.B.—The above letter I had begun to write to Chatterton on his redemanding his MSS., but not chusing to enter into a controversy with him, I did not finish it, and, only folding up his papers, returned them.

HOR. WALPOLE.

Once more concessions must be made to Walpole's defective memory. It has been shown that he was in error as to the exact date of his journey to Paris in the autumn of 1769; also, in the one letter we have *officially* from him to Chatterton—that is to say, wafered, addressed in his handwriting, and postmarked—he misdated the second edition of his own *Anecdotes of Painting*; and therefore, by the same token, it is not altogether unlikely that he may, in perfect good faith, have believed that he had burnt the draft of his final letter, only to rediscover it, years later, among other long-forgotten papers, in some rarely opened drawer.

But even allowing for this, and for the intervention of Gray and Mason, something is yet wanting. The transition from the silken civilities of the book-lined study to the harsher and more critical atmosphere of the headmaster's room is too violent to be accepted without mental reservations. For on being brought face to face with those letters Chatterton had written to him so long ago, letters Walpole doubtless imagined to have disappeared for ever, but which now rose to confront him, like a spectre from the past, out of the pages of Barrett's *History*, might it not have occurred to him that there was nothing to prevent his own two answers to the poet from being exhumed and published hereafter, either by Barrett or some other meddling busy-body? Until now his *Vindication* had sounded plausible enough, but if his first response to Chatterton, abounding in expressions of deferential credulity, should ever be set on record for all the world to read, what would become of his claim to be regarded by posterity as a literary *connoisseur* and a man of impeccable taste? The urgent need of some document that might in some part redress this possible evil, and act as an additional prop to the *Vindication* is, if purely conjectural, at least clearly apparent. Moreover, its motive is less far to seek than the motive underlying that very incriminating invitation to Rousseau which, history tells us, was never tendered by Frederick the Great.

* * *

Chatterton's repulse at the hand of Walpole rankled deeply, and put him more than ever out of countenance with his life at Lambert's and among his Bristol friends. His indiscreet boastings, on the strength of Walpole's temporary acceptance of his services—or the implication of that temporary acceptance—had now to be paid for at a heavy rate of interest. One can imagine that when the high-flown scheme collapsed, Catcott and Burgum might be trusted to stress their commiseration with a certain ironical fervour, and that the Juvenile Club, no less exempt from petty meannesses and jealousies than are most of such *coteries*, would add their quota of slyly administered pricks and barbs. And the fact that Chatterton himself was fully convinced that Walpole's dismissal of him was actuated not so much by qualms as to the genuineness of his manuscripts as from contempt of his poverty, must have immeasurably increased his humiliation. There was no hope of a further appeal. No means, at the moment, of easing his situation. Satire was the only weapon by which he could hit back at the man who had so ill-used him, and henceforth, whenever an opening presented itself, divining that Walpole had a horror of ridicule, he attacked him in the Press.

D *

In the *Middlesex Journal*, describing an imaginary exhibition of pictures, and making great play with a real or imagined association between Walpole and Kitty Clive, the actress, he writes:

No. 12. A Piece of Modern Antiquity, by Horace Walpole. This is no other than a striking portrait of the facetious Mrs. Clive. Horace, finding it too large to be introduced into his next edition of *Virtu*, has returned it on the town.

Again, in *The Advice; Addressed to Miss M—— R—— of Bristol*, the lady, doubtless the Miss Rumsey of the letter to Baker at Charlestown, is reminded of the transience of youth, and the poem continues:

> *To keep a lover's flame alive*
> *Requires the genius of a Clive,*
> *Or Walpole's mental taste.*

And further references occur in two separate contributions to *The Town and Country Magazine*, where his victim appears as Horatio Otranto, in *The Polite Advertiser*, and as Baron Otranto, in *The Memoirs of a Sad Dog*, while in the burletta, *A Woman of Spirit*, there is a passing allusion to Horatio Trefoil.

But the most scathing denunciation of all is to be found in those lines—with a queer hiatus towards the end, where the poet's inspiration seems to have run out—dashed off in white-hot fury immediately after the return of his manuscripts:

> *Walpole! I thought not I should ever see*
> *So mean a Heart as thine has proved to be;*
> *Thou, who, in Luxury nurs'd behold'st with Scorn*
> *The Boy, who Friendless, Penniless, Forlorn,*
> *Asks thy high Favour,—thou mayst call me Cheat—*
> *Say, didst thou ne'er indulge in such Deceit?*

Who wrote Otranto? But I will not chide,
Scorn I will repay with Scorn, and Pride with Pride.
Still, Walpole, still, thy Prosy Chapters write,
And twaddling Letters to some Fair indite,—
Laud all above thee,—Fawn and Cringe to those
Who, for thy Fame, were better Friends than Foes
Still spurn the incautious Fool, who dares——

*   *   *   *   *   *   *

Had I the Gifts of Wealth and Lux'ry shared,
Not poor and Mean—Walpole! thou hadst not dared
Thus to insult. But I shall live and Stand
By Rowley's side—when Thou art dead and damned.

THOMAS CHATTERTON.

1769.

I intended to have sent the above to Mr. Walpole but my sister persuaded me out of it.   T. C.

It was fated that life should give Chatterton few opportunities for developing the gentler and more affectionate side of his nature. But it provided him with a fearless strength of character, and an exterior hardness that were proof against most things. And it certainly succeeded in making him a good hater, once his enmity was aroused.

CHAPTER VII

THE ROWLEY POEMS

(PART ONE)

WHATEVER claim to genius Chatterton may be said to have possessed is implicit in the Rowley Poems. In none of his other work, modern verse, political satires, or musical libretti, is there displayed to anything like the same extent that sustained creative impulse, rising out of the depths of some inner spiritual consciousness and crying instinctively for utterance, which alone distinguishes all memorable and lasting achievement.

Aware, even in early childhood of certain innate qualities which separated him from the rest of his companions, of a mysterious fire that burned within him, of strange incommunicable ecstasies and despondencies that came and went without apparent reason, of vague dissatisfied longings which preyed upon him like a half-voluptuous pain, it was but natural that he should attempt to crystallize his dreams into concrete shape, and still more natural that the church of St. Mary Redcliff, and William Canynges, the church's benefactor, should present themselves as the outward symbols of his secret creed.

In a Warton Lecture, given at the British Academy in 1930, W. Macneile Dixon draws an illuminating contrast between the awakening of poetic sensibility in Warton and Gray and the dawn of a similar development in Chatterton:

I have said that Warton's sympathies with things medieval were aroused, as Gray's were aroused, by their poetic values.

Both had learning. They lived and moved, the one at Oxford, the other at Cambridge, among ancient colleges, the visible monument of a bygone time. They were men of cultivated taste, connoisseurs, accustomed to sample literary and artistic flavours as they sampled vintages. They had but to look round them with speculative eyes. We cannot wonder that the romances took their fancy, or that Gothic architecture, its soaring and majestic structures, awoke their interest in such creations, unique in style, mysteriously wrought, and that they should ask themselves what thoughts were here enshrined, or what manner of men were their builders. Chatterton's passion was by contrast a species of miracle. It had no roots in knowledge or travel. It descended upon him in early infancy like a fire from heaven. It drove him to unremitting and solitary labours. So far from sharing his visions, probably not a boy in England could have so much as found any meaning in his religious fervour for antiquity. And a religious fervour it may justly be called.

The "fire from heaven" had, however, sundry terrestrial elements as well. Subjoined to it were hereditary influences reaching back for well over a century and terminating collaterally in that sexton uncle, Richard Phillips, who was at all times willing to let him have access to St. Mary's. The sexton uncle, too, would surely have a store of fables and legends to impart, and one pictures the youthful Chatterton eagerly drinking in tales of Simon de Bourton, the Canynges, and all that was known, or might still more effectively be invented, concerning the knights, merchants, and monkish personages, whose bones lay mouldering beneath the flagstoned pavements of the church. So the stiff recumbent forms, carved in marble, or outlined in black upon great slabs of worn and polished brass, became an integral part of the boy's existence, casting the same sort of glamour over his imagination as the fairy heroes and heroines of Hans Andersen and the brothers Grimm were wont to exercise upon the children of an earlier generation than our own. And gradually the idea of a sleeping antique world which waited but the wave of a magician's wand, or some abstruse juggling with Time, to bring it once more into robustious and colourful life, began to evolve itself in his mind.

Already, then, almost before he was capable of writing a single line of poetry or prose, chance had provided him with the perfect setting and the ideal central figure for a romance of the Middle Ages. The nucleus was there, though as yet he was too young to envisage it as more than a dimly formulated dream. Not until he had read as deeply as circumstances allowed into the history of the church and the city, not until he had gone to Colston's, perhaps not until he had come into possession of what remained of the Redcliff parchments, did the vision become sharply focused, or did he perceive how he might link up the story of St. Mary's, William Canynges, and Bristol in the days of the Wars of the Roses, with himself. Then came the metamorphosis of his own personality into that of Thomas Rowley, secular priest of St. John's. The acquisition of the name of Rowley may have been in some degree accidental, or it may actually have appeared on one of the documents surviving from the raid on "Mr. Canynges' Cofre," but, like most of the ingredients used by Chatterton in his antique writings, it was not without an obscure foundation in truth.

In 1772, two years after the poet's death, Barrett, writing to Dr. Ducarel, remarks:

I have been taking all methods to inquire into the name, family, burial, &c., of Rowley, but I have not, I fear, succeeded: though I have met with an inscription of one Tho. Rowley,[1] who served bailiff when Mr. Canynge was Mayor and Sheriff of Bristol soon after. But he was a merchant, and lies buried in St. John's Church, in this city. Query, if he ever took priest's orders as his friend Mr. Canynge did? The date is 1478, four years only after the death of Mr. Canynge.

[1] The name on the brass referred to is spelt Rouley.

Now Chatterton, with his propensity for probing into the dark corners of ancient buildings, may very well have happened upon the identical memorial brass, and swiftly recognized its potentialities. Here was a real-life character who would fit his purpose admirably; exactly the period that he wanted, and bearing a Christian name fortuitously coinciding with his own. That the brass made further reference to the said Thomas Rouley's wife, Margaret, who had died in the year 1470, and also supplied a list of twelve children—six boys and six girls—was a disconcerting addition to the genealogical equipment of one who was to be converted into a celibate priest; but his ever fertile powers of invention were qualified to over-ride even greater discrepancies than these; few of his fellow townsmen had the leisure or the inclination to indulge in antiquarian researches, and hence the risks he ran of ultimate discovery did not worry him overmuch.

*   *   *

The Rowley Poems are something more than a collection of pseudo-archaic verse. Behind them is a deliberate and painstaking effort to reconstruct the manners, the customs, and the civic and ecclesiastical spirit of the fifteenth century in England. Apparently unwilling to let the poems speak for themselves, Chatterton invents copious explanatory notes, an imaginary correspondence between Rowley and Canynges, and to *The Storie of William Canynge* appends a biographical narrative in Rowleian prose which was intended to give unity and verisimilitude to what was, for so young a mind, a truly epic conception.

A wealth of information is vouchsafed regarding the two chief protagonists, and, in the prose version of *The Storie of William Canynge*, it is Rowley who tells the life-histories of Canynges and himself.

Thomas Rowley, born at Norton Malreward, in

Somersetshire, was an ardent Yorkist, and parish priest of St. John's. From his boyhood upwards he had been on intimate terms with the Canynges family. He and William were schoolfellows at the Carmelite Priory which had formerly stood on the site of Colston's, and had worn the long blue habit and yellow stockings of the Bristol Blue Coat School. There, as Rowley relates, "began the kindness of our lives. Our minds and kinds were alike, and we were always together." William Canynges was an intellectual, a visionary, and a generous dispenser of bounties—a very different person from his elder brother, Robert, their father's favourite, who was "greedy of gain and sparing of alms." Fortune, however, favoured William, for both his father and brother died in the same year, leaving him in full and undisputed possession of their united wealth, and this just at a time when Rowley had taken orders and might appropriately be appointed his friend's chaplain and confessor. But the services rendered by Rowley to his benefactor were by no means limited to the discharge of his spiritual offices alone; Canynges found another employment for him, and one for which he was eminently suited, namely to travel the country, first in search of drawings, and afterwards to collect old manuscripts.

"I gave my hande," he tells us, "and he told mee I must goe to all the abbies and pryorys, and gather together auncient drawyings, if of anie account, at any price. Consented I to the same, and pursuant sett out the Mundaie following for the minster of our Ladie and Saint Goodwyne, where a drawing of a steeple, contryvd for the belles when runge to swaie out of the syde into the ayre, had I thence; it was done by Syr Symon de Mambrie, who, in the troublesomme rayne of kyng Stephen, devoted himselfe, and was shorne."

In the course of his journeyings Rowley visited Cirencester, Peterborough, Coventry, York, Durham, and even crossed over to Ireland—"wheere ys twayne of your Famylie buryed"—and everywhere he encountered the most gratifying successes.

On Canynges he bestowed many of his own poetical compositions which were rewarded by a profuse liberality that was far in excess of anything Chatterton himself had received in return for the work he had given to Barrett and Catcott. Indeed, it is impossible not to suspect the presence of a purely contemporaneous back-hander in the incident, as set forth by Rowley:

I gave master Canninge my Bristow tragedy, for which he gave me in hands twentie pounds, and did praise it more than I did think my self did deserve, for I can say in troth I was never proud of my verses since I did read master Chaucer; and now haveing nought to do, and not wyling to be ydle, I went to the minster of our Ladie and Saint Goodwin, and then did purchase the Saxon manuscripts, and sett my self diligentley to translate and worde it in English metre, which in one year I performed and styled it the Battle of Hastyngs; master William did bargyin for one manuscript, and John Pelham, an esquire of Ashley, for another.—Master William did praise it muckle greatly, but advised me to tender it to no man, beying the menn whose names were therein mentioned would be offended. He gave me 20 markes, and I did goe to Ashley, to master Pelham, to be payd of him for the other one I left with him.

But his ladie being of the family of the Fiscamps, of whom some things are said, he told me he had burnt it, and would have me burnt too if I did not avaunt. Dureing this dinn his wife did come out, and made a dinn to speake by a figure, would have oversounded the bells of our Ladie of the Cliffe; I was fain content to get away in a safe skin.

Shortly after the deaths of his father and brother, William Canynges removed for a while to Gloucester, where he married Johanna Hathwaie, but, his young wife dying in childbirth, he returned to the family mansion in Bristol—"the greete rudde House neere the waterre"— and here he gathered about him an assemblage of all those who practised, or were interested in, literature and the fine arts, foremost among whom were John Carpenter, Bishop of Worcester, John a Iscam, a canon of the monastery of St. Augustine in Bristol, Sir Charles Baldwin, a Lancastrian Knight, Sir Thybbot Gorges, a country esquire, Sir Alan de Vere, and John a Dalbenie.

On the vigil of the Epiphany, "1432," Canynges opened his house as a Masonic Lodge, inaugurating the occasion by an address on The Arts in Relation to Trade, and in a letter to Rowley, who was still away on his archæological tour at the time, he says: "The Freers did enlarge, the gentlemen attende and the councylmen felle asleepe." But banquetings, learned debates, political discussions, and the general interchange of ideas, did not constitute themselves the only diversions; amateur theatricals were high in favour, and Rowley's dramatic pieces, *Ælla*, *Goddwyn*, and *The Parlyamente of Sprytes*, this last specially written to commemorate the dedication by Carpenter of the church of "Our Lady of Redclefte," were given their first public performances at the Red Lodge, the casts being made up of various members of the household.

Rowley, on his return from his wanderings, had a "house on the hyll," where "the ayer was mickle keen," yet he was ever the close companion, adviser, and spiritual confessor of Canynges, and for many years—for upwards of thirty, if the chronology of his priestly biographer is to be trusted—the civic life of the merchant prince, with its five successive mayoralties, its extensive shipping interests —according to William of Worcester, the authentic Canynges was owner of ten ships and gave employment to a hundred artificers on land—his munificent donations towards the restoration and completion of St. Mary Redcliff, moved spaciously side by side with that other and more satisfying existence shared with the intellectual community he had founded.

But at the height of his prosperity he met with a sudden serious misfortune, in that he was commanded by King Edward IV to enter into a marriage that was repugnant to him. And now Rowley takes up the burden of the tale once more:

In the year kyng Edward came to Bristow, master Canninge send for me to avoid a marriage which the kyng was bent upon between him and a ladie he ne'er had seen, of the familee of the Widdevilles: the danger was nigh, unless avoided by one remidee, an holie one, which was, to be ordained a son of holy church, being franke from the power of kynges in that cause, and cannot be wedded. Mr. Canninge instantly sent me to Carpenter, his good friend, bishop of Worcester, and the Fryday following was prepaird and ordaynd the next day, the daie of St. Matthew, and on Sunday sung his first mass in the church of our Ladie, to the astonishing of kyng Edward, who was so furiously madd and ravynge withall, that master Canninge was wyling to give him 3000 marks, which gave him peace again, and he was admitted to the presence of the kyng, staid in Bristow, partook of all his pleasures and pastimes till he departed the next year. . . .

Finally, having outwitted and afterwards conciliated the King, Canynges renounced the world, retiring to the College of Westbury, where he lived in pious seclusion until his death in 1474. The fate of Rowley is less certain. For a time at least he seems to have continued to live in Bristol, exchanging his house on the hill for a more commodious residence by the Tower, to which he removed his chattels and "lived warm." From his own pen we are given a glimpse of his increasing age and infirmities:

And now grown auncient I was seized with great pains, which did cost me mickle marks to be cured off. Master William offered me a cannon's place in Westbury College, which gladly I had accepted but my pains made me stay at home.

The weight of years and the consequent enfeeblement of his mind, however, would appear to have played strange tricks with his memory, for elsewhere, referring to his relations with his old friend and patron, he remarks:

Wyth hym I lyved at Westburie six yeeres before he died, and bee nowe hastenynge to the grave mieselfe.

*   *   *

The first of the antique poems is *Elinoure and Juga*, alleged by Thistlethwaite, as previously stated, to have been in existence as early as the summer of 1764. Attention has already been drawn to the echoing cadences of **Gray** in this simple and charming piece, wherein two maidens, "sisters in sorrow," sit by the banks of the Rudborne, a stream near St. Albans, lamenting the probable fates of their lovers, who are absent at the Wars of the Roses. The story is told, with a touching and very youthful artlessness, in the form of a dramatic ballad, and that gift for creating an effective background, which was to become so salient a feature of all the poet's later work, is even now strongly in evidence:

JUGA.

When murky clouds do hang upon the gleam
Of waning moon, in silver mantles dight;
The tripping fairies weave the golden dream
Of happiness which flieth with the night.
Then (but the Saints forbid!) if to a sprite [1]
Sir Richard's form is lyped, [2] *I'll hold distraught,*
His bleeding clay-cold corse, and die each day in thought.

ELINOURE.

Ah! woe-bemoaning words! What words can shew?
Thou polished river, on thy bank may bleed
Champions, whose blood will with thy waters flow,
And Rudborne stream be Rudborne stream indeed!

[1] Spirit.   [2] Wasted away; *liposychy,* a small swoon.

Haste, gentle Juga, trip it o'er the mead,
To know, or whether we must wail again,
Or with our fallen knights be mingled on the plain.

So saying, like two levyn-blasted trees,
Or twain of clouds that holdeth stormy rain;
They movèd gently o'er the dewy mees,[1]
To where Saint Alban's holy shrines remain.
There did they find that both their knights were slain.
Distraught, they wandered to swoll'n Rudborne's side,
Yellèd their lethal knell, sank in the waves, and died.

*   *   *

The Unknown Knyght, or *The Tournament*, sent, according to George Catcott, to Baker, and referred to in Chatterton's letter to Charlestown, dated 6th March 1768—"THE TOURNAMENT I have only one cento of, which I send herewith; the remainder is entirely lost"—is a piece of spirited descriptive writing, running into 108 lines, in the same *genre* as the longer and more important poem, *The Tournament, an Interlude,* which presumably followed later. The opening lines of *The Unknown Knyght* are full of bustle and expectancy and show a nice sense of "period."

The Mattin-bell had sounded long,
The Cocks had sung their morning song,
When lo! The tuneful Clarion's sound,
(Wherein all other noise was drown'd)
Did echo to the rooms around,
And greet the ears of Champyons strong;
"Arise, arise from downy bed,
For sun doth 'gin to shew his head!"

[1] Meads (wrongly).

Then each did don in seemly gear,
What armour each beseemed to wear,
And on each shield devices shone,
Of wounded hearts and battles won,
All curious and nice each one;
With many a tassell'd spear;
And, mounted each one to his steed,
Unwist, made ladies' hearts to bleed.

But the poem ends in a hurried, inconclusive manner, and lacks the sustained dramatic interest of *The Tournament*, seeming to stand in relation to it as might a rough sketch to a finished drawing.

*   *   *

The Tournament: an Interlude appears in the copy-book that contains the De Bergham Pedigree, and was probably in some part inspired by Chatterton's desire to provide the pewterer with an ancestor of a hardier and more combative type than the fourteenth century poet who was "the greatest ornament of his age," since Syr Johan de Berghamme figures prominently in the lists. The main theme, however, is concerned with Syrre Symonne de Byrtonne and the foundation of St. Mary Redcliff. In one of the "old" parchments produced by Chatterton, and doubtless intended to be a key to the poem itself, are given various biographical notes relating to Syrre Symonne; how, for example, he was born on the eve of the Annunciation, "M.C.C.XXXXXXI," was "desyrabelle of aspect," and in his youth much given to tourneying, "abstayned from marryage," was "myckelle learned," built himself a palatial house in the Isle of Wight, was ever "fullen of almsdeeds and was of the poor beloved." Then comes a spirited description of the tournament, following closely the content of the verses, telling how King Edward I "kept his Chrystmasse (of 1285) at Brightstowe," with a company of strong and valiant knights, "who established a three days jouste on Sayncte Maryes Hylle." The poem is a joyous affair of glancing spears, bright primary colours, and swift head-long encounters. It opens with the entrance of a herald.

HERALD.

The tournament begins; the hammers sound;
The coursers run about the measured field;
The shimmering armour throws its sheen around;
Quaint fancies are depicted on each shield.

First to appear in the arena is Syrre Symonne de Bourtonne,[1] chafing with impatience to begin the fray; there is a slight delay, and then the King enters, attended by Syrr Hugo Ferraris, Syrr Ranulph Nevylle, Syrr Lodovick de Clynton, Syrr Johan de Berghamme, and other knights, heralds, minstrels, and servitors. At the King's command the proceedings are ushered in by a minstrel's song, in praise of William the Conqueror's prowess in hunting, after which ensues the serious business of the day, and the contests are hot and furious. De Bourtonne engages in single combat with Nevylle and Ferraris, who successively fall before his lance. De Berghamme and de Clynton next face each other, and de Clynton falls. Then the two victors, de Bourtonne and de Berghamme, wrestle for supremacy, and de Berghamme is unhorsed. At this juncture a strange knight rides into the lists, claiming the right to do battle. Five of Edward's knights are pitted against him, and all are overthrown.

---

[1] The name is spelt de Byrtonne in the biographical fragment, and de Bourtonne in the poem. Variations also occur in the ancient spelling of the word *Sir*—which is given as Syr, Syrr, and Syrre.

Whereupon, de Bourtonne, by virtue of his three victories, challenges the unknown knight, vowing that if his former feats of arms are crowned by yet another success, he will build a church on this very spot to commemorate his triumphs in the field.

> By thee, Saint Mary, and thy Son, I swear,
> That in what place yon doughty knight shall fall
> Beneath the strong push of my outstretched spear,
> There shall arise a holy church's wall,
> The which in honour, I will Mary call,
> With pillars large, and spire full high and round.
> And this I faithfully will stand to all,
> If yonder stranger falleth to the ground.
> Stranger, be boune; [1] I champion you to war.
> Sound, sound the slogans, to be heard from far.
> (BOURTONNE and the STRANGER fight. STRANGER
> falls.)

KING. The morning-tilts now cease.

HER. Bourtonne is King.

> Display the English banner on the tent;
> Round him, ye minstrels, songs of achments [2] sing;
> Ye heralds, gather up the spears besprente; [3]
> To king of tourney-tilt be all knees bent.
> Dames fair and gentle, for your loves he fought;
> For you the long tilt-lance, the sword he shente; [4]
> He jousted, having only you in thought.
> Come, minstrels, sound the string, go on each side,
> Whilst he unto the king in state doth ride.

The rhythm now changes, the martial spirit giving place to a softer and more beguiling tone, and the scene closes with a second minstrel's song, extolling the pleasures of

---

[1] Ready.
[2] Achievements; but misspelt.
[3] Sprinkled about.
[4] Spoilt, broke.

rest and relaxation, once the stern demands of honour have been satisfied.

*   *   *

Battle of Hastings, purporting to be the work of Turgot, a Saxon monk of the eleventh century, translated by Rowley —though the reader has already been made aware how Chatterton confessed to Barrett that he had written the first part of it himself—is one of the earliest and longest of the Rowley Poems; Part One containing fifty-six ten-line stanzas and one broken stanza of four lines; Part Two, seventy-two ten-line stanzas. Each part begins with an invocation, that of Part One being:

> *O Christ, it is a grief for me to tell,*
> *How many a noble earl and valorous knight*
> *In fighting for King Harold nobly fell,*
> *All slain in Hastings field in bloody fight.*
> *O sea! our teeming donor had thy flood*
> *Had any fructuous entendèment,*[1]
> *Thou wouldst have rose and sunk with tides of blood,*
> *Before Duke William's knights had hither went;*
> *Whose coward arrows many earlès slain,*
> *And 'brued the field with blood, as season rain.*

Harold and William of Normandy severally harangue their troops, the English King strikes the blow, the struggle to repel the invaders commences, and instantly one is struck by the savage zest and exultancy with which the poet lays about him; for despite the precocious maturity of his mind, and his frequent flashes of undeniable genius, Chatterton, at this period of his life, seems to have had a thoroughly normal and boyish passion for strife, violent untrammelled action, and gore that "smoked in puddles on the dusty plain." By far the greater portion of this

---

[1] Fertile understanding, *i.e.* useful knowledge.

turgid and bloodthirsty composition is devoted to "close-ups" of desperate, hand-to-hand encounters, in which one or other, or preferably both, the combatants are slain. The affrighted air resounds to the din of battle-axes, the hiss of arrows, the thunder of horses' hooves, and the groans of the wounded and dying. All is unbelievable carnage and confusion. The poem ends abruptly—but the fighting still goes on.

In Part Two, the invocation is to Truth—"immortal daughter of the skies"—and for a spell there is a welcome lull in the hostilities.

> *And now the grey-eyed morn with violets drest,*
> *Shaking the dewdrops on the flowery meads,*
> *Fled with her rosy radiance to the west.*

But the early morning quietude is of short duration. Hardly is the sun fully risen, before Harold:

> *His mighty arm, decked with a manchyn[1] rare;*
> *With even hand a mighty javelin peised,[2]*
> *Then furious sent it whistling through the air.*
> *It struck the helmet of the Sieur de Beer.*
> *In vain did brass or iron stop its way;*
> *Above his eyes it came, the bones did tear,*
> *Piercing quite through, before it did allay;[3]*
> *He tumbled, screeching with his horrid pain;*
> *His hollow cuishes[4] rang upon the bloody plain.*

Once more the conflict rages; but now, amid the general insistence upon butchery and the lust for destruction, there come compensating glimpses of the varying moods and aspects of the countryside and, when the exploits of the knight Adhelm are dilated upon, we

---

[1] Sleeve.   [2] Poised.   [3] Stop (wrongly).
[4] Armour for the thighs.

are given a sudden, unexpectedly gracious picture of Kennewalcha, the wife he has left behind him:

> *Taper as candles laid at Cuthbert's shrine,*
> *Taper as elms that Goodricke's abbey shrove;* [1]
> *Taper as silver chalices for wine,*
> *So taper were her arms and shape y-grove.* [2]
> *As skilful miners by the stones above*
> *Can ken what metal is contained below,*
> *So Kennewalcha's face, y-made for love,*
> *The lovely image of her soul did shew. . . .*

All too soon, however, the idyll of Adhelm and Kennewalcha is dispersed. The atmosphere darkens, the sanguinary tide of war rolls onward, death and annihilation stalk on every side, and the last stanza closes with Harold still alive, and the fate of the day as yet undecided.

*   *   *

No greater contrast to the wild horrors of *Battle of Hastings* could be found than the dignified restraint and disciplined economy of expression which place *Bristowe Tragedie, or The Dethe of Syr Charles Bawdin* high on the list of Chatterton's poetical achievements. Two years after the poet's death, *Bristowe Tragedie* was published separately by Newbury, in St. Paul's Churchyard, when it did not escape the watchful eye of Horace Walpole, who, on 25th May 1772, wrote to Mason:

Somebody, I fancy Dr. Percy, has published a dismal, dull poem called The Execution of Sir Charles Bawdin, and given it for one of the Bristol poems called Rowley's—but it is a still worse counterfeit than those which were first sent to me.

But Walpole was notoriously deficient in literary taste, the old grievances still rankled, and he was not likely to

---

[1] Rowleian for shrouded.   [2] *Y-graven*; shaped, formed.

miss putting a spoke in the wheel of Rowley and Chatterton whenever an opportunity for doing so occurred. There is, indeed, no trace of anything dismal or dull in the poem. The subject is pitiful and tragic enough, but the arrest of Sir Charles Bawdin, a brave Lancastrian knight, on a charge of high treason; the unavailing appeal of William Canynges to Edward IV, himself in Bristol at the time, for clemency and justice on the prisoner's behalf; the parting of Sir Charles from his sorrowing wife; the procession to the scaffold, witnessed by the King in person from a neighbouring building; and the culminating scene of execution and dismemberment, are all projected in a strong, clear, wintry light, and conceived in a spirit of heroic fortitude and freedom from exaggeration that are fully in keeping with the highest romantic traditions. The character of the hero is beautifully drawn, and nothing could exceed the moving simplicity of the lines in which, having learnt that Canynges' efforts to save him have failed, Sir Charles prepares to meet his death.

> "*My honest friend, my fault has been*
> *To serve God and my prince;*
> *And that I no time-server am,*
> *My death will soon convince.*
>
> *In London city was I born,*
> *Of parents of great note;*
> *My father did a noble arms*
> *Emblazon on his coat.*
>
> *I make no doubt but he is gone*
> *Where soon I hope to go;*
> *Where we for ever shall be blest,*
> *From out the reach of woe:*
>
> *He taught me justice and the laws*
> *With pity to unite;*

And eke he taught me how to know
The wrong cause from the right.

He taught me with a prudent hand
To feed the hungry poor,
Nor let my servants drive away
The hungry from my door.

And none can say but all my life
I have his wordès kept;
And summed the action of the day
Each night before I slept.''

Nor does his courage waver, or his belief in his own
integrity desert him, when on his way to the gallows he
passes the King, seated in state at the window of the great
minster; he remains proudly and inflexibly defiant to the
end.

"Thou thinkest I shall die to-day;
I have been dead till now,
And soon shall live to wear a crown
For aye upon my brow:

Whilst thou, perhaps, for some few years
Shalt rule this fickle land,
To let them know how wide the rule
'Twixt king and tyrant hand:

Thy power unjust, thou traitor slave!
Shall fall on thy own head——"
From out the hearing of the king
Departed then the sledde.

King Edward's soul rushed to his face,
He turned his head away,
And to his brother Gloucester
He thus did speak and say:

> *" To him that so-much-dreaded death*
> *No ghastly terrors bring,*
> *Behold the man! He spake the truth,*
> *He's greater than a king!"*

Then comes the falling of the headsman's axe, the quartering of the dead body so that, in conformity with the barbarous custom of the period, it might be exposed to public obloquy in various parts of the town, the severed head being hoisted to the top of the cross in High Street; and lastly, the poet's bitterest, most ironic shaft of all:

> *Thus was the end of Bawdin's fate:*
> *God prosper long our king,*
> *And grant he may, with Bawdin's soul,*
> *In heaven God's mercy sing!*

> *   *   *

In *The Storie of William Canynge*, Rowley, now advanced in years, is discovered, lost in reverie, by the side of a stream:

> *Beside a brooklet as I lay reclined,*
> *List'ning to hear the water glide along,*
> *Minding how thòrough the green meads it twined,*
> *Awhilst the caves responsed its muttering song,*
> *At distant rising Avon to be sped,*
> *Mingled with rising hills, did show its head;*
> *Engarlanded with crowns of osier weeds*
> *And wreaths of alders of a bercie [1] scent,*
> *And sticking out with clod-agested [2] reeds,*
> *The hoary Avon shew'd dire semblamente,[3]*
> *Whilst blataunt [4] Severn, from Sabrina clepde,[5]*
> *Roars flemie [6] o'er the sandès that she heap'd.*

---

[1] An unexplained word.
[2] Heaped up.
[3] Appearance (but right spelling is semblaunt).
[4] Noisy.
[5] Named.
[6] Frightened (wrongly).

Dreaming to the accompaniment of these sylvan sights and sounds, Rowley's mind turns back to "the hardy champions knowen to the flood;"—to Ælla, Warden of Bristol, and to holy Wareburghus, "as fair a saint as any town can boast."

> *I see his image walking through the coast;*
> *Fitz-Harding, Bithricus, and twenty moe [1]*
> *In vision 'fore my phantasy did go.*

Suddenly, while he is thus half-bemused, there rises from the water the form of a maiden:

> *Whose gentle tresses moved not to the wind;*
> *Like to the silver moon in frosty neete,[2]*
> *The demoisel did come, so blithe and sweet.*

> *No broided[3] mantle of a scarlet hue,*
> *No shoe-peaks plaited o'er with riband-gear,*
> *No costly paraments[4] of woden[5] blue,*
> *Naught of a dress, but beauty did she wear;*
> *Naked she was, and lookéd sweet of youth,*
> *All did bewryen[6] that her name was Truth.*

Recalling his priestly vow, and mindful of the crucifix he carried in his pocket, Rowley looked upon her "with eyne as pure as angels do, and did the every thought of foul eschew." Whereupon the maiden tells him how—

> *"Full many champions and men of lore,*
> *Painters and carvellers[7] have gained good name,*
> *But there's a Canynge to increase the store,*
> *A Canynge who shall buy up all their fame.*
> *Take thou my power, and see in child and man*
> *What very nobleness in Canynge ran."*

---

[1] More.   [2] Night (Scottish).   [3] Embroidered.   [4] Apparel.
[5] Dyed with wode—a coined word.   [6] Meant for reveal.   [7] Carvers.

Rowley's reverie deepens, and in an ecstasy he is carried back to the days of Canynges' birth, from which moment he traces the life of his patron through all its phases; his childhood, youth, manhood, marriage; the deaths of his father and brother; his inheritance of their wealth; the chantry he built to redeem their souls; the provision he makes for his younger brother, John, who becomes Lord Mayor of London; the untimely death of his wife, Johanna; his share in the glories of St. Mary Redcliff; until, in the closing stanza, he is roused—his dream-journey through Time accomplished—by the ringing of a distant bell:

> *I saw the myndbruch* [1] *of his noble soul*
> *When Edward menacèd a second wife,*
> *I saw what Pheryons* [2] *in his mind did roll;*
> *Now fixed from second dames a priest for life.*
> *"This is the man of men," the vision spoke;*
> *Then bell for evensong my senses woke.*

The Storie of William Canynge is incomparably the finest of all the shorter Rowley Poems. From the first line to the last the mood of remoteness, of spiritual detachment, is consistently maintained, and the whole composition moves with a lovely grave serenity rarely equalled and, within its self-prescribed limits, assuredly never surpassed in English poetry.

*   *   *

Englysh Metamorphosis, the title obviously suggested by the *Metamorphoses* of Ovid, resolves itself into a Rowleian variation of stanzas 5–19, Canto X, of the Second Book of Spenser's *Faerie Queene*, dealing with the legendary manner

---

[1] "A hurting of worship or honour."
[2] A mistake for pheons—from "*Pheon*, the barbed head of a dart or arrow."
—Bailey.

in which the river Severn came by its name. In the Rowley version there are slight modifications of spelling in regard to two of the principal characters: Locrine, the King, and Sabrina, his natural daughter by Estrild, remain unchanged; but the Spenserian Queen, Guendolene, is converted into Guendoline, and the wanton, Estrild, euphoniously transposes a consonant and becomes Elstrid. The poem opens in much the same spirit as the original, with an account of the savage and unenlightened· state of the country, described in *The Faerie Queene* as: "Unpeopled, unmannured, unprovd, unpraysd;" the arrival from over the seas of Brutus, who is acclaimed Emperor; the dawn of a primitive civilization; and the succession, after a "twain of twelve years," of Locrine. The Locrine of Rowley, though he repels an invasion of the Huns, is of a gentler, less heroic temper than Spenser's Locrine; but he is equally susceptible to the allurements of Elstrid, in whom:

> *The morning tinge, the rose, the lily flower,*
> *In ever-running race, on her did paint their power.*

Neglecting his loyal and blameless wife, Locrine is oblivious of everything, save his infatuation for Elstrid, on whom he fathers the child, Sabrina.

> *They lived soft moments to a pleasant age;*
> *Oft wandering in the coppice, dell, and grove,*
> *Where no one's eyes might their disport engage;*
> *There did they tell the merry loving fage,*[1]
> *And crop the primrose flowers to deck their head;*
> *The fiery Guendoline, in woman-rage*
> *Assembled warriors to revenge her bed;*
> *They rose; in battle was great Locrine sleene;*
> *The fair Elstrida fled from the enragèd queen.*

[1] A merry tale.—Bailey.

E

Elstrid and her love-child, the mother disguised as a youth in armour, and calling herself Vincent, hide themselves in the Western hills, but Guendoline sends in pursuit of the fugitives a giant knight, who tears up a mountain and flings it at them. Olympus, however, is indulgent:

> *The gods, who knew the actions of the wyghte,*
> *To lessen the sad hap of twain so fair,*
> *Hollow did make the mountain by their might.*
> *Forth from Sabrina ran a river clear,*
> *Roaring and rolling on in course bysmare:* [1]
> *From female Vincent shot a ridge of stones,*
> *Each side the river rising heavenwere;* [2]
> *Sabrina's flood was held in Elstrid's bones.*
> *So they are called; the gentle and the hind* [3]
> *Can tell, that Severn's stream by Vincent's rock's*
>   *y-wrynde.* [4]

Nor does the fantasy end here. Spenser had been satisfied with one metamorphosis, that of Sabrina into the river bearing her name; Rowley, on the other hand, with scarcely any denigration of existing literary values, contrives to bring off a hat-trick, for in addition to the miracle of St. Vincent's Rock, he arrests the giant knight on his homeward journey, overwhelms him by "ruddy lightning," and transforms him into Snowden!

*　　*　　*

The *Songe to Ælla; To John Ladgate;* and *Lines Composed by John Ladgate, a Priest in London;* form a small composite group of their own. By John Ladgate is meant John

---

[1] Meandering, devious.
[2] Heavenward (wrongly).
[3] Peasant.
[4] Covered (wrongly).

Lydgate (1370?–1450?), a Benedictine monk of Bury St. Edmunds, the contemporary and disciple of Chaucer, whose name Chatterton repeatedly misspells both here and elsewhere. Lydgate was the author of *Troy Book; Storie of Thebes; Falls of Princes;* and also, in a much gayer and more satirical strain, of such minor works as *Mumming at Hereford*, *A Ditty of Woman's Horns* (a lampoon directed against the extravagant head-dresses worn by court ladies in the Middle Ages) and *London Lickpenny*. In the present instance Rowley has professedly forwarded a copy of the *Songe*, with ten extra lines of verse, to Lydgate, explaining somewhat tritely that since they must now engage in what he calls a "bouting match"—

> *This is my 'formance, which I now have writ,*
> *The best performance of my little wit.*

To which Lydgate, having read the *Songe* and greatly admired it, replies by sending in return five stanzas of appreciation, briefly sketching the history of poetry from Homer, Virgil, Merlin, Alfred, and Turgotus, to Chaucer and Stone—or Stowe, as he evidently prefers to misname him—rounding off with:

> *Now Rowley in these murky days*
> *Lends out his shining lights,*
> *And Turgotus and Chaucer lives*
> *In ev'ry line he writes.*

As for the *Songe to Ælla*, it is a Pindaric ode to the Saxon hero, stirring and forceful, the emotional tensity ever mounting upwards until the final and most dynamic line of all is reached. To quote from the poem would be to detract from this exciting cumulative quality, and therefore it may be more fittingly given in full.

SONGE TO ÆLLA

Lord of the Castle of Bristol in Days of Yore.

I

Oh thou, or what remains of thee,
Ælla, the darling of futurity,
Let this my song bold as thy courage be,
As everlasting to posterity.

II

When Dacia's sons, whose hairs of blood-red hue,
Like kingcups bursting with the morning dew,
Arranged in drear array,
Upon the lethal day,
Spread far and wide on Watchet's shore;
Then didst thou furious stand,
And by thy valiant hand
Didst sprinkle all the meads with gore.

III

Drawn by thy weapon fell,
Down to the depths of hell
Thousands of Dacians went;
Bristolians, men of might
Then dared the bloody fight,
And acted deeds full quaint.

IV

Oh, thou, where'er (thy bones at rest)
Thy sprite to haunt delightest best,

Whether upon the blood-embruèd plain,
  Or where thou ken'st from far
  The dismal cry of war,
Or sèest some mountain made of corse of slain;

V

Or seest the hatchedd [1] *steed,*
  Y-prancing o'er the mead,
And neigh to be among the pointed spears;
  Or, in the black armour stalk'st around
  Embattled Bristol, once thy ground,
And glowest, ardurous [2] *on the Castle steeres;* [3]

VI

Or fiery round the minster glare, [4]
  Let Bristol still be made thy care;
Guard it from foemen and consuming fire;
  Like Avon's stream, ensyrke [5] *it round,*
  Nor let a flame enharm the ground,
Till in one flame all the whole world expire.

*   *   *

The Worlde, attributed not to Rowley but to William Canynges, displays all the familiar signs and tokens of a miniature Morality. The characters are A Father (strongly resembling the elder Canynges in his covetous greed for "ruddy gold") and six Minstrels. The Father summons the Minstrels into his presence, and confides to them his anxieties concerning his young son, who is starting out in the world:

---

[1] Covered with achievements; from Bailey's *Hatchments*.
[2] Burning brightly (coined word).   [3] Castle stairs.
[4] False grammar for glarest, or dost glare.   [5] Encircle (wrongly).

> *Ye minstrels, warn him how with rede* [1] *he stray*
> *Where gilded vice doth spread his mascill'd* [2] *snare;*
> *To getting wealth I would he should be bred.*.. . .

In obedience to their master's behests, the Minstrels thereupon appear, .one by one, in the guise of various human failings; the first as Interest, the second as an Idle Deceiver, the third as Pride, the fourth as Usury, the fifth as Vice, the sixth as Death. Each declaims a stanza frankly revealing his own baseness, yet containing a scratch of uncongenial ethical protest scarcely concealed beneath its shrouded claws. That of Vice, for example, being:

> *Vice I am called, on gold full oft I ride,*
> *Full fair unto the sight for aye I seem;*
> *My ugliness* [3] *with golden veils I hide,*
> *Laying my lovers in a silken dream.*
> *But when my untrue treasures have been tried,*
> *Then do I shew all filthiness* [4] *and rou,* [5]
> *And those I have in net would fain my gripe eschew.* [6]

Death is even more uncompromising:

> *I am great Death; all ken me by the name,*
> *But none can say how I do loose the sprite;*
> *Good men my tardying delay do blame,*
> *But most rich usurers from me take a flight;*
> *Mickle of wealth I see, where'er I came,*
> *Doëth my terror* [7] *mickle multiply,*
> *And maketh them afraid to live or die.*

---

[1] Counsel, good advice.
[2] Full of meshes; from Bailey's *Mascle* (in heraldry) a short lozenge, voided, representing the mesh of a net.
[3] C. has "Ugsomeness.".   [4] C. has "Horrowness"—mean, base.
[5] An old form of rough.   [6] Escape from—correctly used.
[7] C. has "Ghastness."

Needless to remark, such is not the counsel the old man seeks; the last arrow strikes so nearly home that, badly shaken but still unregenerate, he bursts out furiously:

> *How! villain Minstrels, and is this your rede?*
> *Away, away! I will not give a curse.*[1]
> *My son, my son, of this my speech take heed,*
> *Nothing is good that bringeth not to purse.*

[1] Professor Skeat, in his footnotes to this poem, has: "Kerse is old English for *cress*; hence "not worth a kerse" meant, originally, "not worth a cress." "It is very improbable, however," he adds, "that Chatterton knew this."

THE ROWLEY POEMS

(Part Two)

Of the three Eclogues—*Robert and Raufe, Nygelle,* and *Manne, Womanne, Syr Rogerre*—the first portrays, in a duologue between two shepherds, Robert and Raufe, the poverty and suffering which are the inevitable concomitants of war; and there is a deeply felt and universal poignancy in Robert's lament for the loss of his former possessions.

> *Oh! I could wail my kingcup-deckèd mees,*[1]
> *My spreading flocks of sheep of lily white,*
> *My tender apples,*[2] *and embodied*[3] *trees,*
> *My parker's grange,*[4] *far-spreading to the sight,*
> *My cuyen*[5] *kine, my bullocks strong in fight,*
> *My gorne*[6] *emblanchèd with the comfreie*[7] *plant,*
> *My flower-Saint-Mary*[8] *shooting with the light,*
> *My store of all the blessings Heaven can grant;*
> *I am duressèd*[9] *unto sorrow's blow,*
> *I, hantenèd*[10] *to the pain, will let no salt tear*
> *flow.*

Apart from the intrinsic worth of the poem, which is rich in simple, moving imagery, and has a desolate,

[1] Rowleian for *meads*.
[2] C. has *applynges*.
[3] Bulky—well-grown.
[4] Park-keeper's farm.
[5] Tender; but there is no such word.
[6] Apparently a contraction of *garden*.
[7] Bailey has "*Comfrey,* an excellent wound-herb."
[8] A periphrasis for Marygold.
[9] Hardened.
[10] Accustomed.

haunting music of its own, the change of heart in the poet, even if it be but a momentary change, is psychologically interesting. For Chatterton, like many another chronicler of heroic deeds, was prone to see one side of the picture only, and to overlook the fact that, while dying warriors might be translated to a glittering Valhalla beyond the clouds, where they remained, in accordance with age-old tradition, immortal, triumphant, and secure, their martial glories none the less insistently called for payment, and fell, a grievous back-breaking burden on those who were left behind. Seldom has the lot of the unhappy survivor, condemned to build up his shattered world anew, been depicted with a starker realism. One reads the poem feeling it might have been written yesterday.

In the second Eclogue, *Nygelle*, the period shifts to the times of the Crusades. In a manner reminiscent of the brilliant, microscopic exactitude of those backgrounds which one sees through doors and windows in paintings by the Italian Primitives, there is a series of word-pictures, describing the return of Nygelle's father from the Holy Land, and his exploits on the field of battle against the Saracens. As always, the visual aspect of the theme is strongly emphasized, and a vivid glimpse is furnished of the armada on its homeward voyage, with its panoply of flags and pennons and brightly coloured heraldic emblems, riding gallantly on the dark waters:

> *The red y-painted oars from the black tide,*
> *Carved with devices rare, do shimmering rise;*
> *Upswelling do they shew in dreary* [1] *pride,*
> *Like gore-red estells* [2] *in the eve-mirk skies;*

[1] *i.e.* terrible.
[2] Stars; old French *estoile*.

The name-depicted [1] shields, the spears arise,
Aye like tall rushes on the water-side;
Along from bark to bark the bright sheen flies;
Swift-sped [2] delights do on the water glide.
Sprites of the blest, and every saint y-dead,
Pour out your pleasance on my father's head.

The last two lines, with one slight variant, are used as a refrain at the end of every stanza, excepting the final one, and the poem closes with the joyful reunion of father and son.

The third Eclogue—*Manne, Womanne, Syr Rogerre*—is purely and simply an English Pastoral. In this small work precisely the right "folk" atmosphere is caught; the writing is forthright, naïvely humorous, and refreshingly free from any taint of self-conscious artifice. A man and a woman meet by chance on the way to a haymaking. All around them the early morning sun lights up the quiet country landscape, yet neither is altogether in tune with the fair promise of the day. It is the woman who first voices her inner dissatisfactions, for she complains:

How hard is my doom to wurch [3]
Great is my woe;
Dame Agnes, who lies in the church
With birlet [4] gold,
With gilded aumeres,[5] strong, untold,
What was she more than me, to be so?

Just then, Syr Rogerre, who is also a priest, and for whose hayfields they are bound, appears in sight, and presently the man accosts him with:

[1] "Rebused shields; a herald term, when the charge of the shield implies the name of the bearer."—(Note by Chatterton).

[2] C. has "Sweft-kerv'd."   [3] Work.   [4] Bailey has "Birlet, a coif or hood."

[5] "Borders of gold and silver, on which was (*sic*) laid thin plates of either metal countercharged, not unlike the present spangled laces."—(Note by Chatterton).   "But," adds Professor Skeat, "he was simply misled by Bailey's '*Aumere*, a welt, skirt, or border.' The meaning of *aumere* is, however, a purse."

All-a-boon, Sir Priest, all-a-boon!
By your priestship, now say unto me;
Sir Gaufrid the knight, who liveth hard by,
Why should he than me be more great,
In honour, knighthood, and estate?

The priest, however, true to type, has his theological stock-in-trade ready to command. He discourses on the precarious tenure upon which all human life is held, and goes on to add:

Thou workest; well, can that a trouble be?
Sloth more would jade thee than the roughest day.

Superficially the man agrees. His portion is less circumscribed than the woman's; he is not without certain consolations which he enumerates cheerfully; his songs at the plough; his long "jub" of ale; his light promiscuous loves; his holidays on Saints' Days, when, to the music of the minstrel, he foots it with his comrades on the green; and yet the faint sting of an undeserved inferiority persists.

And so Syr Rogerre resorts once more to his spiritual emollients and, with better heart than logic, clinches the argument thus:

Hast thou not seen a tree upon a hill,
Whose unlist [1] *branches reachen far to sight?*
When furious tempests [2] *do the heaven fill,*
It shaketh dire, in dole and much affright,
Whilst the poor lowly floweret, humbly dight,
Standeth unhurt, unquashèd by the storm.
Such is a picte [3] *of life; the man of might*
Is tempest-chafed, his woe great as his form;
Thyself, a floweret of a small account,
Wouldst harder feel the wind, as thou didst higher mount.

[1] Unbounded, boundless, huge (wrongly).
[2] C. has "Fuired unwers"; from Bailey's "Fuir, fury," and a contraction of *unweather*, *i.e.* tempest, as in Dutch.   [3] Picture (wrongly).

There remain *The Romaunte of the Cnyghte*, which was supposed to have been written by Henry Burgum's ancestor, John de Burgham; *The Merrie Trickes of Lay-myngetowne*, attributed to John a Iscam; *A Chronycalle of Brystowe*, "wrote bie Raufe Chedder, Chappmanne, 1356;" *On Happienesse*, *The Gouler's Requiem*, and the epigram, *Onne John A Dalbenie*, all three purporting to come from the pen of William Canynges; *Fragment* and *Warre*, "by John, Seconde Abbotte of Seyncte Austyns Mynsterre;" a number of minor Rowley compositions, including his translations of the imaginary works of the two Saxon bishops, Ecca of Hereford, and Elmer of Selseie, which formed part of the *Historie of Peyncters yn Englande* instalment that was sent to Horace Walpole; and three important dramatic pieces—*The Parlyamente of Sprytes*, the unfinished tragedy of *Goddwyn*, and the tragedy of *Ælla*.

The Parlyamente of Sprytes is described as "An Interlude, Played by the Carmelite Friars at Master Canynge's great house, before Master Canynge and Bishop Carpenter, on dedicating the church of *Our Lady of Redclefte*." Obviously it is an early work, and though it may be said, after its own fashion, to accomplish the purpose for which it was written, namely the glorification of the church which obsessed the poet's young imagination, it is in no wise comparable, either in conception or in execution, with *Goddwyn* and *Ælla*.

The piece opens with an "Introduction by Queen Mab," written by "J. Iscamme," beginning:

> When from the earth the sun's hulstrèd,[1]
> Then, from the floweret's straught[2] with dew,
> My liege men make you awhapèd,[3]
> And witches then their witchcraft do.

---

[1] "*Hulstered*, hidden, retired."—Bailey.
[2] Stretched.
[3] "*Awhaped*—amazed."—Bailey.

Then rise the sprites ugsome [1] *and rou,* [2]
And take their walk the churchyard [3] *through.*

In regard to the second line, Chatterton, with that transparent artfulness, which is truly and rather attractively characteristic of him, adds the following footnote: "I think this line is borrowed from a much better one of Rowley's, viz., 'Like kynge cuppes brasteynge wyth the mornynge dew.' The reason why I think Iscam guilty of the plagiary is, that the 'Songe to Ælla' from whence the above line is taken, was wrote when Rowley was in London, collecting of drawings for Mr. Canynge to build the church, and Iscam wrote the above little before the finishing of the church." By such ingenuous devices was the Rowley legend given, in his eyes at least, a more solid and enduring basis.

Immediately after the *Introduction* follows an Address, *To John Carpenter, Bishop of Worcester* (*By Rowleie*), wherein the prelate is apostrophized as being:

> *Learned as Beauclerc, as the Confessor*
> *Holy in life, like Canynge charitable,*
> *Busy in holy church as Vavasour,*
> *Slack in things evil, in all good things stable,*
> *Honest as Saxons were, from whence thou'rt sprung,*
> *Though body weak, thy soul for ever young.*

And then the spirits of the departed great ones—a strange and heterogeneous assemblage—defile processionally before the spectators. First comes Nimrod, conjured up not so much by virtue of his skill as a mighty hunter, but on the strength of his having been the fabled builder of the Tower of Babel; next, for no discoverable reason,

[1] Ugly. Bailey has "*Ugsumness*, terribleness."
[2] "*Rou*, ugly, froward."—Bailey.
[3] C. has *letten*, from Bailey's Litten, as Church-litten, a churchyard.

appears a chorus of Assyrians; who in turn give place to Ælla (here spelt Elle), Bythrycke, Byrton (a new spelling of Simon de Bourton's name), Segowan, Fitz-Hardynge, Framptone, Gaunte, A Knight Templar, and Lamyngeton.

The Spirit of Bythrycke cries out in rapt astonishment:

> *What wondrous monument, what pile is this,*
> *That binds in wonder's chain entendèment?* [1]
> *That doth aloft the airy skyën kiss,*
> *And seemeth mountains, joined by cement,*
> *From Goddès great and wondrous storehouse sent.*
> *Full well mine eyes advise* [2] *it cannot be,*
> *That man could rear of such a great extent*
> *A church so huge yet handsome* [3] *as we see.*
> *The scattered* [4] *clouds, disparted, from it fly,*
> *'Twill be, Iwis,* [5] *to all eternity.*

One by one the spirits sing their praises of the newly-risen church, and the Spirit of Ælla brings the pageant to a close with a timely tribute to the piety and munificence of Canynges himself:

> *When Michael's trump shall sound to inmost land,*
> *Affright the wicked, and awaken all;*
> *Then Canynge rises to eternal rest,*
> *And finds he chose on earth a life the best.*

* * *

The tragedy of *Goddwyn* survives merely as a fragment, a fair copy of which is written out in a thin copy-book, once in the possession of George Catcott, into which had also been transcribed in the poet's handwriting the three Eclogues, the whole being headed: "Eclogues and other

---

[1] Intelligence; the understanding.　　[2] C. has "Arede."
[3] C. has "Bausyn fetyve"; where the former word is Bailey's "*Bawsin*, big, gross; and the latter a misprint for Bailey's "*Fetise*, handsome, spruce."
[4] C. has "Flemed."　　[5] Certainly.

Poems by Thomas Rowley, with a Glossary and Annotations by Thomas Chatterton."

The play has a *Prologue* of twelve lines, "made bie William Canynge," and the "Persons Represented" are set forth as follows:

> Harolde, by T. Rowleie, *the Author*.
> Goddwyn, by Johan de Iscamme.
> Edwarde, by Sir Thybbot Gorges.
> Alstan, by Sir Alan de Vere.
> Kynge Edwarde, by Master Willyam Canynge.

> Others by Knights and Minstrels.

The action of the play concerns itself with the ever-growing ascendancy of Norman influence in Britain at the time of Edward the Confessor. The opening scene discloses Goodwyn and Harold, father and son, restive under the Norman oppression. Harold, young, brave, headstrong, and intensely nationalist in his sympathies, inveighs against the King's weakness, his partiality towards the foreign nobles, and the firm hold they have obtained upon his mind. Goddwyn, while fully alive to the country's danger, counsels patience.

GOD. *Await the time, when God will send us aid.*
HAR. *No; we must strive to aid ourselves with power.*
      When God shall send us aid! 'tis bravely prayed!
      Must we thus cast away the livelong hour?
      Thus cross our arms, and not to live dareygn,[1]
      Unburlèd, undelievre, unespryte?[2]
      Far from my heart be fled that thought of pain,
      I'll free my country, or I'll die in fight.

---

[1] Attempt, endeavour; from Bailey's "*Darraign*, to attempt, to challenge."
[2] An obvious parody of Shakespeare's line—"unhouseled, disappointed, unaneled." It was intended to mean—"Unarmed, unactive, spiritless."

Though his sister is married to Edward, Harold is bound by no ties of kinship or of self-interest; for, when reminded of this circumstance, he exclaims:

> *Aye, I know she is his queen;*
> *Albeit, did she speak her foemen fair,*
> *I would destroy her comely seemlykeen,*
> *And fold my bloody anlace in her hair.*

Under the pressure of Harold's bitter and merciless invective, Goddwyn eventually agrees that the time has come for drastic measures; nevertheless, he is strongly averse to his son's suggestion that the King should be dethroned, providing that Edward will consent "to yield the spoils, and only wear the helm," and the scene closes with Harold about to set out for the West, in order to enlist the services of the powerful earls of Mercia and Coventry, whom he undertakes to bring to Goddwyn's castle, where it is proposed they shall hold a council of war.

The second scene begins with a brief encounter between the King and Queen. The Queen, somewhat lackadaisically, complains of the "broided strangers," who are all too prevalent at court, and warns her husband that the people are disturbed and resentful. But the King, weak though he may be in matters politic, is apparently quite capable of managing his domestic affairs. Peremptorily he dismisses her, telling her that he wishes to spend his time in prayer. Hardly has she gone before Sir Hugh, a Norman knight, appears on the scene. He is the bearer of bad tidings, yet he delivers them with the utmost resourcefulness. The treasury is exhausted, and fresh taxation is out of the question. Harold, when approached upon the subject, has struck Sir Hugh across the face, "Saying, 'Go bear that message to the king.'" Goddwyn, too, has refused to pay further tribute. Sir Hugh contrives, whilst blackening the characters of his enemies, to ingratiate himself with his Royal master, declaring that the Saxons are "Unworthy such a marvel of a king!" Edward is easily beguiled, and promises the knight that if he will help him with his prayers, he will give him twenty mancas (marks), a twain of hamlets for himself and his heirs, and that all the Normans shall be fed from his lands.

The scene ends with the departure of the King and Sir Hugh. And then, suddenly, without the slightest preparation, as it were out of silence and emptiness, crashes, like a prolonged fanfare of trumpets, the magnificent Saxon *Chorus to Liberty*:

When Freedom, dressed in bloodstained vest,
　　To every knight her warsong sung,
Upon her head wild weeds were spread,
　　A gory weapon by her hung.
　　　She dancèd on the heath,
　　　She heard the voice of death.

Pale-eyed Affright, his heart of silver hue,
　　In vain essayed her bosom to acale.[1]
She heard, unscared, the shrieking voice of woe,
　　And sadness in the owlet shake the dale.
　　　She shook the armèd spear,
　　　On high she raised her shield,
　　　Her foemen all appear,
　　　And fly along the field.

Power, with his head out-stretched into the skies,
　　His spear a sunbeam, and his shield a star;
E'en like two burning meteors rolls his eyes,
　　Stamps with his iron feet, and sounds to war.

---

[1] To chill; but *acale* is an adverb, meaning *in a chill*; Bailey has "*Acale*, cold."

She sits upon a rock,
She bends before his spear,
She rises from the shock,
Wielding her own in air.

Hard as the thunder doth she drive it on,
Wit, closely wimpled, guides it to his crown;
His long sharp spear, his spreading shield is gone,
He falls, and falling, rolleth thousands down.
War, gore-faced War, by Envy armed, arist,[1]
His fiery helmet nodding to the air,
Ten bloody arrows in his straining fist——

*   *   *

And here, abruptly as it burst into being, the wild music ceases. Whether Chatterton simply abandoned the play, when inspiration failed him, and turned to something else; or whether he actually completed it, and the manuscript by some mischance got lost, it is of course impossible to say. Sir Daniel Wilson is of the opinion that the prologue in itself furnishes strong circumstantial evidence that *Goddwyn* was carried through to the end; whilst E. H. W. Meyerstein points out that the inclusion of two characters, Edwarde and Alstan, neither of whom appears in this the only available portion, would seem to argue that further dramatic developments were at least in contemplation. On the other hand, Sir Hugh, whose scene with the King occupies thirty-seven lines out of the play's sum-total of two hundred and twenty, is not mentioned in the *dramatis personæ* at all. Certain it is that one long dramatic poem, *The Apostate*, is known to have disappeared, and was thought to have been destroyed by the poet himself during his last hours in Brooke Street;

---

[1] Bailey has "*Arist*, he arose"; which is wrong, since *arist* is a mere contraction of *ariseth*, the present tense.

hence it is not outside the bounds of reasonable conjecture that the remainder of *Goddwyn*, granted that the piece ever existed in its entirety, may have suffered a similar fate.

*   *   *

Ælla was first printed, in Tyrwhitt's edition, from a folio manuscript supplied by George Catcott, who had written across the top of it: "Chatterton's own transcription, 1769."

That its author considered his tragedy to be all and even more than he had claimed for it in his letter to James Dodsley is abundantly proved by the manner in which the piece is presented. In no other instance were all the resources of Chatterton's natural bent for showmanship so skilfully exploited. The approach to the main building is planned on the most grandiose architectural lines. Before the outer façade is exposed to view, the chastened visitor is required to pass through three separate literary fore-courts; the first, *An Epistle To Mastre Canynge on Ælla;* the second, a *Letter to Dygne Mastre Canynge;* and the third, an *Entroductionne.*

Incidentally, the first of these supplementary productions contains testimony sufficient to have blown the whole edifice sky-high, had any of the lynx-eyed pedants of the latter part of the eighteenth century, or the first two decades of the nineteenth, possessed an elementary knowledge of his national literature. But it so happened that, although the age could boast a plentiful crop of classical scholars of the finest attainments, home products were consistently neglected, and apparently among those who battled for and against the authenticity of Rowley, and wrote books and pamphlets with long-winded and provocative titles upon the subject, there was not one who was aware that the only kind of dramatic performances extant in the fifteenth century were the Mystery and

Miracle Plays acted in churches, and that any sustained attempt at a more secular form of entertainment was practically unheard of until nearly a hundred years later. And so the priest was allowed to declare, unchallenged:

> *Plays made from holy tales I hold unmeet,*
> *Let some great story of a man be sung;*
> *When as a man we God and Jesus treat,*
> *In my poor mind we do the Godhead wrong.*

Sentiments, which, however admirable in themselves, were wholly foreign to what would have been Rowley's own mental outlook, and still further removed from the prevailing spirit of the times.

Even the title-page of *Ælla* displays a notable intensification of the Rowleian idiom:

ÆLLA:

A TRAGYCAL ENTERLUDE, OR DISCOORSEYNGE
TRAGEDIE, WROTENN BIE
THOMAS ROWLEIE;
Plaiedd Before Mastre Canynge, atte
Hys Howse Nempte The
Rodde Lodge;
Alsoe Before The Duke of Norfolck
Johan Howard.

On this occasion, as before, the actors were recruited from the stock company of amateurs at the Red Lodge.

PERSONNES REPRESENTEDD.

Ælla, bie Thomas Rowleie, Preeste, the Aucthoure.
Celmonde . . . Johan Iscamm, Preeste.
Hurra . . . . Syrr Thybbotte Gorges, Knyghte.
Birtha . . . . Mastre Edwarde Canynge.

Odherr Partes bie Knyghtes, Mynstrelles, &c.

The first scene is laid in Bristol, on the wedding morn of Ælla, Warden of Bristol Castle, and his lovely Saxon bride, Birtha. The stage, on the rising of the curtain, is empty, save for Celmonde, Ælla's friend, who has presumably escaped from the marriage ceremony, unable to bear it any longer, since he is himself secretly in love with Birtha. In a soliloquy with which the play opens, he discloses his hopeless passion and the base and treacherous thoughts which it engenders:

> *Ah! Birtha, why did Nature frame thee fair?*
> *Why art thou all that pencil can bewreene?[1]*
> *Why art thou not as coarse as others are?*
> *But then—thy soul would through thy visage sheene,[2]*
> *That shimmers on thy comely semlykeene,[3]*
> *Like nutbrown clouds, when by the sun made red,*
> *Or scarlet, with choice linen cloth ywreene;[4]*
> *Such would thy sprite upon thy visage spread.*
> *This day brave Ælla doth thine hand and heart*
> *Claim as his own to be, which ne'er from his must part.*
>
> *And can I live to see her with anere?[5]*
> *It cannot, must not, nay, it shall not be!*
> *This night I'll put strong poison in the beer,*
> *And him, her, and myself, at once shall sle.[6]*
> *Assist me, Hell! let devils round me 'tend,*
> *To slay myself, my love, and eke my doughty friend.*

Disturbed by the approach of Ælla and Birtha, he retires, and the lovers, now safely married, make their appearance. Ælla pours out his heart's devotion upon Birtha, telling her that never, even when the Danes were

---

[1] Probably is intended to mean *express*, but *bewrien* in Chaucer is an infinitive mood, and means *to reveal, discover*.
[2] Shine.
[3] An invented word, due to Bailey's "semeliheed," seemliness, comeliness.
[4] Covered. But the true form is *ywryen*, and it really means concealed.
[5] False spelling for another.   [6] Rowleian for Slay.

in full flight before his advancing army, has he known such joy as he is experiencing now, and after having received in return her own confession of happiness, he adds:

> But had my actions stretched the roll of fate,
> Plucked thee from hell, or brought heav'n down to thee,
> Laid the whole world a footstool at thy feet,
> One smile would be sufficient meed for me.
> I am love's borrow'r, and can never pay,
> But be his borrower still, and thine, my sweet, for aye.

To which Birtha replies:

> Love, do not rate your services so small,
> As I to you, such love unto me bear;
> For nothing past will Birtha ever call,
> Nor on a food from heaven think to cheer.
> As far as this frail brittle flesh will spare,
> Such, and no further, I expect of you;
> Be not too slack in love, nor over-dear;
> A small fire than a loud flame proves more true.

Their mutual protestations are interrupted by the return of Celmonde—now completely master of himself and voluble in his good wishes and congratulations—attended by a troop of minstrels. He bids the minstrels discourse, and there follow, in swift succession, three pastoral ballads; the first a duet between a man and a woman; the second sung by three male voices; and a third, a *Minstrel's Song*, written not by Rowley, but by Sir Thybbot Gorges, and therefore, as E. H. W. Meyerstein suggests, probably intentionally inferior in quality. But the first two are so filled to overflowing with sheer, instinctive lyrical beauty, with tender humanity, and simple love and understanding of the English countryside, that it is astonishing they should not be more widely known. The eighteenth century can show nothing more perfect of their kind.

Scarcely has the singing ceased than a messenger enters
with news of a fresh invasion by the Danes who, under the
joint leadership of Magnus and Hurra, are already closing
in upon the town of Wedĕcester. All gaiety and movement
die out on the instant. Summoned, on the very brink of
the fulfilment of his happiness, to battle with the opposing
forces, Ælla is torn betwixt love and duty. In vain Birtha,
using every feminine sophistry, implores her newly-made
husband to stay with her and to send Celmonde in his
stead to repulse the Danes. Ælla is sorely tempted; for a
moment he seems to waver; but in the end, discipline and
his own conscience prove too strong to be overborne. He
rushes from Birtha, calling as he goes:

> Birtha, adieu; I may not here obaie.[1]
> I'm flying from myself in flying thee.

While she, pursuing him, cries:

> O Ælla, husband, friend, and loverde,[2]
> He's gone, he's gone, alas! perchance he's gone for aye.

And as at the commencement of the scene, Celmonde is
once more left the central figure on the stage; impatient to
plunge into action with Ælla, yet for a space held motion-
less by dark dissatisfactions, and still darker hopes.

The scene now changes to Watchet, where Magnus,
Hurra, and a High Priest, with part of the Danish Army,
are gathered together. At the instigation of Magnus, the
High Priest invokes the gods of battle, falls down, and
afterwards rises to exclaim:

> Thus say the Gods; "Go, issue to the plain,
> For there shall heaps of mighty men be slain."

[1] Evidently with the sense of *abide*; but there is no such word. Speght
wrongly has "Obay, abide."
[2] Lord.

Then ensues a fierce and protracted quarrel between the two leaders. Magnus accuses Hurra of cowardice, calling down physical maledictions upon him in much the same manner as that in which Prospero threatens Caliban with "old cramps" and aches in his bones. Nor is Hurra far behind them when it comes to invective, and the altercation rages until it is silenced by the separate entrances of two messengers, each of whom brings tidings of the arrival of Ælla and his army, and the consternation their presence is spreading through the Danish ranks.

The third scene, which takes place the next morning, is set "Near Watchet." It opens with an impassioned address to his men by Ælla, which is none the less moving and effective because it quite patently derives from Henry V's speech in a similar emergency outside the walls of Harfleur. Indeed, so dynamic are its rhythm and patriotic intensity that, rhetorically speaking, it may fairly be said to hold its own against anything in the dramatic literature of our own or any other European country. Of the seven ten-line stanzas it is here possible only to quote four; but these speak eloquently enough.

> *Ye Christians, do as worthy of the name,*
> *These spoilers of our holy houses slea;* [1]
> *Burst like a cloud from which doth come the flame,*
> *Like torrents, gushing down the mountains, be.*
> *And when along the green their champions flee,*
> *Swift as the red consuming lightning-brand*
> *That haunts the flying murderer o'er the lea,*
> *So fly upon these spoilers of the land.*
> *Let those that are unto their vessels* [2] *fled*
> *Take sleep eterne upon a fiery flaming bed.*

---

[1] Rowleian for *sle*, to slay.

[2] C. has "battayles"; apparently it means *little boats*, from the O.E. *bate*, a boat.

Let coward London see her town on fire,
And strive with gold to stay the spoiler's hand;
Ælla and Bristol have a thought that's higher,
We fight not for ourselves, but all the land.
As Severn's eagre [1] *layeth banks of sand,*
Pressing it down beneath the running stream,
With horrid din engulfing the high strand,
Bearing the rocks along in fury breme, [2]
So will we bear the Dacian army down,
And through a storm of blood will reach the champion's
     crown.

If in this battle luck deserts our gare, [3]
To Bristol they will turn their fury dire;
Bristol, and all her joys, will sink to air,
Burning perforce with unaccustomed fire.
Then let our safety doubly move our ire,
As wolves, wide-roving for the evening prey,
Seeing the lamb and shepherd [4] *near the briar,*
Doth th' one for safety, th' one for hunger slay.
Then when the raven croaks upon the plain,
Oh! let it be the knell to mighty Dacians slain!

Like a red meteor shall my weapon shine,
Like a strong lion-cub I'll be in fight,
Like falling leaves the Dacians shall be slain,
Like loudly-dinning stream shall be my might.
Ye men who would deserve the name of knight,
Let bloody tears by all your paves [5] *be wept;*

[1] The "eagre" (Chatterton has *hyger*) or "bore" of the Severn is a large and swift tide-wave which sometimes flows in from the Atlantic ocean with great force.

[2] Furious.

[3] Cause; from confusion with Bailey's "*gare*, to cause."

[4] Chatterton has *shepster*, which means a female sheep-shearer; but he meant shepherd.

[5] Daggers; a word purely invented from observation of Bailey's "*pavade*, a dagger."

> *To coming times no pencil e'er shall write,*
> *When England had her foeemn, Bristol slept.*
> *Yourselves, your children, and your fellows cry,*
> *Go, fight in honour's cause, be brave, and win or die.*

Instantly the cry of defiance is echoed all along the lines, and the episode closes with the appearance of the Danish troops on a stretch of rising ground, and the din and uproar of battle.

The battle itself is indicated in a series of short broken scenes. Three Danes enter, running away from the Saxons, and are met by Hurra who, urging the necessity for sounding a quick retreat, exposes the boastful Magnus as the real weakling, careless in regard to the disposition of his men, and preoccupied only by qualms for his own safety. Celmonde next enters, recounting the progress of the fight, Ælla's valour and brilliant gifts of leadership, and the death of Magnus, caught in the act of escaping from the field, and dispatched by the Saxon warrior's spear. But Celmonde's whole-hearted admiration for his chief is not proof against the baser side of his nature, or the torments that prey upon his mind. Ælla is wounded, both armies are momentarily spent, and Celmonde calls his squire, ordering him to

> *Prepare a flying horse,*
> *Whose feet are wings, whose pace is like the wind——*

Then, left alone, he thus communes with himself:

> *. . . The qualities I from my parents drew*
> *Were blood and murder, mastery and war;*
> *These will I hold to now, and heed no moe* [1]
> *A wound in honour than a body-scar.*
> *Now, Ælla, now I'm planting of a thorn,*
> *By which thy peace, they love, thy glory, shall be torn.*

[1] More.

From Watchet the scene reverts to Bristol. Here Birtha
and Egwina, her maid, are discovered. Birtha bewails
the absence of her husband, and Egwina, to revive her
mistress's drooping spirits, calls in the minstrels to sing
to her. They sing the lovely ballad, *Oh! Sing unto My
Roundelay*, with its Ophelia-like refrain of—

> *My love is dead,*
> *Gone to his death-bed,*
> *All under the willow-tree—*

which is probably the best-known of all Chatterton's
lyrical poems. Birtha hears them patiently to the end;
but their music cannot stay her fears or lift the heaviness
from her heart.

Thence the action moves with brief suddenness to
Watchet, where a glimpse is afforded of Ælla, chafed by
his wounded and helpless condition, yet none the less
determined to ride to Bristol, so that, if he needs must die,
he may at least do so within the sight of Birtha's eyes and
the sound of her voice; after which there is a "flash-back"
to Bristol, and from now onwards the tragedy moves
rapidly towards its appointed end. Celmonde thrusts his
way into Birtha's presence, breaks the news to her that
Ælla, mortally wounded, is lying at Wedëcester, and
persuades her, without giving any hint of her intention to
Egwina or the rest of the household, to accompany him
on horseback to her husband's side. On the road to
Wedëcester, when night has fallen, he decoys her into a
wood, and once there, believing himself to be secure from
any chance of his plans miscarrying, he confesses his love
for her, and attempts to possess her by force. Birtha,
wholly taken by surprise, and aghast at the horror of her
situation, repulses him and screams aloud for help. Her
cries are heard by Hurra and a detachment of Danish

soldiers, who have taken shelter in the darkness of the trees. They rush to her rescue, a furious encounter takes place between them and the now desperate and frustrated Celmonde who, after having killed several of the soldiers, is himself slain by Hurra. Birtha then reveals her identity as the wife of Hurra's sworn enemy; but he, chivalrous even in defeat, offers her honourable conduct back to Bristol.

The last scene is laid once more in Bristol Castle, on the morning of the following day. Ælla has returned only to learn from Egwina of his wife's flight during the preceding night with a stranger. At first he cannot believe his ears, but when the maid's story is corroborated by another servant, he cries:

> *Oh! speak no more; my heart flames in its hest.*
> *I once was Ælla, now am not his[1] shade.*
> *Had all the fury of misfortune's will*
> *Fall'n on my bannèd head, I had been Ælla still.*
>
> *This only was unarmed, of all my sprite:*
> *My honour, honour, frowned on the soft[2] wind*
> *That steekèd[3] on it; now with rage I'm pight;[4]*
> *A furious tempest is my tortured mind.*
> *My honour yet some driblet joy may find,*
> *To the Dane's wounds I will another give.*
> *When thus my glory and my peàce is rynde,[5]*
> *It were a cowardice to think to live.*
> *My servants, unto every asker tell,*
> *If nobly Ælla lived, as nobly Ælla fell!*
>
> (*Stabs his breast.*)

[1] C. has *yttes*, a word not used in early English, and not suitable here.
[2] C. has *dolce*, from Bailey's "*Dolce*" (in Musick Books) signifies soft and sweet.
[3] Stole (on Chatterton's authority only). Hence *steeked on* is *stole upon*.
[4] Plucked, tortured; a wrong meaning.
[5] Rowleian for *ruined*.

So saying, he stabs himself, and while yet conscious appoints a new warden of the castle in one, Coernyke, just as Birtha and Hurra arrive. Nothing can now save Ælla's life, but he is allowed the consolation of knowing that Birtha has not swerved in her allegiance to him, and that he dies with his honour still unstained. There is a poignant leave-taking between the two ill-starred lovers, and Birtha falls senseless across her husband's body, as the curtain descends on Coernyke's final apostrophe:

> What? Ælla dead? And Birtha dying too?
> So fall the fairest flowerets of the plain.
> Who can unfold the works that heaven can do,
> Or who untwist the roll of fate in twain?
> Ælla, thy glory was thy only gain,
> For that, thy pleasure and thy joy was lost.
> Thy countrymen shall rear thee on the plain
> A pile of stones,[1] as any grave can boast.
> Further, a just reward [2] to thee to be,
> In heaven thou sing of God, on earth we'll sing of thee.

The play, so far as is known, has never been publicly performed. In all probability, its extreme shortness—it comprises but 1,244 lines, and the whole text might be contained, with half a scene to spare, within the first two acts of *Hamlet*—rendered it, since it requires an elaborate production and a large number of supernumeraries, somewhat impracticable for stage purposes. Yet it moves swiftly, gathering interest and significance as the plot unfolds itself; the chief protagonists have a queer, arresting vitality of their own; and the characterization is clear and forthright, especially in the case of Celmonde, who is no

[1] C. has "A pyle of carnes," not being aware, it would appear, that a *cairn* is the pile itself.
[2] C. has *amede*, which is a wrong spelling for *mede*, *i.e.* Meed, reward.

mere stock-figure of villainy, but a subtly drawn personality, who has just, by some inner spiritual flaw, missed
the heroic perfection of the Ælla he betrays. Every effect
that the poet strives for he captures with the ease of an
assured craftsmanship, an unerring sense of selection, and a
masterly economy of means.

It is, of course, idle to speculate upon what might or
might not have happened, had Chatterton's own tragedy
not supervened before he had attained to the full meridian
of his powers. But if he could conceive and execute a play
of the calibre of *Ælla*, between the ages of sixteen and
seventeen, it would not appear unreasonable to prophesy
that, given another thirty years of life, he might have
restored to the theatre something of the lustre it has lost
since the days of Elizabeth and James I, and which it seems
unlikely ever to acquire again.

CHAPTER VIII

MARKING TIME

(1769–1770)

DURING the progress of the Walpole correspondence, though, towards the end of July, he must have begun to be assailed by doubts as to its successful issue, he could still write in a light-hearted, egotistical strain to his relative, Mr. Stephens, of Salisbury:

CORN STREET, BRISTOL. *July* 20, 1769.

SIR,

If you think Vanity is the Dictator of the following Lines, you will not do me Justice. No, Sir, it is only the desire of proving myself worthy your Correspondence, has induced me to write. My partial Friends flatter me, with giving me a little uncommon share of Abilitys, tis Mr. Stephens alone whose good Sense disdains Flattery, whom I must appeal to. It is a Maxim with me that compliments of friends are more dangerous than railing of Enemys. You may inquire, if you please, for the Town and Country Magazines, wherein all signed D. B. and Asaphides are mine. The Pieces called Saxon are originally and totally the product of my Muse; tho I should think it a greater Merit to be able to translate Saxon. As the sd Magazine is by far the best of its Kind I shall have some Pieces in it every Month and if I vary from my said Signatures, will give you notice thereof. Having some curious Anecdotes of Paintings and Painters I sent them to Mr. Walpole Author of the Anecdotes of Painting, Historic Doubts, and other Pieces well known in the learned World. His answer I make bold to send you. Hence began a Literary Correspondence, which ended as most such do. I differed with him in the age of a MS he insists upon his superior Talents, which is no proof of that Superiority. We possibly may publickly engage in one of the periodical Publications tho' I know not who will give the onsett: of my proceedings in this Affair I shall make bold to acquaint you. My next Correspondent of Note is Dodsley, whose Collection of modern and antique Poems are in every Library. In this City my principal Acquaintance are—Mr. Barrett, now writing at a vast expence An Ancient & modern History of Bristol a task more difficult than the cleansing the Augean Stable many have attempted but none succeeded in it, yet will this Work when finished please not only my fellow-Citizens, but all the World—Mr. Catcott, Author of that excellent Treatise on the Deluge and other Pieces to enumerate which would Argue a supposition you was not acquainted with the Literary World. To the studys of these Gentlemen I am always admitted, and they are not below asking my Advice in any matters of Antquity. I have made a very curious Collection of Coins and Antiques. As I cannot afford to have a gold Cabinet to keep them in I commonly give them to those who can. If you can pick up any Roman Saxon English coins or other Antiques, even a sight of them would highly oblige me.

Then the letter concludes with those recommendations as to the quartering of Mr. Stephens's arms, and the short disquisition upon the origin of his family, already quoted on a previous page, the poet signing himself:

I am, yr very hble Servt,

THOS. CHATTERTON.

All that he said about *The Town and Country Magazine* was literally true. The paper, a new monthly periodical, had made its first appearance in January 1769; he had been a constant contributor to its pages since the second number, and *Elinoure and Juga*, the only one of the Rowley Poems he ever saw in print, was published in the May issue. That he received no remuneration of any kind, either for the poem itself or for the other articles and sketches accepted by Hamilton, the editor of the magazine, was, for the moment, a minor consideration, what counted for most was the realization that he was breaking new ground, and reaching a wider section of the public than had been possible heretofore.

But the end of the year found him restless and despondent, once more painfully aware of his servitude, at variance with everything and everybody around him except his own family, and casting about in his mind for some expedient, however, desperate, that might help to set him free.

By now the bulk of the Rowley Poems must have been completed. Yet how could it profit him to have built up the Rowley-Canynges Saga, poem by poem, if it were fated to remain indefinitely upon his hands, or in those of Barrett and Catcott, hidden away from the world? Indeed it would almost seem as if his own long-continued faith in Rowley was gradually diminishing, for more and more, as the months went on, he employed his leisure in writing satirical pieces, after the manner of Churchill— then at the height of his fame—dealing with current topics of the day, and lampooning the frailties and absurdities of all who had incurred his displeasure. By this means he was enabled to get rid of some of his accumulated spleen, and also such material—facile, easily written, and as easily forgotten—was less difficult to dispose of than his antique verse, and therefore more likely to advance the two main objects he had in view; namely, the forcing of himself upon the attention of the public, and the eventual earning of a regular income by his pen.

Towards the middle of August a minor tragedy had occurred that was not without its ultimate repercussion on Chatterton's own life. Peter Smith committed suicide at the age of twenty-one. He had been one of the young Bristol poetasters, but had drifted into bad company, frittered away his opportunities, and was in consequence so severely reprimanded by his father that he went up-stairs to his room and killed himself. Quite unjustifiably

F

Chatterton's influence was held to be indirectly responsible for this calamity, though he had never been in the habit of seeing anything like so much of Peter as he did of William, who was one of his most inseparable friends. As a matter of fact, under the impression that William had been the victim, he at once wrote an *Elegy*, inveighing against the whole Smith family—"brother, father, and sisters"—for their cruelty to the deceased, concluding with the line: "O may his crying blood be on your heads!" and afterwards adding a postscript: "Happily mistaken, having since heard from good Authority, it is Peter."

Then, on 1st November, Phillips, the usher at Colston's, died, and another *Elegy*—to the "Immortal shadow of my much-loved friend!"—called for composition. Apparently Phillips had left Colston's shortly after Chatterton, and as his death took place at Fairford, in Gloucestershire, one is led to infer that they could not have met for some time. But whatever might be the depth and extent of their relationship, the thought of one, so near his own age and so closely bound to him by early recollections, snatched out of life in the fulness of his young manhood, must have affected Chatterton profoundly, especially when following so swiftly on Peter Smith's suicide and coinciding with a period during which existence held for him nothing but emptiness and gloom.

Yet the loss of Phillips brought with it a new friend in Michael Clayfield, a distiller, who had known Phillips well, and to whom Chatterton had applied—in verse—for further information concerning the usher's last illness, and also for confirmation of a rumour then circulating about the city that the illness had proved fatal. Between the poet and Clayfield an intimacy soon arose. Clayfield possessed a library which he placed at the disposal of the other, lent him books on astronomy, took a warm and sympathetic interest in his work, and throughout the few

months that were left to them in which to enjoy each
other's society, showed himself unselfishly devoted to
Chatterton's best interests.

There was, however, very little that Clayfield could do.
For Chatterton the times were so badly out of joint that
no singly directed effort could possibly have put them right
again. Under the pressure of his misfortunes his mind had
become warped, his temper more sullen and intractable
than ever. In a sudden fit of pique, taking offence at some
slighting reference to his poetry, he fell foul of the Rev.
Alexander Catcott. Their association must always have
been rather perilously poised, for in character, disposition,
and outlook they were the direct antitheses of one another.
The Vicar of Temple Church had inherited much of the
pedagogic pomposity of his late father, the Rev. Alexander
Stopford Catcott, who had been headmaster of the Bristol
Grammar School. He was an earnest, industrious man,
but his eyes gave him constant trouble, and he was obliged
to have those works on theology and geology—which were
his chief preoccupations—read aloud to him in his study,
which was fitted up like a museum with shells, fossils,
and specimens of all kinds of mineral formations. Of his
brother George's infatuation for Rowley he thoroughly
disapproved, for he had the greatest antipathy to poetry,
considering its influence, particularly on those who
indulged in the writing of it, to be definitely evil; a belief
which he now probably felt had been amply vindicated by
what had happened to Peter Smith, and might yet happen
to William. And in December, Chatterton, who could
not bear to hear his mistress abused, had retaliated by
composing a rhymed *Epistle to the Rev. A. Catcott*, accompanied by the following prefatory note:

Dec. 20*th*, 1769.—Mr. Catcott will be pleased to observe that
I admire many things in his learned Remarks: this Poem is an
innocent Effort of Poetical Vengeance, as Mr. Catcott has done

me the honour to criticise my Trifles. I have taken great Poetical Libertys, and what I dislike in Verse possibly deserves my approbation in the plain Prose of Truth—The many Admirers of Mr. Catcott may, on Perusal of this, rank me as an Enemy: but I am indifferent in all things; I value neither the Praise or Censure of the multitude.

> *What strange infatuations rule mankind!*
> *How narrow are our projects, how confined—*

was a trenchant beginning, though, emanating from a boy just turned of seventeen, not exactly calculated to appeal to the Vicar, and when the poet went on to gibe with much gusto at his antagonist's foibles, contradict him flatly on nice points of doctrine, accuse him of deficiencies in logic, and presently to make mincemeat of his pet theory—which he was never tired of expounding and in defence of which he had written a portentous *Treatise*— that Noah's flood was to be explained geologically by the internal waters of the earth arising and dissolving the entire world, and that this phenomenon should be accepted in a literal, and not merely in an allegorical sense, by all who truly professed themselves Christians, one can hardly wonder at the reverend gentleman's recoil. He was an expert on the subject. He had given every moment of his spare time to it. He had examined the two "druidical temples" at Abury and Stonehenge, as well as the mines and caves of Derbyshire and Cornwall, and he was perfectly convinced that his findings were correct.

The attack had been launched, perhaps, less from a desire to do real mischief than from a boyish impulse to show off. Fearing that he might have gone too far, how-ever—which he certainly had—he ventured on an apology, and tried to excuse his outspokenness by saying that he had an unlucky way of railing and, when the strong fit of "satyre" was on him, he spared neither friend nor foe. But the Rev. Alexander was not to be conciliated; he took it all as solemnly as he did the Deluge, and Chatterton found that henceforward, to him at any rate, the doors of the Vicarage were closed.

The worst of it was, of course, that the house had been a very useful one, where he had met people who were intelligent and of much better social standing than were the average run of his Bristol friends. Moreover, to have forfeited the right to go there of his own free will argued a serious loss of prestige.

*　　　*　　　*

In *The Epistle*, the Rev. Thomas Broughton, Vicar of St. Mary Redcliff, also came in for much incidental rough handling, and as he was said to have been at one time helpful and kindly disposed towards Chatterton, which may well have been the case considering the Chatterton family's long association with the church, we may safely conclude that there must have ensued another estrangement here. Nor was disapprobation confined to the clergy alone. The older and more respectable citizens shook their heads, and murmured among themselves that the poet was a wild undisciplined youth, who knew a lot of queer people and, mistaking what was simply a hatred of self-sufficiency and hypocrisy in high ecclesiastical places for a contempt of religious principles, began to label him a free thinker and an open and avowed enemy to all established law and order.

And from his principles they passed onwards to his morals. It would have been convenient could they have accused him of being a drunkard, but, curiously enough, though Barrett had tempted him to drink and he had constantly before him the none too edifying spectacle of George Catcott who, less ascetic than his clerical brother, was not above spending a convivial evening now and then at Lewellin's ale-house and staggering home in the small hours, Chatterton still remained faithful to the glass of water and the sparing diet that was all he could ever be induced to partake of from the time he had been a small boy.

But he was handsome, reckless, manly in his bearing, looked years older than he really was, had an insatiable zest for and curiosity about life that not all the hard knocks he had received from it could sensibly diminish, and women had always attracted him. Women then were the one weak joint in his armour, as those who wished to blacken his reputation while he lived, and his memory after his death, were not slow to find out.

That he got a bad name was largely his own fault. His sense of fighting for a bare existence against tremendous odds, of being pitted against an older generation that was either blind to, or mortally afraid of, beauty in any shape or form, of being despised for his empty pockets, and of being tolerated by those immediately above him only so long as he respected their prejudices and made an effort to behave himself, brought out all that was naturally rebellious in him, so that the dreamer, the child idealist who had peopled the silent spaces of St. Mary's with heroic visions of the Middle Ages, was overlaid by that obverse side of his dual personality—the sharp-witted, cynically-minded young man of the world, who might have been twin-brother to Tom Jones. To show how little he cared what was said or thought about him, he flaunted public opinion, boasted of his promiscuities, and greatly fancied himself in the *rôle* of a local Don Juan. Precocious in all ways, in sex experience as in everything else, this was precisely the sort of exhibitionist attitude one would have expected him to adopt. Probably had he been more abandoned than he actually was, he would have kept silent about his occasional lapses, and thus the fact that he was ever almost tiresomely anxious to portray himself as a little monster of iniquity is in itself his best defence.

"Till his fifteenth year he was remarkably indifferent to females," his sister Mary, who afterwards became Mrs. Newton, declares to Sir Herbert Croft.

Yet at fifteen he could write, giving rein to an adolescent touch of exaggeration, to his friend Baker that he had been violently in love these three and twenty times since the other's departure, take a humorous tilt at cuckoldry in passing, and finish up, in one of his enclosures, *Journal Sixth*, with ten lines of verse that throw so scarifying a light on the seamier aspects of drunkenness and incontinence that they have been expunged from several of the later editions of his collected works. Even Mrs. Newton cannot dismiss the problem as though it were non-existent, for she adds:

He would frequently walk the Colledge green with the young girls that statedly paraded there to shew their finery. But I realy believe he was no debauchee (tho some have reported it) the dear unhappy boy had faults enough I saw with concern that he was proud and exceedingly impetuous but that of venality (*sic*) he could not be justly accused with.

The voluble Thistlethwaite had also a word or two in point to say:

The opportunities a long acquaintance with him afforded me, justify me in saying that while he lived in Bristol he was not the debauched character represented. Temperate in his living, moderate in his pleasures, and regular in his exercises, he was undeserving of the aspersion.

Foremost among the dissentient voices is that of the Rev. Dr. Michael Lort who, in relation to Chatterton, may be claimed by E. H. W. Meyerstein as his own especial discovery, since to the earlier biographers he is apparently quite unknown. In Mr. Meyerstein's admirable *Life of Thomas Chatterton*, there appears a transcription of certain notes in manuscript, made by Dr. Lort within eight years of Chatterton's death, all of which are designed to bring the poet into still further disrepute.

Existing testimonies, such as Lambert's in regard to his apprentice's regularity in business and punctuality in returning to the house of an evening, are ruthlessly swept aside, and the evidence of Mrs. Newton and Thistlethwaite is rejected as too partial—that of a sister and a friend; whereas in reality it was a mutual mistrust, the one for ever being anxious to know at first hand what tricks the other might be up to, rather than a sympathetic community of interests, which formed the tie between Chatterton and Thistlethwaite, and therefore, though Mrs. Newton might plausibly be tempted to sketch in the awkward parts of her narrative as lightly as possible, Thistlethwaite was not in the least likely to be handicapped by any such qualms. Among Dr. Lort's observations are:

Chatterton's Bristol acquaintance of the most abandoned sort.
Regularity of his attendance not true, he was sometimes about at nights, and not in the best of company.
It is certain that much of his time was spent in the company of disreputable young men.
Profligacy equal to his abilities.

Mr. Meyerstein describes Dr. Lort as a painstaking and unobtrusive antiquary, which he may well have been, but one cannot help feeling that his strictures would have carried more weight had they been less overwhelmingly directed in Chatterton's disfavour, without the smallest hint of clemency or understanding anywhere, and also had Dr. Lort himself not been a personal friend and admirer of Horace Walpole, and of the latter's most frequent correspondent, the Rev. William Cole. Mason, as well, is in the offing, and somehow one gets an impression of a very hostile little clique, which wrote far too many letters and gossiped far too much. Likewise, it must not be forgotten that towards the close of his life, Chatterton had so unmercifully, and often unjustifiably, satirized the clergy that any sledgehammer bludgeonings issuing from that quarter became essentially unsound.

Conceivably something about midway between Dr. Lort's denunciatory thunderbolts and J. H. Ingram's milk-and-watery halo—for in *The True Chatterton* Chatterton is consistently depicted as most untruly chaste—would perhaps fairly meet the case. At Miss Maria Rumsey— that "female Machiavel"—he had obviously cast an appraising eye, but Miss Rumsey stood on the threshold of marriage with the detested Fowler, while her would-be suitor was only fifteen. Then there are the ladies apostrophized in verse: Miss Bush, Miss Clarke, Miss C——m, of Bristol, the urban Fanny of the Hill, the rustic Biddy of the Dale, and, in addition to these, a fresh bevy of beauty, concerning whose welfare, as we shall presently see, he makes solicitous inquiries when writing home from London. "Safety in numbers" is the time-worn adage that most readily presents itself to the mind. Yet there still survive two letters of the greatest import, which strongly suggest that his dalliance was not always so innocent, or so superficially conducted, as might have been supposed.

The first of the letters is emphatically the more sinister, and would certainly seem to savour rather of the cloven hoof than of the milk-and-watery halo. Part of it is written in a kind of tortured and loosely-rhyming doggerel, and the lady, deficient in spelling and completely disregardful of punctuation, is plainly in no very amiable mood:

> Sir,
>   l send my Love to you and
> Tell you Thiss if you prove Constant I
> not miss but if you frown and torn a way
> I can make Cart of better Hay pray Excep
> of me Love Hartley an send me word Cartingley

F *

Tell me how maney ouncs of Gre'n Ginger
Bread can show the Baker of Honiste
   My house is not bilt with Stavis I
not be Coarted by Boys nor Navis
I Haive a man an man shall Haive me.
if I whaint a fool I send for the
   if you are going to the D
I wish you a good Gonery.

This by itself is sufficiently startling. But there is another shock to come. For on the back of the sheet of paper on which the above is written, the recipient has paraphrased the gist of the letter in twenty lines of verse, in a manner so starkly and unashamedly Rabelaisian, that as yet no publisher has been found who will risk publishing them as they stand. At the British Museum the folio has been removed (in 1892) from the volume containing a collection of the poet's writings, and discreetly lodged in the office of one of the custodians.

The second letter, preserved in the Bristol Library, is noticeably less illiterate and, in this instance, the sender does not hesitate to sign her name in full.

Sir,
to a Blage you I wright a few Lines to you
But have not the weakness to Believe
all you say of me for you may say as
(erasure) much to other young Ladys for all I now
But I Can't go out of a Sunday with you
for I ham a fraid we Shall be seen toge (ther)
Sir if it agreeable to you I had Take a walk with
you in the morning for I be (erasure) Beliue
we shant be seen a bout 6 a Clock
But we must wait with patient for
there (erasure) is a Time for all Things.

1770
April 3
Esther Saunders.

Below:

There is a time for all things—Except Marriage, my Dear
          And so your hbl Serv[t]
                              T. CHATTERTON,
                                   April 9th.

Also a further endorsement:

> This Affair began Mar. 19th 70
> & broke off April 9th 70—
>   The Young Lady wants to be
>   married and can't keep her own
>   Secrets—

N.B.   Having no great Stomach to the Amour for
        divers good Causes and Considerations she
        therefrom otherwise moving, and having
        been forc'd into Correspondence by the Officiousness
        of B. was very indifferent about it &
        far from being chagrin at dismission
        Had also the pleasure of seeming to break
        first—
  ☞ The Lady is not handsom but a great Fortune
  † Miss W. a very pretty Girl now in Chace.

Nothing perhaps could give one a clearer insight into
Chatterton's psychological mechanism at this juncture
than his reactions to these uncouth, slatternly scrawls.
In them, or rather in their spiritual projections, Dr. Lort
saw the whole picture, instead of what was merely a
component part of it—worked in to lend balance and
diversification to the general design. There was another
feature of which he may not have known, or that may have
escaped his notice—seeing that he was on the look-out for
shadows, not for high-lights—and this was a yellowing
scrap of paper, mounted on vellum and soiled along the
creases, where it had been folded so that Chatterton might
slip it into his waistcoat pocket and carry it about with
him wherever he went. On the scrap of paper he had
written out his creed:

THE ARTICLES OF THE BELIEF OF ME THOMAS CHATTERTON.

That God being incomprehensible it is not required
of us to know the mysterys of the Trinity, &c. &c. &c. &c.
That it matters not whether a man is a Pagan, Turk,
Jew, or Christian if he acts according to the Religion
he professes.
That if a man leads a good moral life he is a Christian.
That the Stage is the best School of Morality
                              and
That the Church of Rome (some tricks of Priestcraft
excepted) is certainly the true Church.

T. CHATTERTON.

Sir Daniel Wilson describes this as "a poor negation of
a creed." But maybe the world was more exacting in its
outward professions of religious belief in 1869 than in the
eighteenth century or to-day. The second article, at any
rate, would seem to embody a broad-minded acceptance
of universal brotherhood, which is, intrinsically, the basis
upon which the doctrines of Jesus Christ are founded.
And if the fourth should appear ambiguous, it must be
explained that in the late seventeen-sixties there had been
several notable Shakespearian productions at the Theatre
Royal, Bristol, where doubtless Chatterton, for the first
time in his experience, had seen the plays publicly performed, as opposed to reading them to himself in private;
and thus he was simply attempting to bring Shakespeare
into line with the *Bible*, as two of the greatest influences at
work for the ultimate perfection of mankind. Nor are the
creed and the rude commentaries any more irreconcilable
than are certain primary colours that, when mixed
together, produce an entirely different colour, which is
none the less complemental to themselves.

In an era when *Tom Jones*, *Peregrine Pickle*, and *Tristram
Shandy* were considered quite suitable for family reading,
the approach to morality, public and domestic, was

much less encumbered by polite evasions than it afterwards became upon the accession of Victoria the Good. Yet even despite a further importation of Germanic rectitude, one suspects that human nature, under the surface, remained unregenerately the same. Indeed, it would almost seem that man, by some singular oversight of Heaven, is not fashioned in the best interests of morality, and the utmost that can be expected from him is that he should keep his appetites under reasonable control.

Chatterton took his pleasures where he found them, as did other apprentices of his age and station; but he was never enslaved by them, never doubted their transience or the stale taste they left behind, and, above all things, he never allowed them to interfere with the two serious preoccupations of his existence, his work and his career. Symbols of dissatisfaction they might truthfully be called, those moth-like flutterings round the candle, not evidences of depravity, as Dr. Lort would have one believe. They brought with them, while they lasted, a fleeting impression of power, of manhood, of physical and mental ascendancy—the only equipment he had for fighting his way through life.

Often he had said that God had brought His creatures into the world with arms long enough to reach anything, if they would be at the trouble of extending them. But nowadays, though he stretched out every bit as eagerly and insistently as ever, there was so much that seemed to be eternally beyond his reach.

CHAPTER IX

PRELUDE TO ADVENTURE

(1770)

THE full cycle of the months had swung round. A new year had dawned—the last he was to know on earth —yet it held out no prospects of an improvement in his circumstances. Things were going from bad to worse. The position at Lambert's was more strained, harder to endure with fortitude, than it had ever been; for the occasional glimpses afforded to him of the amenities of life in better-class families, at the houses of the Smiths, the Catcotts, the Barretts, and the Clayfields, where he was received as a guest and not as a dependent, had increased his repugnance to meals roughly served and vulgarly eaten in his master's kitchen. He talked of ending it all by running away, though, without money or any other kind of resource, he knew that escape by this means was next to impossible; they would only find him, bring him back with ignominy, and, in all probability, lock him up in the Bridewell to teach him a wholesome respect for the conditions under which he was bound. Sometimes he even hinted darkly at self-destruction, a threat which the servants lost no time in passing on to their mistress, the attorney's mother, who was thrown into a state of the utmost nervous anxiety at the idea of anything so dreadful happening, especially if Lambert should chance to be away from home.

While the deaths of Phillips and Peter Smith were still pressing heavily upon his mind, Chatterton had written:

Since we can die but once, what matters it
If rope or garter, poison, pistol, sword,
Slow-wasting sickness or the sudden burst
Of valve arterial in the noble parts,
Curtail the miserys of human life?
Though varied is the Cause, the Effect's the same:
All to one common Dissolution tends.

And always there tore at him that restless impatience, that consciousness of Time still rushing past him and leaving him panting in its wake. It was not even now that he misdoubted his capacity, or his intellectual superiority to those about him. He took a fierce sort of pride in his own gifts, in his power to crystallize his thoughts and emotions into vivid impassioned phrases that shone like jewels spread out in the sun. What drove him well-nigh frantic was the world's indifference to the rich stores of wonder and enchantment that lay heaped up around it; its soulless absorption in trade, in politics, in solving that one problem which was ever foremost in its mind—how to get as much out of life as possible for itself, and give away as little in return. Somewhere surely there must be people who would listen to him, and who would gladly give him the praise and recognition for which he hungered, if only he could get into touch with them, if only he could break away from Bristol and wake up one morning to find himself free. But the bars of his cage were set maddeningly close together; he hurled the whole weight of his will-power against them, yet it was he, not they, who was flung back shaken, bruised, and spent.

But however unfavourable the conditions under which he laboured his output was in no wise impaired, his genius being of that hardy and tenacious order which can be relied upon to flourish in the poorest soil. Short of the simultaneous loss of his hands and his brain, nothing could have prevented him from writing. He wrote at the office, during those days when Lambert was happily out of the way; he wrote upstairs in the bedroom he shared with the footboy, while the rest of the household was asleep, always finding that his pen ran faster, and inspiration was more feverishly alive in him when the moon waxed full.

Now he had altogether forsaken Rowley. The material he was producing at the moment he knew to be second-rate, good enough of its kind, perhaps, and displaying that ingenious glibness that was at once his strength and his weakness; but this was all according to plan. He told himself that it was no use attempting to fly before he had learnt to walk. He must meet the prevailing public taste on its own level, play down to it, if needs be, dress his poor overworked drudge of a muse in the brightest motley, rouge her cheeks, paint her lips, pluck her protesting eyebrows, and set her up like a slave for sale in an Eastern market-place. For "pure" poetry—as Horace Walpole had called it—had fallen on evil days. The activities of Junius, Churchill, and their attendant band of satellite scribes, discharging showers of arrows, whose barbs were dipped in poisoned epigrams, against the Grafton Government, and in defence of the outlawed Wilkes, were the supreme sensation of the hour. Politics held pride of place, and the smaller fry must swim with the tide or be submerged by it. Time enough hereafter to make Clio an honest woman, and to bring Rowley into his own again, when the hue and cry had died down.

One of the first of his non-political, modern poems of 1770 was an African Eclogue, of which he subsequently wrote two more, called *Heccar and Gaira*, and it appeared in *The Court and City Magazine* for February, though the manuscript is actually dated the preceding year. *Heccar and Gaira* was modelled, not wholly successfully, on the *Oriental Eclogues* of Collins. A pale reflection of the original strength and vigour of *Ælla* flickers here and there through the lines; but the local colour—snakes, tigers, macaws, javelins, burning plains, and desert sands—has been applied with too heavy a hand, and the result is oleographic rather than inspired. *February—an Elegy* was also printed in *The Town and Country Magazine* for the same month; and about this time he finished *The Consuliad*, a savage attack upon the Government, Lord Sandwich—thinly disguised as "Twitcher"—and the Duke of Grafton.

> *. . . Like Grafton, too, for every vice renowned—*
> *Grafton to whose immortal sense we owe*
> *The blood which will from civil discord flow;*
> *Who swells each grievance, lengthens every tax,*
> *Blind to the ripening vengeance of the axe—*

On 29th January the Grafton Ministry collapsed, the Duke resigned the premiership, and on 24th February there was published, under the signature of *Decimus*, in *The Middlesex Journal*, a *Letter* to the Duke of G——n, drawn up in the style of Junius, and containing a further tirade against the late Prime Minister, whose private life, no less corrupt than his administration, had long been an open scandal, for latterly he had not even scrupled to place his mistress, the notorious Nancy Parsons, beside him at the head of his table, no matter how decorous might be the rest of the company.

Indeed, the first four months of the year, from January until close upon Easter, were marked by the most amazing fertility. Following on the downfall of Grafton came *Resignation*, a long satirical poem, reviewing the crisis from a "Patriotic" angle; and this was succeeded by the even longer *Kew Gardens* (comprising parts of *The Whore of Babylon*, and several shorter pieces) in which that very unpopular lady, the Dowager Princess of Wales—reputed to keep her son, the King, in leading-strings, and to be dangerously susceptible to the fascinations of Lord Bute— was figuratively all but flayed alive. In *Resignation* Chatterton keeps more or less strictly to his central theme, but in *Kew Gardens* such purely local characters as Burgum, Catcott, Broughton, and so forth, whose names were utterly unknown in London, are naïvely introduced cheek by jowl with all the leading social, literary, and political celebrities of the day; yet the piece, as a whole, is animated by a glancing, keen-edged malice, and a brilliant certainty of attack, that place it deservedly high among the ephemeral productions of its class.

Some time in March he sent the first instalment of *Kew Gardens* to Edmunds, the editor of *The Middlesex Journal*, with a note to the effect that

"Mr. Edmunds will send the author, Thomas Chatterton, twenty of the Journals, in which the above poem (which I shall continue) shall appear, by the machine, if he thinks proper to put it in; the money shall be paid to his orders."

Plainly he did not expect payment for the right of publication, and was even ready to defray the cost of the copies forwarded for his own use.

Probably, anticipating that the appearance of *Kew Gardens* might be delayed, he decided to strike yet another blow at the Dowager Princess, composed an Open Letter to her, and dispatched it also to Edmunds.

This was on the Tuesday of Holy Week. Then suddenly, after a long spell of intensive writing, of smouldering discontent, and of acute anxiety concerning his future, events took a violently dramatic turn. Always he had been hard pressed for money, but now, with a number of small debts mounting up against him, he found himself without a penny in the world. It must be borne in mind that he had nothing on which he could count save the wholly

inadequate pocket-money his mother, by stinting herself
and her household, could just manage to allow him, and
that however sparingly he lived there was paper to be
bought, books, which were far more important to him
than food, to be borrowed from the circulating libraries,
and the postage on his manuscripts to be franked, this last
being in itself no inconsiderable matter in those days. In
his difficulties he thought of Burgum, who was a coarse
though not ill-natured man, begged him to lend him
sufficient to tide him over, but at the last moment Burgum
refused to help him in any way at all.

The next thing that happened was that Lambert found,
lying about the office, a letter addressed in Chatterton's
handwriting to Clayfield, which he opened and read. In
it Chatterton declared that he was at the end of his tether,
that he could no longer bear the burden of his joyless,
frustrated existence, and that by the time the letter
reached its destination he would have killed himself.

Thoroughly alarmed and incensed, yet realizing that
his own intervention was likely to be worse than useless,
Lambert instead of forwarding the letter to Clayfield, had it
conveyed to Barrett, who, the attorney evidently thought,
had more influence and authority over Chatterton than
any one else. Barrett thereupon sent for the poet and,
according to his own account: "Questioned him closely
upon the occasion in a tender and friendly manner, but
forcibly urged on him the horrible crime of self-murder,
however glossed over by our present libertines, blaming the
company and principles he had adopted. This betrayed
him into some compunction, and by his tears he seemed to
feel it. At the same time he acknowledged he wanted for
nothing, and denied any distress upon that account."

Here one is sensible of suppressions on both sides;
Barrett, willing enough to pour out good counsel by the
bushelful, but putting his questions as to what might be

the root of the trouble very cautiously, so that he should not be committed to assistance of any more substantial kind; Chatterton, bewildered as to how his letter had fallen into alien hands, sullen and mistrustful, taking refuge in tears of mingled pride and exhaustion, and resolutely shutting down his mind.

In any case, the interview between them must have been inconclusive, at least in so far as Chatterton was concerned, for, still unable to understand by what means Barrett had learnt of his intention to commit suicide—unless, indeed, as he appears to think, the letter, unbeknown to himself, was posted or sent to Clayfield, and that Clayfield and Barrett had subsequently met and discussed its contents—he wrote to the surgeon on the following evening:

SIR,

     Upon recollection, I don't know how Mr Clayfield, could come by his Letter, as I intended to have given him a Letter but did not. In regard to my Motives for the supposed rashness, I shall observe, that I keep no worse Company than *myself*: I never drink to Excess, and have, without Vanity, too much Sense to be attached, to the mercenary retailers of Iniquity. No; It is my PRIDE, my damn'd, native, unconquerable Pride, that plunges me into Distraction. You must know that 19-20th of my Composition is Pride I must either live a Slave, a Servant; to have no Will of my own, no Sentiments of my own which I may freely declare as such;—or DIE—Perplexing Alternative! But it distracts me to think of it—I will endeavour to learn Humility, but it cannot be here. What it may cost me in the Trial Heaven knows!—I am

Y^r much Obliged, unhappy
hble Ser^t.

T. C.
Thursday Even^g

*   *   *

The next day being Good Friday, Lambert's office was presumably closed. On the Saturday, Chatterton, doubtless having the place to himself, employed his time in composing his Last Will and Testament, that strange admixture of mockery, bitterness, and poignant sincerity, the discovery of which was directly responsible for bringing about a consummation he had been striving towards ever since his failures with Dodsley and Walpole—the cancellation of his indentures, and his final severance from Bristol.

The Will, written out in the poet's careful copperplate handwriting, and now preserved in the Bristol Museum, is worded thus:

> All this wrote bet 11 & 2 oclock
> Saturday in the utmost Distress of Mind

NOTA BENE

In a dispute concerning the Character of David it was argued that he must be a holy Man from the Strains of Piety that breathes thro' his whole works—Being of a contrary Opinion and knowing that a great Genius can affect every thing—endeavoring in the foregoing Poems to represent an Enthusiastic Methodist intended to send it to Romaine & impose it upon the infatuated World as a Reality but thanks to Mr Burgum's Generosity I am now employ'd in matters of more Importance.

> Burgum I thank thee thou hast let me see
> That Bristol has impress'd her Stamp on thee
> Thy genrous Spirit emulates the May'rs,
> Thy gen'rous Spirit with thy Bristol's pairs
> Gods! what would Burgum give to get a name
> And snatch his blund'ring Dialect from Shame
> What would he give to hand his Mem'ry down
> To times remotest Boundary—a Crown.
> Would you ask more? his swelling Face looks blue
> Futurity he rates at Two pounds Two.
> Well Burgum take the Laurel to thy brow
> With a rich saddle decorate a Sow
> Strut in Iambics totter in an Ode
> Promise and never pay & be the Mode

Catcott for thee: I know thy heart is good
But ah! thy Merit's seldom understood
Too bigotted to Whimsys which thy Youth
Receiv'd to venerate as Gospel Truth
Thy Friendship never could be dear to me
Since all I am is opposite to thee
If ever obligated to thy Purse
Rowley discharges all; my first chief Curse
For had I never known the antique Lore
I ne'er had ventur'd from my peaceful Shore
To be ye wreck of promises and hopes
A Boy of Learning and a Bard of Tropes
But happy in my humbler Sphere had mov'd
Untroubled unrespected unbelov'd

To Barrett next—He has my Thanks sincere
For all the little Knowledge I had here
But what was Knowledge could it here succeed
When hardly twenty in the Town can read
Could Knowledge bring in In'trest to maintain
The wild Expences of a Poet's Brain
Disinterested Burgum never meant
To take my Knowledge for his Gain Per Cent
When wildly squand'ring every thing I got
On Books and Learning and the Lord knows what
Could Burgum then my Critic, Patron, Friend,
Without security attempt to lend
No! that would be imprudent in the Man
Accuse him of Imprudence if you can
He promis'd I confess and seem'd sincere
Few keep an honorary Promise here,
I thank thee Barrett; thy Advice was right
But twas ordain'd by Fate that I should write
Spite of the Prudence of this prudent Place
I wrote my Mind nor hid the Author's face
Harris e'er long (when reeking from the Press
My Numbers make his self-importance less)
Will wrinkle up his Face and damn the Lay
And drag my Body to the Triple Way
Poor superstitious Mortals! wreak your hate!
Upon my cold remains.

This is the last Will and Testament—of me Thomas Chatterton of the City of Bristol being sound in Body or it is the Fault of my last Surgeon—The Soundness of my Mind the Coroner and Jury are to be judges of—desiring them to take notice that the most perfect Masters of Human Nature in Bristol distinguish me by the Title of the Mad Genius therefore if I do a mad action it is conformable to every Section of my Life which all savoured of Insanity.

Item. If after my Death which will happen tomorrow night before 8 oClock being the feast of the resurrection, the Coroners & Jurors bring it in Lunacy I will and direct that Paul Farr Esqr & Mr Jno Flower do at their joint Expence Cause my Body to be interred in the Tomb of my Fathers and raise the Monument over my Body to the Height of 4 feet 5 Inches placing the present Flat stone on the Top & adding six Tablets. . . .

Then follow inscriptions in French, Latin, and English, in memory of real and imaginary ancestors, occupying three of the tablets.

The fourth, printed in Roman characters, reads:

To the Memory of Thomas Chatterton. Reader Judge not: if thou art a Christian, believe that he shall be Judged by a Superior Power, to that Power only is he now answerable. . . .

The fifth and sixth tablets are devoted to heraldic achievements, and then the Will proceeds as follows:

And I will and direct that if the Coroners Inquest bring it in— Felo de se the s^d Monument shall be notwithstanding erected —And if the s^d Paul Farr & Jno Flower have Souls so Bristol-lish as to refuse this my Bequest they will transmit a Copy of my Will to the Society for supporting the Bill of Rights whom I hereby empower to build the said Monument according to the aforesaid Directions. And if they the said Paul Farr & Jno Flower should build the said Monumt I will and direct that the Second Edition of my Kew Gardens shall be dedicated to them in the following Dedication —To Paul Farr & John Flower Esq^rs this Book is most humbly dedicated by the Author's Ghost—

Item. I give and bequeath all my Vigor and Fire of Youth to Mr George Catcott being sensible he is in most want of it—

Item. From the same charitable motive I give and bequeath unto the Revd Mr Camplin Senr all my Humility. To Mr Burgum all my Prosody & Grammar likewise one Moiety of my Modesty, the other moiety to any young Lady who can prove without blushing that she wants that valuable Commodity. To Bristol all my Spirit and Disinterestedness parcells of goods unknown on her Key since the days of Canynge and Rowley. Tis true a Charitable Gentleman one Mr Colston smuggled a Considerable quantity of it, but it being prov'd that he was a Papist the worshipful Society of Aldermen endeavor to throttle him with the Oath of Allegience—I leave also my Religion to Dr Cutts Barton Dean of Bristol hereby impowering the Subsacrist to strike him on the head when he goes to Sleep in Church—My Powers of Utterance I give to the Reverend Mr Broughton hoping he will employ them to a better Purpose than reading Lectures on the immortality of the Soul—I leave the Revd Mr Catcott some little of My freethinking that he may put on the Spectacles of reason and see how vilely he is duped in believing the Scripture literally. I wish he and his Brother would know how far I am their real Enemy but I have an unlucky way of railing and when the strong fit of Satyre is on me Spare neither Friend nor Foe. This is my Excuse for what I have said of them elsewhere. I leave Mr Clayfield the sincerest thanks my Gratitude can give and I will and direct that whatever any Person may think the Pleasure of reading my Works worth they immediately pay their own valuation to him since it is then become a lawful Debt to me & to him as my Executor in this Case—I leave my Moderation to the Politicians on both Sides the Question—I leave my Generosity to our present Right Worshipful Mayor Thomas Harris Esqr—I give my Abstinence to the company at the Sheriffs annual feast in General more particularly to the Aldermen—

Item. I give and bequeath unto Mr Mat. Mease a Mourning Ring with this motto Alas! poor Chatterton—Provided he pays for it himself.

Item. I leave the young Ladys all the Letters they have had from me assuring them that they need be under no Apprehensions from the Appearance of my Ghost for I dye for none of them.

Item. I leave all my Debts in the whole not five Pounds to the Payment of the Charitable and generous Chamber of Bristol On Penalty if refused to hinder every Member from ever eating a good Dinner by appearing in the form of a Bailiff—If in Defiance of this terrible Spectre they obstinately persist in refusing to discharge my Debts Let my two Creditors apply to the Supporters of the Bill of Rights.

Item. I leave my Mother & Sister to the protection of my Friends if I have any

Executed in the presence of Omniscience
this 14th day of April 1770

T. CHATTERTON.

Codicil.—

It is my Pleasure that Mr Cocking & Miss Farley print this my Will the first Saturday after my Death

T. C.

*   *   *

The fact that the basic idea underlying the Will was not original, but derived from a similar satirical document drawn up by Samuel Derrick, a Master of Ceremonies at Bath, and published in the July 1770 number of *The Town and Country Magazine*, wherein the poet, as a fellow contributor, must have seen, read, and remembered it, has led several of Chatterton's later biographers to misdoubt the genuineness of that distress of mind upon which he lays so much emphasis at the beginning of his own composition. But the rancour against Bristol rings true, and the tone throughout is consistently one of blank and unutterable disillusionment.

The Will and the letter to Clayfield have been described as hoaxes, devised for no other purpose than to force Lambert's hand—desperate expedients, however, would be nearer the mark. For by this time there was no questioning the disordered state of Chatterton's mind. He wrote to Barrett that he was being distracted and he meant quite literally what he said. His position in Bristol chafed and humiliated him past all endurance, he had come to loathe his environment to such an extent that he felt himself subtly poisoned by the very air he breathed, hence he was ready to snatch at any shift or contrivance which might serve to secure him independence of thought and action.

Whether he actually intended to make an end of himself is a more debatable point. Probably not. Whenever he was seized by those black moods of rebellion and hopelessness, whenever melancholy bore down upon him in a solid, palpable wall, and he was like an abject creature crawling in a small circle of darkness, turning round and round upon himself, the thought of suicide was always recurrently present in his brain. But he was too young, too strong, too interested in life as it *might* and *should* be, to regard self-destruction other than as a last resort—as a loaded weapon that he carried about with him in case he was attacked and overpowered. And while London, still largely unexploited, seemed to promise golden harvests that might one day be his, he had every incentive to hold out a little longer even yet.

Perhaps if both the Will and the letter to Clayfield had failed . . . But the Will did not fail. It was found, as the letter had been found, and Lambert's household was filled with consternation. Old Mrs. Lambert was beside herself. Veiled menaces conveyed to her at second-hand, were disturbing enough; but those same menaces set down on paper, signed, and sealed, were more than flesh and blood could stand. True not a word in disparagement of herself or her son was to be found in the whole mad rigmarole; but that belike was thanks to pure accident; it simply so chanced that the boy had overlooked them in his insensate hatred of every one else. And, anyway, it was all too evident that he had meant to bring the scandal of his own criminal propensities upon their home. Ever since she had first set eyes on him he had been a source of constant vexation to her, sowing discord in the kitchen, giving himself a hundred airs and graces, making more trouble than he was worth.

So she ran on, until Lambert, perceiving that only by drastic action from him could domestic harmony be restored, turned furiously round on his apprentice and told him to pack up and clear out. There was no need to repeat the order twice. Almost before the words had left his lips, Chatterton was through the door, up the stairs, and bundling together his few possessions, some of which, including rough drafts of poetry and his father's Book of Magic, he forgot and left behind.

All the heavy forebodings that had oppressed him during the last six months or so had lightened and melted into the fresh spring air. Now he could begin life over again— without hampering restrictions—give his undivided energy to the one thing that meant everything in the world to him. At home fears for his welfare, and maybe even reproaches, would be waiting for him; but he knew he could soon allay them, for when he chose to be sanguine, light-hearted, and persuasive no one could resist him.

Besides, his chance had come. He believed in himself, in his high destiny, in his power to wrest success from the indifferent Gods, in defiance of the entire planetary system.

The road to London was open before him and nothing could impede his triumphal progress.

At long last he was free.

CHAPTER X

SHOREDITCH

(1770)

ANXIOUS though he was to turn his back on Bristol and to launch out upon that more varied and adventurous career, whose success he looked on as a foregone conclusion, Chatterton had not compelled Lambert to dismiss him without having first made such inquiries as might seem to justify his taking a step from which, once taken, there could be no withdrawal.

In *Love and Madness*,[1] Mrs. Newton says:

A few months before he left Bristol he wrote letters to several booksellers in London, I believe, to learn if there was any probability of employment there, but that I can't affirm as the subject was a secret at home.

Thistlethwaite, however, is much more positive, for in his letter to Dean Milles, he declares:

---

[1] *Love and Madness*, by Sir Herbert Croft, published in 1779, was a novel written in the form of letters, founded on an illicit love affair between Martha Reay, an actress, the mistress of Lord Sandwich, and James Hackman, an unbalanced and neurotic clergyman, who shot her dead at the stage-door of Drury Lane Theatre, and was afterwards sentenced to be hanged. The affair created a profound sensation, and by adroitly contriving that Miss Reay should express a desire to be told the whole unhappy story of Chatterton (details of which were duly supplied by her lover) the author was enabled to introduce a second theme of topical interest, for by this time the *Rowley Poems* had already appeared in Tyrwhitt's edition, and speculations as to their authenticity were very much in the air. All unsuspectingly many facts relating to Chatterton were furnished by Mrs. Newton, and Croft, though a clergyman himself, managed, by various shifts and deceptions, to possess himself for a while of the letters written by the poet to his mother and sister, whose feelings may be imagined when they discovered that their private correspondence had been printed in a work of this kind. Mrs. Chatterton, indeed, wrote and protested against such outrageous treatment and, according to Southey, was rewarded by a "present" of ten pounds.

The printers finding him of advantage to their publications, were by no means sparing of their praises and compliments; adding thereto the most liberal promises of assistance and employment should he choose to make London his place of residence.

There is also a story—which Sir Daniel Wilson stigmatizes as "apocryphal"—that when Thistlethwaite questioned the poet as to his plans, he airily replied:

My first attempt shall be in the literary way; the promises I have received are sufficient to dispel doubt; but should I, contrary to my expectations, find myself deceived, I will, in that case, turn Methodist preacher: Credulity is as potent a deity as ever, and a new sect may easily be devised. But if that too should fail me. my last and final resource is a pistol.

Which, if it be not genuine Chatterton, is at least a quite brilliant piece of improvisation, even down to the inevitable suggestion of suicide, held in reserve, as an emergency trap-door exit.

Indubitably many a young man of his period had set forth from Scotland, from Ireland, or from the wilds of the English provinces, to battle against the drudgery, the poverty, and the endless heartbreaking treacheries and disappointments that awaited the unknown beginner in the purlieus of Fleet Street and the neighbourhood of Paternoster Row, with fewer sound eggs in his basket. He was quick-witted, knew the value of his good looks, his ingratiating manners (when he could serve his own ends by being ingratiating) and his plausible and persuasive tongue. He could handle men older than himself and bring them to believe in his capabilities; and, what was just as important, he could turn his hand to anything in the journalistic line, catching the characteristic note of whatever writers were most in favour with the public, and yet remaining essentially himself. Two qualities only were missing from his equipment—humility and patience—

these, and a still more intangible element, which the successful so often refuse to acknowledge as luck.

*   *   *

For a week after leaving Lambert's he roved the city at large, making such preparations as were needful for his coming departure, taking insouciant farewells of all those impressible maidens to whom he had referred so cavalierly in his Will, and cutting a brave figure amongst the more stay-at-home members of the Juvenile Club, whose general attitude towards the dream and the business was to keep each in a separate water-tight compartment and, not altogether unwisely, to attend to the business first. Chatterton rather grandly pitied them, deplored their lack of initiative, but promised to act as their literary agent when he got to town. His stock of prestige had bounded up again, and he was happier than he had been since the days of the Walpole disaster.

Walpole was now almost lost sight of in the rising glory of Wilkes. Wilkes was a personality after the poet's own heart; a man with courage, high spirits, a scintillating wit, and a magnificent, if occasionally unscrupulous, tenacity of purpose, beside whom the lesser activities of Walpole, his intellectual pernicketyness, his tea-cup prattle, and his Gothic stained-glass-window affectations seemed very small beer indeed.

During the course of seven chequered years, ever since the outcry raised in Court and Ministerial circles by his attack on the King in No. 45 of *The North Briton*, and the subsequent suppression of that paper, Wilkes had fought alone and undismayed against the most powerful faction in the country, playing off each successive Administration against the one that had preceded it, widening the original issue to embrace the legality of General Search Warrants, Parliamentary Privilege, his own obscene poem, the *Essay on Woman*, and the public's right to elect and return its own representatives to the House of Commons; so that, finally, after a long exile abroad and twenty-two months' imprisonment, he had emerged from the King's Bench Prison, the idol of the people, and certainly in their eyes the greatest political hero history had ever known. Nothing could have exceeded the ovations he received on his release. Busts and statues of him, in china, bronze, and marble, decorated the chimney-pieces of half the houses in London. His portrait and his crest, surmounted by a cap of liberty, were to be seen in every shop-window. "Wilkes and Liberty" was chalked on all the walls and pavements; and devices, in which the figure 45 was prominently displayed, found a ready sale as brooches, pins, bracelets, and other feminine adornments.

And on 17th April, the day that saw the end of his captivity, a grand dinner was held at the Crown in Bristol in honour of the Patriot, at which those who had been his chief supporters were regaled with forty-five pounds of meat, forty-five tankards of ale, forty-five bowls of punch, and forty-five pipes of tobacco. Curiously enough, Wilkes's enlargement occurred practically at the same time as Chatterton's own, and in the months that followed, though there is no evidence of any accredited meeting between them, the same influences operated upon their lives, and their fates, while never actually converging, were destined for a space to run side by side.

*   *   *

The fact that circumstances forced him to rely upon his older friends, the very people he had so roundly abused in his writings of late, for financial assistance—the money to defray the cost of his fare to London and a small surplus to support him until he had had time to look round—

must have been somewhat damaging to his self-esteem. But the chances were that he looked upon the purse which had been subscribed for him, containing about five pounds in all—or five guineas would perhaps be more exact, since Barrett tells us that most of his friends contributed a guinea apiece—not as a gift, but as a temporary loan that could be paid back later, when he was properly established and had found a steady market for his work. As for the friends themselves, they probably felt that their personal idiosyncrasies and private concerns would stand less risk of being exposed, with impish twists and distortions, if the young author's disturbing talents were deflected to pastures new. And Henry Burgum and the Rev. Alexander Catcott, at any rate, may have thought the removal of so stormy a petrel was cheap at the price.

Dusk had fallen on the 24th of April, and a thin penetrating mist was drifting through the ill-lighted streets, when Chatterton started out from his native Bristol, which he was never to see again. Never before had he been farther away from home than a whole day's ramble in the surrounding country, and now, although the other passengers, muffled to the eyes in shawls and greatcoats, were grumbling at the unwonted severity of the weather, he at least was undaunted by the prospect of those hardships which the more experienced travellers asserted were surely lying in wait for them, and longed to get his partings over so that he might sample the novelties and excitements of the road. While the luggage was being loaded up, he cheered his mother and sister with gallant promises of all he hoped to be able to do for them in the near future, and received in return affectionate messages to be conveyed to certain relatives who lived in London, as well as the strictest injunctions to take good care of himself. Soon, however, the bustling preparations were completed, the passengers took their places, and he, after some last

rather harrowing embraces, leapt into the basket—an
uncomfortable contraption slung on to the back of the
coach—to which he had consigned himself for cheapness'
sake. The carriage-lamps were lit, the horn re-echoed its
note of warning, the ostlers sprang back from the horses'
heads, the driver cracked his whip, and the coach lurched
forward over the cobblestones and out through the wooden
archway. The great adventure had begun.

He reached London on the following afternoon, and the
next day wrote to his mother to tell her that he was safely
settled and how he had fared on the journey.

LONDON. April 26, 1770.

DEAR MOTHER,

Here I am, safe, and in high spirits.—To give you a
journal of my tour would not be unnecessary. After riding in
the basket to Brislington, I mounted the top of the coach, and
rid easy; and was agreeably entertained with the conversation
of a quaker *in dress*, but little so in personals and behaviour.
This laughing friend who is a carver, lamented his having sent
his tools to Worcester, as otherwise he would have accompanied me to London. I left him at Bath, when finding it
rained pretty fast, I entered an inside passenger to Speenhamland, the halfway stage, paying seven shillings: 'twas lucky I
did so, for it snowed all night, and on Marlborough downs the
snow was near a foot high.

At seven in the morning I breakfasted at Speenhamland,
and then mounted the coach-box for the remainder of the day,
which was a remarkable fine one.—Honest gee-ho compli-
mented me with assuring me that I sat bolder and tighter than
any person who ever rid with him.—Dined at Stroud most
luxuriantly, with a young gentleman who had slept all the
preceding night in the machine; and an old mercantile genius
whose school-boy son had a great deal of wit as the father
thought, in remarking that Windsor was as old as *our Saviour's
time*.

Got into London about 5 o'Clock in the evening—called
upon Mr. Edmonds, Mr. Fell, Mr. Hamilton, and Mr.
Dodsley. Great encouragement from them; all approved of
my design; shall soon be settled.—Call upon Mr. Lambert,

G

shew him this, or tell him, if I deserve a recommendation, he would oblige me to give me one—if I do not, it would be beneath him to take notice of me.   Seen all aunts, cousins—all well—and I am welcome.   Mr. T. Wensley is alive and coming home.—Sister, grandmother, &c. &c. &c. remembered.—

I remain,

Your dutiful son,

T. Chatterton.

Of the relatives to whom he was welcome, we are given only this solitary glimpse, and then, with the exception of a further reference to a cousin, they rather tantalisingly disappear from view.   There was, however, another relation, on his mother's side, apparently a distant cousin, Mrs. Ballance, the widow of a sea-faring man, who lodged at the house of Mr. Walmsley, a plasterer, in Shoreditch, and it was with her that Chatterton went to live on his arrival in town.   The Walmsley family were four in number, the plasterer himself, his wife, a niece of about seventeen years old, and a nephew between fourteen and fifteen.   Chatterton, queerly fated until the last weeks of his life never to have a room of his own to sleep in, shared a bedroom with the nephew who, from all accounts, suffered as much, if not more, from his bedfellow's nocturnal industry as the footboy at Lambert's had done.

Exactly how the newcomer responded to this humble domestic environment does not transpire.   Doubtless he had indulged in dreams of untrammelled freedom, and to find himself fenced in by well-meaning relations, bent on keeping him under their watchful eyes, must have been a heavy strain on his none too tractable nerves and temper.   Mrs. Ballance, a motherly, simple-minded creature, developed a habit of calling him "Cousin Tommy," which put his back up at once.   He asked her indignantly if she had ever heard of a poet being called Tommy?   To which

she answered that she knew nothing of poets, and only
wished he would not set up for a gentleman—a retort that
cut him to the quick.

But in general his thoughts were occupied with more
important things, and so long as he had a place where he
could write, and a door that he could close behind him, he
cared for little else. Whether he actually set out on his
round of business calls directly he reached London, or
whether he waited till the next morning, as it would seem
more reasonable to suppose, he lost no time in making
personal contacts with those editors who already had some
knowledge of his work. Hamilton, of *The Town and Country
Magazine*, to which for upwards of a year he had contributed regularly, had offices at St. John's Gate,
Clerkenwell; Edmunds, of *The Middlesex Journal*, who
knew him as "Decimus" of Bristol, was in Shoe Lane;
Fell, of *The Freeholder's Magazine*, in Paternoster Row; and
Dodsley, of *The Annual Register* (and ill-omened *Ælla*
memory) was farthest away, in Pall Mall.

One by one, he interviewed and disposed of them all,
and his youth, his eagerness, his engaging candour, his
perfect address and self-possession, must have taken them
completely by surprise. It would be safe to assume that
Fell was the most encouraging. For Fell was one of those
shifty, down-at-heel Grub Street twisters that Wilkes had
a gift for collecting round him—to do his dirty work. For
some time past Fell had sailed as near to the wind as might
be, championing the cause of the City and the People
against the predatory encroachments of the King and his
Ministers; and now, on the verge of bankruptcy and
imprisonment, he was only too willing to exploit a forceful
if inexperienced pen, and to pour out liberal promises of
benefits to be reaped hereafter, when the political crisis
was over and his own position stabilized again.

*　　　*　　　*

The first of the London poems was *The Exhibition: A Personal Satyr*, a crude and unsavoury production, treating of the appearance of a Bristol clergyman, charged with indecent behaviour, before a tribunal of doctors. Quite apart from the unpleasantness of the theme, the composition is imbued throughout with the worst kind of schoolboy pruriency, the church is castigated with a lack of restraint that borders almost on anti-religious mania, and one is left wondering how the mind which had conceived the steel-bright integrity of the martial parts of *Ælla* and the fresh, spontaneous loveliness of *The Storie of William Canynge*, could even momentarily, have descended to such depths of cheap vulgarity and ineptitude. To himself it must have been obvious that no editor, especially at a time when official surveillance was increasing in strictness week by week, would have risked his liberty and reputation by publishing the poem as it stood. Indeed, it is hard to determine what Chatterton's motive could have been in writing it, unless at the back of his mind, he had some confused recollection of the public commotion caused by the still more unprintable *Essay on Woman*, which he must have heard of, for all the world had heard of it (but could not possibly have seen) and wanted to go one better than Potter and Wilkes, its reputed authors.

A transcription from the original manuscript of *The Exhibition*, now in the possession of the Bristol Library, has been made by Esther P. Ellinger, and the poem was published, *in extenso*, in the United States of America, in 1930, as a pendant to Miss Ellinger's short yet lucid psychological monograph on the poet. In this country, however, save for a bowdlerised version presented by John Ingram, in Appendix B, of *The True Chatterton*, wherein, owing to the deletion of, roughly, a hundred and sixty lines out of a total of four hundred and forty, all meaning, continuity, and intention are lost in a multiplicity of blanks and dots, the work has been, perhaps deservedly, suppressed. The utmost that can be said in its favour is that, by virtue of Chatterton's amazing fluency, the writing of it occupied only three misspent days. It was begun on the 1st and finished on the 3rd of May.

Happily, in *Narva and Mored*, the second of the African Eclogues, which followed immediately after, we are back once more on normal ground. This poem, and its fellow, *The Death of Nicou*, Chatterton, when speaking of his modern work, described as "the only two pieces I have the vanity to call poetry," and they appeared successively in *The London Magazine* for May and June. *Narva and Mored*, though unworthy of comparison with the best of Rowley, is nevertheless a distinct advance on the earlier *Heccar and Gaira*; the subsidiary ornamentation is as elaborate as ever, but here it does not retard the action and, with an easy mastery of technique, the pace and rhythm of the primitive love tale accelerate as it progresses, so that the imagination is borne breathlessly onwards to the last dramatic line.

These two poems, *The Exhibition* and *Narva and Mored*, and a number of political articles in the popular form of open letters to various notabilities, designed for *The Middlesex Journal*, were his main preoccupations up to the 6th of May, on which date he wrote his second letter home to Bristol:

SHOREDITCH, LONDON. *May 6th*, 1770.

DEAR MOTHER,

I am surprized that no letter has been sent in answer to my last. I am settled, and in such a settlement, as I would desire. I get four guineas a month by one magazine: shall engage to write a history of England and other pieces, which will more than double that sum. Occasional essays for the daily papers would more than support me. What a glorious prospect! Mr. Wilkes knew me by my writings since I first corresponded with the booksellers here. I shall visit him next week, and by his interest will ensure Mrs. Ballance the Trinity House.[1]   He affirmed that what Mr. Fell had of mine could not be the writings of a youth: and expressed a desire to know the author.   By the means of another bookseller I shall be introduced to Townshend and Sawbridge.   I am quite familiar at the Chapter Coffee-house, and know all the geniuses there. A character is now unnecessary; an author carries his character in his pen.   My sister will improve herself in drawing.   My grandmother is, I hope, well.   Bristol's mercenary walls were never destined to hold me—there, I was out of my element; now I am in it—London! Good God! how superior is London to that despicable place Bristol!—here is none of your little meannesses, none of your mercenary securities which disgrace that miserable Hamlet.—Dress, which is in Bristol an eternal fund of scandal, is here only introduced as a subject of praise; if a man dresses well, he has taste; if careless, he has his own reasons for so doing, and is prudent.   Need I remind you of the contrast?   The poverty of authors is a common observation, but not always a true one.   No author can be poor who understands the arts of booksellers.—Without this necessary knowledge, the greatest genius may starve; and, with it, the greatest dunce live in splendor.   This knowledge I have pretty well dipped into. The Levant, man of war, in which T. Wensley went out, is at Portsmouth; but no news of him yet.—I lodge in one of Mr. Walmsley's best rooms.   Let Mr. Cary copy the letters on the other side, and give them to the persons for whom they are designed, if not too much labour for him.

I remain, yours, &c.

T. CHATTERTON.

P.S.—I have some trifling presents for my mother, sister, Thorne, &c.
Sunday Morning.

Also enclosed was a note to Mr. T. Cary:

I have sent you a task.   I hope no unpleasing one.   Tell all your acquaintance for the future to read the *Freeholder's Magazine*.   When you have anything for publication, send it to me, and it shall most certainly appear in some periodical

---

[1] The Trinity House was a charitable foundation which supplied grants to the widows of deserving seamen.

publication. Your last piece was, by the ignorance of a cor-
rector, jumbled under the considerations in the acknowledgments. But I rescued it, and insisted on its appearance.

Your friend,

T. C.

Direct for me, to be left at the Chapter Coffee-house,
Paternoster row.

On the back of his mother's letter, in order to save
additional postage, were messages to be copied out by
Cary, and delivered to the persons to whom they were
addressed, Kator, William Smith, Mease, Rudhall, and
others; written in confirmation of his having agreed to
look after their literary interests in London, demanding
that they should send him any material they happened
to have ready for the Press, and enjoining, as in the case of
Cary, that they read *The Freeholder's Magazine*, in which
his own most spirited essays in political invective were
due to appear.

Already, after but ten days of his new and ardently
longed for existence, he was posing as one to whom all
doors flew open at the slightest touch, and pledging
himself to undertakings which he had neither the influence
nor the ability to perform. Already, too, he was beginning
to feel the need for dressing up facts, for taking the truth,
or what he hoped might pass muster for the truth, and
handling it as if it had been a damp ostrich feather, shaking
it and fluttering it out in the gentle warmth of an all too
mobile imagination. He must have the *best* room at
Walmsley's, which could only have been a workman's
dwelling in a comparative slum. Not satisfied with
Wilkes, he drags in Wilkes's staunchest supporters in the
City Party, Townshend and Sawbridge. And lastly, of
course, it is necessary that he should have at his finger-
ends the technique of imposing his personality on those
editors and booksellers who were likely to be of use to him.

In fine, the instinct which, in the days of his youthful absorption in St. Mary Redcliff, had driven him to conjure up a secondary world that was braver and lovelier than the one in which he lived, and to use this world as a cunningly painted drop-scene let down between himself and the sordid actualities of life, was once more subconsciously at work.

The letters to his mother and sister are the one guide we possess as to his thoughts, feelings, and actions from day to day in London, and the attitudinizings, the exaggerations, the fantastic claims to distinction, which are displayed in every other line of them, are perfectly logical and consistent if they are viewed as an extension of the original Rowley impulse, manifesting itself in an unfamiliar form. And since we know that he was ever most self-assertive when he had nothing to assert, it is a simple matter to estimate, in an inverse ratio to his exultancy, the varying levels of that tide of disillusionment which was at last to sweep him far beyond his depth. It has been contended that the letters were written for the sole purpose of throwing dust in the eyes of his anxious family and keeping the Doubting Thomases of Bristol at bay; to some extent, of course, they were, yet always, full in the foreground, is the unquiet, restless figure of Chatterton— trying most desperately to convince himself.

*   *   *

By the time he wrote to his mother again, eight days later, the first of his setbacks had occurred. Fell, who had told him that Wilkes admired his writings and, as likely as not, by way of further bait, had promised to arrange a meeting between the poet and his idol, was now, through eleventh-hour Ministerial intervention, safely housed in the debtors' wing of the King's Bench. Edmunds, too, had been prosecuted by the Government for spreading seditious propaganda in *The Middlesex Journal*, and was committed to Newgate. Chatterton made light of these happenings, and when he went to visit Fell in prison, used the address as a heading to his letter, in order, one supposes, to startle his family, while instead of his usual "Dear Mother," he began "Dear Madam"—presumably to enhance the dramatic effect. What he does not seem to have realized, or chose perhaps to ignore, was that the steps taken by Lord Bute and his emissaries against the two editors were but the forerunner of a systematic muzzling of the "Patriot Press," which was bound to bring panic and disintegration in its wake. However, whether he was alive to, or oblivious of, his own danger, it was part of his policy to paint his London life in the brightest colours, and no hint of the approaching storm is allowed to ruffle the pages he sends home.

KING'S BENCH, for the present, *May* 14, 1770.
DEAR MADAM,

Don't be surprized at the name of the place. I am not here as a prisoner. Matters go on swimmingly: Mr. Fell having offended certain persons, they have set his creditors upon him, and he is safe in the King's Bench. I have been bettered by this accident: His successors in the Freeholder's Magazine, knowing nothing of the matter, will be glad to engage me, on my own terms. Mr. Edmunds has been tried before the House of Lords, sentenced to pay a fine, and thrown into Newgate. His misfortunes will be to me of no little service. Last week being in the pit of Drury-Lane Theatre, I contracted an immediate acquaintance (which you know is no hard task to me) with a young gentleman in Cheapside; partner in a music shop, the greatest in the city. Hearing I could write, he desired me to write a few songs for him: this I did the same night, and conveyed them to him the next morning. These he showed to a doctor in music, and I am invited to treat with this doctor, on the footing of a composer, for Ranelagh and the gardens. *Bravo, hey, boys, up we go!—* Besides the advantage of visiting these expensive and polite places, gratis: my vanity will be fed with the sight of my name

G*

in copper-plate, and my sister will receive a bundle of printed songs, the words by her brother. These are not all my acquisitions: a gentleman who knows me at the Chapter, as an author, would have introduced me as a companion to the young Duke of Northumberland, in his intended general tour. But alas! I speak no tongue but my own!—But to return once more to a place I am sickened to write of, Bristol. Tho', as an apprentice none had greater liberties, yet the thoughts of servitude killed me: now I have that for my labour, I always reckoned the first of my pleasures, and have still, my liberty. As to the clearance, I am ever ready to give it; but really I understand so little of the law, that I believe Mr. Lambert must draw it. Mrs. L. brought what you mention. Mrs. Hughes is as well as age will permit her to be, and my cousin does very well.

I will get some patterns worth your acceptance; and wish you and my sister would improve yourselves in drawing, as it is here a valuable and never-failing acquisition.—My box shall be attended to; I hope my books are in it—if not, send them; and particularly Catcott's Hutchinsonian jargon on the Deluge, and the M.S. Glossary, composed of one small book annexed to a larger.—My sister will remember me to Miss Sandford. I have not quite forgot her; though there are so many pretty milliners, &c. that I have almost forgot myself.— Cary will think on me: upon inquiry, I find his trade dwindled to nothing here. A man may very nobly starve by it.—Miss Rumsey if she comes to London, would do well, as an old acquaintance, to send me her address.—London is not Bristol —we may patrole the town for a day, without raising one whisper, or nod of scandal: if she refuses, the curse of all anti-quated virgins light on her: may she be refused, when she shall request! Miss Rumsey will tell Miss Baker, and Miss Baker will tell Miss Porter, that Miss Porter's favoured humble servant though but a *young* man, is a very old lover; and in the eight and fiftieth year of his age: but that, as Lappet says, is the flower of a man's days, and where a lady can't get a young husband, she must put up with an old bed-fellow. I thought Miss Singer, I am very sorry to say it, in a very bad way: that is, in a way to be married.—But mum—Ask Miss Suky Webb the rest; if she knows, she'll tell ye.—I beg her pardon for revealing the secret; but when the knot is fastened, she shall know how I came by it.—Miss Thatcher may depend upon it, that, if I am not in love with her, I am in love with nobody else: I hope she is well; and if that whining, sighing, dying, pulpit-fop, Lewis, has not finished his languishing lectures, I hope she will see her amoroso next Sunday.—If Miss Love has no objection to having a crambo song on her name published, it shall be done.—Begging pardon of Miss Cotton for whatever has happened to offend her, I can assure her it happened without my consent. I did not give her this assurance when in Bristol, lest it should seem like an attempt to avoid the anger of her furious brother. Inquire, when you can, how Miss Broughton received her billet. Let my sister send me a journal of all the transactions of the females within the circle of your acquaintance. Let Miss Watkins know, that the letter she made herself ridiculous by, was never intended for her; but for another young lady in the neighbourhood, of the same name. I promised before my departure to write to some hundreds, I believe; but, what with writing for publications, and going to places of public diversion, which is as absolutely necessary to me as food, I find but little time to write to you. As to Mr. Barrett, Mr. Catcott, Mr. Burgum, &c. &c. they rate literary lumber so low, that I believe an author, in their estimation, must be poor indeed! But here matters are otherwise; had Rowley been a Londoner, instead of a Bristowyan, I could have lived by copying his works.—In my humble opinion, I am under very few obligations to any persons in Bristol; one, indeed, has obliged me, but, as most do, in a manner which makes his obligation no obligation.—My youthful acquaintances will not take it in dudgeon that I do not write oftener to them, than I believe I shall: but as I had the happy art of pleasing in conversation, my company was often liked, where I did not like; and to continue a correspondence under such circumstances, would be ridiculous. Let my sister improve in copying music, drawing, and every thing which requires genius: in Bristol's mercantile style those things may be useless, if not a detriment to her; but here they are highly profitable.— Inform Mr. Rhise that nothing shall be wanting on my part, in the business he was so kind as to employ me in; should be glad of a line from him to know whether he would engage in the marine department; or spend the rest of his days, safe, on dry ground.—Intended waiting on the Duke of Bedford, relative to the Trinity House; but his Grace is dangerously ill. My grandmother, I hope, enjoys the state of health I left her in. I am Miss Webb's humble servant. Thorne shall not be

forgot when I remit the small trifles to you. Notwithstanding
Mrs. B's not being able to inform me of Mr. Garsed's address,
thro' the closeness of the pious Mr. Ewer, I luckily stumbled
upon it this morning.

I remain, &c. &c. &c. &c.

THOMAS CHATTERTON.

Monday evenung.

    (Direct for me, at Mr. Walmsley's, at Shoreditch—only.)

Chatterton's expansiveness regarding his love-affairs,
and the frankness with which he discusses sexual matters
in general with his mother and sister, have not escaped
the censorious eyes of certain historians, and it has been
argued that the family must have been more than a little
lax in its attitude towards the minor decencies of life.
But the literature, manners, and personal relationships of
the eighteenth century were singularly free from that
hypocritical worship of the God of Outward Appearances
which was afterwards to become so formidable a bulwark
of the Victorian Age. Also, it must be remembered, the
Chatterton household was, comparatively speaking, quite
a young one; Mrs. Chatterton being only thirty-nine at
this time, although from almost every biography the
impression received of her is that of a patient, hard-
working, sober-minded person, well on in years; Mary
Chatterton had just come of age; and the poet himself
was not yet eighteen. There is, as a matter of fact, a
curious affinity between Chatterton's letters and those of
the adolescent Mozart, written to his sister, Nannerl,
when he was touring the country with his father; as, for
instance:

Tell Mlle. von Molk that I expect the same reward from her
as for the last quartets. She knows what that is. My compliments, pray, to Roxelana, and she is bidden to take tea with
the Sultan this evening. Give my very kindest regards, I beg,
to Miss Mizerl, and tell her she must not doubt my love and

that she is ever before my mind's eye in her entrancing négligée; I have seen many pretty girls here, but no such beauty as she.[1]

For the rest we have, in the King's Bench letter, passing references to two dukes that may at once be discounted as exuberant fictions; the warning postscript that no further correspondence is to be addressed care of the Chapter Coffee-house, where, having little money to spend, he had almost certainly been snubbed by the management and taken himself and his custom elsewhere; the story of the chance meeting with the musical young man in the pit of Drury Lane, which while being "given legs to stand on," was not altogether without a solid substratum of truth, as will be seen hereafter; and the demand that his copy of the Rev. Alexander's Treatise on the Deluge (containing poems of his own in manuscript) and his glossary, should be sent to him, which would seem to imply that he had thoughts of returning at some time or other to his earlier antique manner, although, so far as can be ascertained, he had not, up to the present, made any attempt to dispose of those Rowley poems he had brought with him to London.

*   *   *

During the month of May, he had five political letters in *The Middlesex Journal*; on the 10th, *To The Earl of H——h* (Lord Hillborough, Minister for the American Colonies); on the 15th, *To The P—— D—— of W——s* (a second assault on the Dowager Princess); on the 22nd, *To Lord N——h* (Lord North, the Prime Minister); on the 26th, a political satire, suggesting ideas for that exhibition of sign-paintings (alluded to in Chapter VI) wherein Horace Walpole and Kitty Clive appear; and, on the same date, an open letter, *To The Freeholders of Bristol*.

---

[1] *Mozart*, by Marcia Davenport, p. 54.

Although he worked indefatigably as ever, thrust his way into editorial offices with the genial pertinacity of an American commercial traveller, left no avenue unexplored which might conceivably lead to his advancement, and at first found no difficulty in placing his topical writings with many of the most popular and successful periodicals, his youth, his inexperience, and his fatal readiness to be of service, were unscrupulously exploited and he was grossly underpaid. From his pocket-book it can be estimated what his earnings actually were.

	£	s.	d.
May 2d. Of Mr. Hamilton for Candidate and Foreign Intel.		2	0
Of Mr. Fell for Resigned . . .		10	6
Court and City *gratis* Middlesex Journal 9th London Packet		8	6
Of Mr. Fell Middlesex Journal	,,	,,	,,
16th Songs Mr. Hamilton		10	6
(And on another page):			
Recd. to May 23 of Mr. Hamilton for Middlesex	1	11	6
Recd. of B.	1	2	3
Of Fell for Consuliad		10	6
	£4	15	9

Another entry is a sum of £10, 17s. 6d., "Due from others," which may, or may not, have been imaginary and conceived in the same spirit as the ironical bill made out to Catcott, in the days of the poet's apprenticeship to Lambert; at any rate, there is no evidence of Chatterton's having received it; and also there are further entries, of two shillings, one shilling and sixpence, and sixpence, as money lent. Thus a month's constant labour had brought him no more than four pounds, fifteen shillings and nine-pence; the door of what had promised to be a lucrative side-line in political journalism was now on the point of closing against him, yet there is no very perceptible falling off in his gay, inconsequent fluency and self-importance, when he writes to his sister from Tom's Coffee-house, to which he had apparently migrated from the Chapter, at the end of the month.

TOM'S COFFEE HOUSE, LONDON. *May 30*, 1770.
DEAR SISTER,

There is such a noise of business and politicks, in the room, that my inaccuracy in writing here, is highly excusable. My present profession obliges me to frequent places of the best resort. To begin with, what every female conversation begins with, dress. I employ my money now in fitting myself fashion-ably; and getting into good company; this last article always brings me in interest. But I have engaged to live with a gentle-man, the brother of a Lord (a Scotch one indeed) who is going to advance pretty deeply into the bookselling branches; I shall have lodging and boarding, genteel and elegant, gratis: this article in the quarter of the town he lives in, with worse accommodations, would be 50 l. per annum. I shall have, likewise, no inconsiderable premium: and assure yourself, every month, shall end to your advantage: I will send you two silks this summer: and expect, in answer to this, what colours you prefer. My mother shall not be forgotten. My employment will be in writing a voluminous history of London, to appear in numbers the beginning of next winter: as this will not, like writing political essays, oblige me to go to the Coffee-house; I shall be able to serve you the more by it. But it will necessitate me to go to Oxford, Cambridge, Lincoln, Coventry, and every Collegiate Church near; not at all disagreeable journeys, and not to me expensive. The Manuscript Glossary, I mentioned in my last, must not be omitted. If money flowed as fast upon me as honours, I would give you a portion of 5000 l. You have doubtless heard of the Lord Mayor's remonstrating and addressing the King: but it will be a piece of news to inform you that I have been with the Lord Mayor on the occasion.

Having addressed an essay to his Lordship, it was very well received; perhaps better than it deserved; and I waited on his Lordship, to have his approbation, to address a second letter to him on the subject of the remonstrance, and its reception. His Lordship received me as politely as a citizen could: and warmly invited me to call on him again. The rest is a secret.— But the devil of the matter is, there's no money to be got of this side the question. Interest is of the other side. But he is a poor author who cannot write on both sides. I believe I may be introduced (and, if I am not, I'll introduce myself) to a ruling power in the court party. I might have a recommendation to Sir George Colebrooke, an East India director, as qualified for an office no means despicable; but I shall not take a step to the sea, whilst I can continue on land. I went yesterday to Woolwich, to see Mr. Wensley; he is paid to-day. The artillery is no unpleasing sight; if we bar reflection; and do not consider how much mischief it may do. Greenwich Hospital and St. Paul's Cathedral are the only structures which could reconcile me to any thing out of the gothic. Mr. Cary will hear from me soon: multiplicity of literary business must be my excuse.—

I condole with him, and my dear Miss Sandford, in the misfortune of Mrs. Carty: my physical advice is, to leach her temples plentifully: keep her very low in diet: as much in the dark as possible. Nor is this last prescription the whim of an old woman: whatever hurts the eyes, affects the brain: and the particles of light, when the sun is in the summer signs, are highly prejudicial to the eyes; and it is from the sympathetic effect, that the head ach is general in summer. But, above all, talk to her but little, and never contradict her in any thing. This may be of service. I hope it will. Did a paragraph appear in your papers of Saturday last, mentioning the inhabitants of London's having opened another view of St. Paul's, and advising the Corporation, or vestry of Redclift, to procure a more compleat view of Redclift church? My compliments to Miss Thatcher; if I am in love, I am; tho' the devil take me, if I can tell with whom it is; I believe I may address her in the words of Scripture, which no doubt she reveres; if you had not plowed with my heifer (or bullock rather), you had not found out my riddle. Humbly thanking Miss Rumsey, for her complimentary expression, I cannot think it satisfactory. Does she, or does she not, intend coming to London? Mrs O'Coffin has not yet got a place; but there is not the least doubt but she will in a little time.

Essay writing has this advantage, you are sure of constant pay; and when you have once wrote a piece, which makes the author enquired after, you may bring the booksellers to your own terms. Essays on the patriotic side, fetch no more than what the copy is sold for. As the patriots themselves are searching for a place, they have no gratuities to spare. So says one of the beggars, in a temporary alteration of mine, in the Jovial Crew.

> *A patriot was my occupation,*
> *It got me a name, but no pelf;*
> *Till, starv'd for the good of the nation,*
> *I begg'd for the good of myself.*
> > *Fal, lal, &c.*

> *I told them, if 'twas not for me,*
> *Their freedoms would all go to pot,*
> *I promis'd to set them all free,*
> *But never a farthing I got.*
> > *Fal, lal, &c.*

—On the other hand, unpopular essays will not even be accepted: and you must pay to have them printed, but then you seldom lose by it—Courtiers are so sensible of their deficiency in merit, that they generally reward all who know how to daub them with an appearance of it. To return to private affairs.—Friend Slude may depend upon my endeavouring to find the publications you mention. They publish the Gospel Magazine here. For a whim I write in it: I believe there are not any sent to Bristol; they are hardly worth the carriage; Methodistical and unmeaning. With the usual ceremonies to my mother and grandmother: and sincerely, without ceremony, wishing them both happy; when it is in my power to make them so, they shall be so; and with my kind remembrances to Miss Webb, and Miss Thorne, I remain as I ever was,

Yours, &c. to the end of the chapter,

THOMAS CHATTERTON.

P.S.—I am this minute pierced through the heart by the

black eye of a young lady, driving along in a hackney coach.—
I am quite in love: if my love lasts till that time, you shall hear
of it in my next.

It is hardly necessary to say that neither the History of
London, nor the gentleman about to enter pretty deeply
into the bookselling branches, was heard of again, and
when Chatterton moved to another lodging, which he
presently did, it was not to the house of the Scottish
Lord's brother that he went. His dealings with William
Beckford, Lord Mayor of London, however, were perfectly genuine, and anything but simply a piece of bright
and pretentious fictional embroidery inserted to draw
attention away from the coarseness of the general texture.
As yet the affair was in a transitional stage, but the contact,
whether in reality a personal or an impersonal one is of
secondary importance, had assuredly been made, and was
soon to produce reactions that one moment promised him
the material security towards which he had been struggling
so steadfastly and so manfully, and the next plunged him
into a dark inferno of despair from which he was never
afterwards wholly to emerge.

For by the end of May he knew that the odds were
mounting up against him, that his position would shortly
become untenable, and that, if he was to keep himself
from going under altogether, something drastic would
have to be done.

In this spring of 1770, there was no man, save possibly
John Wilkes, who stood higher in the public estimation
than the Lord Mayor. Throughout the protracted
guerilla warfare between Wilkes and the Government,
relative to Wilkes's expulsion from the House of Commons,
Beckford had thrown himself heart and soul into the fray,
upholding Wilkes and the right of the Middlesex electors
to return their own representative to Parliament. Wilkes,
first elected for Middlesex on 28th March 1768, had been

repeatedly unseated during the subsequent elections, although invariably coming from the poll with a majority overwhelmingly in his favour. From the commencement of the proceedings the King and his chief advisers had blundered all along the line; even, on 13th April 1769, going so far as to put forward a candidate of their own, one Colonel Lawes Luttrell, who was promptly defeated; Wilkes gaining 1143 votes to the Colonel's 296. Whereupon, nothing daunted, the Government ignored the count, falsified the returns, insisted that Wilkes's victory was null and void, and finally had the effrontery to declare the beaten candidate duly elected, on the score that he *ought* to have been elected.

The outcome of this high-handed and unconstitutional behaviour was that, in the same month, the King was presented with a "Petition of the Freeholders of Middlesex," boldly complaining of "the odious and vexatious claims of the Crown," and beseeching his Majesty "to banish from your Royal favour for ever those evil and pernicious counsellors who have endeavoured to alienate the affections of your Majesty's subjects;" and this was followed in July by a second petition, prescribed by the Lord Mayor and sheriffs, and couched in even more opprobrious terms.

The Court, however, in pursuance of its general policy of never taking action until it was forced to do so, and then completely losing its head, affected to ignore the matter, and, after a while, it appeared to have been forgotten.

But on Wilkes's release from prison the old dissensions broke out once more. The City suddenly discovered that it had been passed over and insulted, and decided to press for an unconditional answer from the King. And so, after several abortive attempts to secure an audience, Lord Mayor Beckford, accompanied by a large retinue of

aldermen and common councillors, set out on 14th March
—actually a month before the Patriot's liberation—from
Guildhall for St. James's Palace, and having been ushered
into the royal presence, presented "The Address, Remonstrance, and Petition of the City of London."

This time the facts of the case were set forth more
unequivocally than ever. Indeed, so strongly was the
petition worded that the Common Sarjeant, in reading
it aloud, stumbled and lost his place, and the Town Clerk
had to take the scroll away from him and finish reading
it himself. The King's brow was clouded; he said that he
was much concerned to listen to language that was dis-
respectful to him, injurious to his Parliament, and
irreconcilable to the Constitution; and shocked murmur-
ings rose from the crowd of courtiers grouped around the
throne. Yet the audience ended, as might have been
foreseen, without the smallest advantage being gained on
either side.

Meanwhile, resentment smouldered everywhere. In
May, Lord Chatham, long estranged from Wilkes, but
now from ulterior motives in close alliance with him,
made a vigorous attempt in Parliament to procure the
other's reinstatement, but the motion was negatived.

Then, on 23rd May, Beckford, with public opinion in
the city solid behind him, having drafted out a new
Remonstrance, resolved to repeat what the King afterwards alluded to as "the whole performance" over again.
Accordingly on that day an imposing procession started
out. The King, of course, had had an opportunity of
glancing through the petition beforehand, and while he
admitted that, on the whole, it was less offensive than he
had expected, he decided that he would return "a short,
dry answer." Once in the presence, and the preliminary
formalities disposed of, Beckford stepped forward and read
an address which made it perfectly clear that the people

were determined to abide by the rights and liberties their
fathers had gained at the Revolution, and that they demanded the dissolution of Parliament, and the removal
of the "evil Ministers."

The King, in cold indignant tones, replied:

I should have been wanting to the public, as well as to
myself, if I had not expressed my dissatisfaction at the late
address. My sentiments on that subject continue to be the
same; and I should ill deserve to be considered as the father
of my people, if I should suffer myself to be prevailed upon to
make such an use of my prerogative as I cannot but think
inconsistent with the interest of and dangerous to the Constitution of the Kingdom.

This was obviously tantamount to a dismissal; but
suddenly Beckford, to the consternation of the Court,
approached still nearer to the throne, and burst out into
that impassioned speech which made civic history, and
has been perpetuated in letters of gold on the base of his
statue in Guildhall.

After assuring his Majesty of the unfailing loyalty of
himself and the citizens of London, and begging that he
and his followers might not be sent away "without some
comfort, without some prospect at least of redress," he
went on:

Permit me, Sire, to observe, that whoever has already dared
or shall hereafter endeavour, by false insinuations and sug-
gestions, to alienate your Majesty's affections from your loyal
subjects in general, and from the City of London in particular,
is an enemy to your Majesty's person and family, a violator of
the public peace, and a betrayer of our happy Constitution,
as it was established at the glorious Revolution.

Such a flagrant breach of etiquette was unprecedented,
but the King's obstinacy, which had long since reduced
the issue to a personal conflict between Wilkes and himself,

was more than equal to the occasion. At the word "Revolution" his face flushed an angry red, but he made a supreme effort to maintain his composure, returned no answer whatsoever to the Lord Mayor's importunities, and the audience concluded without any further interruption or disorder, the deputation being permitted to "kiss hands" and withdraw.

Next day the town was seething with excitement. In the streets and the shops, in the clubs and the coffee-houses, everywhere that people congregated together, the great affair of the Remonstrance was the sole topic of conversation. At no other period of Wilkes's stormy career had popular feeling run so high in his favour. He and Beckford were the heroes of the hour.

*   *   *

It will be seen that Chatterton had chosen his moment with characteristic astuteness. His voice, in so vast an uproar, might perhaps be reckoned a small one, but he fully intended that it should be heard. Already he had written a letter, signed "Probus," to the Lord Mayor, championing his defiance of the King, and urging a still more inflexible resistance:

His Majesty's behaviour when he received the complaints of his people (not to redress them, indeed, but to get rid of them, an easier way) was something particular; it was set, formal, and studied. Should you address him again, my Lord, it would not be amiss to tell his Majesty that you expect *his* answer, and not the answer of his Mother and his Ministers.

This was designed for, and eventually appeared in, *The Political Register*. However, before it was set up in type, possibly even before its acceptance for publication, he had sent or taken a copy of it, as we know from his last letter home, to Beckford, who gave it his courteous approval, and consented to have yet another letter on the same subject addressed to him.

With the second letter Chatterton was even more fortunate, for he arranged for it to come out in *The North Briton*. *The North Briton* was a revival of Wilkes's famous paper and, as David Masson tells us, it differed from the ordinary run of newspapers in that it was smaller in size and, instead of being made up of a variety of miscellaneous information, was usually confined to one carefully written essay; the type was clear and elegant, and the paper of a superior quality. William Bingley, its editor and proprietor, was, even in those days, when an unsolicited notoriety was the common lot of the organisers of the Opposition Press, something of an original. In 1768, he had been cited as a witness for the Crown in one of Wilkes's many trials, and, dragged in against his will, he made an oath that unless he was put to the torture he would refuse to utter a word. Impervious alike to threats or arguments, he was arrested for contempt of court and committed to the King's Bench, where he remained for two years, calmly bringing out *The North Briton* every Saturday, and dating it from prison, until at length, early in June 1770, the Government, since Wilkes himself had been set at liberty, decided that there was no object in detaining him any longer. On his release the first thing he did was to start another paper, called *Bingley's Journal, or The Universal Gazeteer*, which, owing to the fact that his case was still fresh in the public mind, achieved a very gratifying measure of success.

As Masson points out, it says much for Chatterton's energy and enterprise that, within a fortnight of Bingley's removal from the King's Bench, he should have established a friendly relationship with him, gained his interest in his work, and been given the whole of one issue of *The North Briton* entirely to himself.

His world, which had been rather heavily overshadowed of late, was irradiated from end to end with dazzling light. His spirits bounded from despondency into exultant belief in himself once more. The difficult corner was turned; from now onwards the road must surely go on mounting steadily upwards. At last he had got the chance he had been praying for, and was in a fair way to make the most of it. All the rest would be plain-sailing. There was nothing more to fear.

And then, on the 21st of June, Beckford died. Overworked, strained to breaking-point by all he had recently undergone, rushing up to London from his country seat of Fonthill Abbey in Wiltshire, he caught a cold, rheumatic fever set in, and he was dead before the shocked and sorrowing world at large had realized that he was ill. The Bingley letter was useless—Chatterton back where he had been at the time of the imprisonment of Fell and Edmunds. Describing the state to which he was reduced by this unlooked-for catastrophe, Mrs. Ballance says: "He was perfectly frantic, out of his mind, and declared he was ruined."

Yet, after a while, he rallied sufficiently to write on the back of the letter that should have appeared in *The North Briton*:

Accepted by Bingley,—set for, and thrown out of, the North Briton, 21 June, on account of the Lord Mayor's death

				£	s.	d.
Lost by his death on this essay	.	.	.	1	11	6
Gained in Elegies	£2	2	0.			
„ „ Essays	3	3	0.	5	5	0
Am glad he is dead by				3	13	6

One *Elegy*, printed in pamphlet form by George Kearsley, of Ludgate Street, on the last day of June, at the price of a shilling, he certainly did write; but the bald statement of figures has a hollow ring about it, and somehow reads less like a joke than an epitaph.

*   *   *

During the later stages of the Beckford negotiations, he allowed a longer time than usual to elapse without writing to Bristol. But on the 19th of June his correspondence with his sister is resumed.

June 19, 1770.

Dear Sister,

I have an horrid cold—The relation of the manner of my catching it, may give you more pleasure than the circumstance itself.—As I wrote very late Sunday night (or rather very early Monday morning), I thought to have gone to bed pretty soon last night: when being half undressed, I heard a very doleful voice; singing Miss Hill's favourite bedlamite song; —the hum-drum of the voice so struck me, that, tho' I was obliged to listen a long while before I could hear the words, I found the similitude in the sound. After hearing her with pleasure drawl for above half an hour, she jumped into a brisker tune, and hobbled out the ever-famous song, in which poor Jack Fowler was to have been satyrized.—"I put my hand into a bush: I pricked my finger to the bone: I saw a ship sailing along: I thought the sweetest flowers to find": and other pretty flowery expressions, were twanged with no inharmonious bray.—I now ran to the window, and threw up the sash, resolved to be satisfied whether or no it was the identical Miss Hill, in propria persona.—But, alas! It was a person whose twang is very well known, when she is awake, but who had drunk so much royal bob (the gingerbread baker for that, you know), that she was now singing herself fast asleep; this somnifying liquor had made her voice so like the sweet echo of Miss Hill's, that if I had not considered that she could not see her way up to London, I should have absolutely imagined it her's.—There was a fellow and a girl in one corner, more busy in attending to their own affairs, than the melody.

(*For some lines this portion of the letter is illegible.*)

. . . the morning) from Marybone gardens; I saw the fellow in the cage at the watch-house, in the parish of St. Giles's; and

the nymph is an inhabitant of one of Cupid's inns of court.—
There was one similitude it would be injustice to let slip. A
drunken fisherman, who sells souse mackerel, and other
delicious dainties, to the eternal detriment of all twopenny
ordinaries; as his best commodity, his salmon, goes off at three
half-pence the piece: this itinerant merchant, this moveable
fish-stall, having likewise had his dose of bob-royal, stood still
for a while; and then joined chorus in a tone which would have
laid half a dozen lawyers pleading for their fees, fast asleep:
this naturally reminded me of Mr. Haythorne's song of

"Says Plato, who oy oy oy should man be vain?"

However, my entertainment, though sweet enough in itself,
has a dish of sour sauce served up in it, for I have a most
horrible weezing in the throat: But I don't repent that I have
this cold; for there are so many nostrums here, that 'tis worth
a man's while to get a distemper; he can be cured so cheap.

June 29th, 1770.
   My cold is over and gone: if the above did not recall to your
mind some scenes of laughter, you have lost your ideas of
risibility.

There is no need to stress the contrast between this and
the earlier letters. All but one of the usual ingredients
are missing, and that which remains—the easy, rather
boisterous, jocularity—is now so high-pitched and exaggerated as to call forth, not an indulgent smile of
amusement at the unshakable buoyancy of youth, but
the liveliest feelings of concern. Here are none of those
improbable encounters with influential strangers that one
has grown to expect; no adventurous schemes for the
future; no sanguine visions of a good time coming, when
the writer would return, laden with riches and honours,
to be a benefactor to his family, the wonder and envy of
his less successful contemporaries, and a triumphant
reproach to those three "small-town" men, Barrett,
Catcott, and Burgum. From beginning to end one is
conscious of vital reservations, of an almost inhuman

detachment. A letter had to be written, the pages could not be sent blank, and so they are filled with the first words that come to hand. There is a drunken brawl outside in the street, which is as good a diversion as any, and as such it all goes down.

Why this mood of stark and unutterable dejection should have fastened upon him, when things were going well, it is hard to determine, unless, as might conceivably have happened, the main portion of the letter and the postscript were written at one and the same time; for the postscript is dated 29th June—eight days after Beckford's death.

He was to recover his mental stability, of course, that goes without saying. All was not lost even yet. Within a week he was to have money in his pockets—as much as he had been in possession of when first starting out from Bristol—the chance of distinction in a new and untried field, the old cocksure note was to crop up in his messages home to the only two people who really believed in him, and, for a while at least, he was to recapture fresh confidence in himself.

Yet these were but intermittent flashes of summer lightning across a darkening sky that, for all his courage, industry, and unswerving resolution, was never more to yield to him the comfort of a clear and untroubled dawn.

CHAPTER XI

BROOKE STREET, HOLBORN

(1770)

Two days after his last despondent letter to his sister, on Sunday, the 1st of July, he is, to all appearances, cured of his distempers, both spiritual and physical, and is writing to Cary again. The greater part of the letter is devoted to a long and not very interesting comparison between two Bristol organists, John Allen and Robert Broderip. Cary has evidently accused the poet of too strong a partiality for Allen at the expense of his rival, and Chatterton takes up more space than is needful rebutting the charge. "Broderip has no taste, at least no real taste." While Allen's relation to music is likened to the builder of St. Mary Redcliff's relation to architecture, than which, from Chatterton, no higher praise could be imagined. Then he branches off into less parochial matters:

A song of mine is a great favourite with the town, on account of the fulness of the music. It has much of Mr. Allen's manner in the air. You will see that and twenty more in print after the season is over. I yesterday heard several airs of my burletta sung to the harpsichord, horns, flutes, bassoons, hautboys, violins, &c., and will venture to pronounce, from the excellence of the music, that it will take with the town. Observe, I write in all the magazines. I am surprised you took no notice of the last London; in that, and in the magazine coming out tomorrow, are the only two pieces I have the vanity to call poetry. Mind the Political Register, I am very intimately acquainted with the editor, who is also editor of another publication. You will find not a little of mine in the London Museum, and Town and Country.

The printers of the daily publications are all frightened out of their patriotism, and will take nothing unless 'tis moderate or ministerial. I have not had five patriotic essays this fortnight, all must be ministerial or entertaining.

I remain, yours, &c.,

T. CHATTERTON.

The burletta was *The Revenge*, written for Marylebone Gardens, which in those days occupied an extensive area to the south of Marylebone High Street, and shared with Ranelagh, in Chelsea, and Vauxhall, on the Surrey bank of the river, almost opposite to Millbank, the reputation of being one of the most popular open-air resorts of the town. On summer evenings, when the two leading theatres of Drury Lane and Covent Garden were closed for the season, crowds of pleasure-seekers, anxious to create for themselves an illusion of urban rusticity, promenaded along gravel paths bordered by multi-coloured lamps, inspected the flower-beds and ornamental shrubberies, loitered by miniature waterfalls, in romantic grottoes, and trellised arbours, sipped tea, chocolate, and more potent beverages, listened to concerts and light operatic performances, and on special gala nights were further enthralled by brilliant displays of fireworks.

As long ago as the autumn of 1769, while he was still at Bristol, Chatterton had written the libretto of a musical play which he called *Amphitryon*—founded on a play of Plautus—whose *dramatis personæ* were divided into "Celestials" and "Mortals"; the celestials embracing Juno, Jupiter, Mercury, and Nox; the mortals, Amphitryon, Alemena, Dorus, Phocyon, Phrygia, and Sosia. This he had brought to London with him, in the hope of being able to dispose of it.

On meeting with his chance acquaintance in the pit of Drury Lane, and being brought into contact with "the doctor in music," who, by an unwonted stroke of good fortune, turned out to be Dr. Samuel Arnold, part-owner of Marylebone Gardens, *Amphitryon*, was shown to him and, presumably at the doctor's suggestion, condensed, partially rewritten, its characters cut down to four, in order to bring the piece within the compass of a small company, and from the earlier version issued *The Revenge*.

One has only to glance cursorily through the libretto of *The Revenge* to appreciate how remarkable was Chatterton's versatility, how sure and unerring his command over his material, his natural aptitude for the effective word and the telling line, his sense of dramatic situation, and the high standard of his general craftsmanship.

The "book" of *The Revenge* is gay, unpretentious, and charming; the plot simplicity itself. Domestic quarrels have arisen between Jupiter and Juno, and Jupiter is about to console himself with Maia, who, though much talked of, does not actually appear in the play. Juno, however, suspects nothing of her husband's intended infidelity, until Cupid, full of resentment towards his master for having tripped him up and laid a thunderbolt across his back, tells her of an assignation made between the other two. He then proposes to get rid of Maia, and to introduce Juno in her stead, and so bring confusion on the clumsy and vindictive "Thunderer." Meanwhile, Bacchus rolls on to the stage, crowned with vine leaves, and bearing a bowl of wine. He tempts Cupid to drink and, when the boy refuses, dashes the contents of the bowl in his face. The young god is furious and swears a second time to be revenged. A darkened scene in the next act makes it easy for Bacchus, now also in love with Maia, to lay siege to her heart by counterfeiting the voice and manner of Jupiter. But the lady is, of course, not Maia but Juno, and when eventually Jupiter himself arrives, the lights go up, and the various conflicting personalities stand revealed, there ensues a wildly farcical and up-

roarious *dénouement*. Then Cupid, his revenge completed
and his wrongs redressed, pours oil on the troubled marital
waters, and all ends happily.

Some of the lyrics are most deftly turned, as, for
example, Jupiter's protest against the uncertain temper of
"the Queen of Heaven," which, even shorn of its musical
setting, seems to contain an inner melody of its own:

> *I fly her embraces,*
> *To wenches more fair;*
> *And leave her wry faces,*
> *Cold sighs, and despair.*

And though the theme is threadbare enough in all
conscience, the poet even manages to infuse freshness
and spontaneity into Bacchus's pæan in praise of the
fermented juices of the vine:

> *Rosy, sparkling, powerful wine,*
> *All the joys of life are thine!*
> *Search the drinking world around,*
> *Bacchus everywhere sits crowned;*
> *Whilst we lift the flowing bowl,*
> *Unregarded thunders roll.*

Air changes.

> *Since man, as says each bearded sage,*
> *Is but a piece of clay,*
> *Whose mystic moisture lost by age,*
> *To dust it falls away;*
> *'Tis orthodox beyond a doubt,*
> *That drought will only fret it;*
> *To make the brittle stuff last out,*
> *Is thus to drink and wet it.*

While, when tempted to drink by Bacchus, there is surely a personal echo of Ingram's *True Chatterton*, in Cupid's reply:

> *Hence, monster, hence! I scorn thy flowing bowl,*
> *It prostitutes the sense, degenerates the soul.*

To which piece of sententiousness Bacchus scornfully retorts:

> *Gadso, methinks the youngster's woundy moral!*
> *He plays with ethics like a bell and coral.*

Again, one seems to catch the voice of Oberon or Puck, and the rustling of leaves in Athenian forests, in Cupid's valedictory lines:

> *For you, ye fair, whose heavenly charms*
> *Make all my arrows useless arms;*
> *For you shall Handel's lofty flight*
> *Clash on the listening ear of night;*
> *And the soft, melting, sinking lay*
> *In gentle accents die away:*
> *And not a whisper shall appear*
> *Which modesty would blush to hear.*

Prefixed to *The Revenge* is the following *dramatis personæ*:

Jupiter	.	.	.	. Mr. Reinhold.
Bacchus	.	.	.	. Mr. Bannister.
Cupid	.	.	.	. Master Cheney.
Juno	.	.	.	. Mrs. Thompson.

But although a reliable series of advertisements dealing with all the entertainments held at Marylebone Gardens throughout the summer of 1770 is still available, there is no trace of *The Revenge* having been performed there during that season, nor at any later period, and Dr. Arnold is said to have stated that, owing to unforeseen difficulties, it was never produced. The manuscript, however, underwent many strange vicissitudes, for after Dr. Arnold's partner, Mr. Luffman Atterbury, had sold it to a Mr. Thomas Egerton, who intended to publish it in book form, it was discovered to be missing from the printing offices. Years went by, nothing more was heard of it, and it was given up for lost, until, in 1827, William Upcott, librarian of the London Institution, ran across it wholly by chance on the counter of a cheesemonger's shop in the city, whence it was rescued and afterwards resold for £150; a sum vastly in excess of anything its author had contrived to earn for himself in all the working years of his life.

In the British Museum is a receipt in Chatterton's handwriting for five guineas—to cover his share in the work.

Receiv'd July 6th; 1770 of Mr Luffman Atterbury, Five Pounds, Five Shillings, being in full for all the Manuscripts contain'd in this Book, of which I am the Author: for which consideration of Five Pounds, Five Shillings I hereby give up my sole right & property in, and the liberty of printing & disposing of the same to the said Luff^n Atterbury only, and in such a manner as he thinks proper—As witness my Hand this 6th Day of July 6th; 1770.

T. CHATTERTON.

Witness—
James Allen.

Hardly was *The Revenge* finished and off his hands than he set himself to write another burletta, for the same company, called *The Woman of Spirit*. This time the period was the then present day, and the characters not mythological, but ordinary flesh-and-blood people. The parts were thus tentatively allotted:

H

Distort	Mr. Bannister.
Counsellor Latitat .	Mr. Reinhold.
Endorse	Master Cheney.
Lady Tempest .	Mrs. Thompson.

Of this there are only two scenes. It was evidently begun and then abandoned, whether from discouragement at the many delays to which the production of *The Revenge* was being subjected, or because other more pressing work demanded his attention, is not known. All that remains of *The Woman of Spirit* is an opening quarrel between the heroine, a lady of quality, who has stooped from her rank to marry Councillor Latitat—wittily described as "a tautology of nothing"—and who is protesting against her house being filled with her husband's senile antiquarian friends; Lord Rust, Horatio Trefoil, Colonel Trajedus, Professor Vase, and Counterfeit, the Jew, that they may "sit upon a brass half-penny, which being a little worn, they agreed, nem. con. to be an Otho!" In the second scene the lady allows herself to be somewhat placated, but only, one suspects, in order that she may presently burst out more disputatiously than ever.

*   *   *

Some time towards the end of June, or at the beginning of July, he left the Walmsleys, and took a top room, under the eaves, in a tall house on the west side of Brooke Street, Holborn, where his landlady was a Mrs. Angel, a sack-, or sacque-maker. The Walmsleys were tenants of Sir Herbert Croft, and when Sir Herbert was collecting material for his *Love and Madness*, he applied to the family and also to Mrs. Ballance, for any personal information they could give him concerning the dead poet. All their testimony—here transcribed from *Love and Madness*—supports that which we have already received from Bristol, and is substantially anti-Lort.

Many of Mrs. Ballance's depositions have found their way into the preceding pages, and of her there remains not much to be said. She maintained that he was

as proud as Lucifer. Upon her recommending it to him to get into some office, when he had been in town two or three weeks, he stormed about the room like a madman, and frightened her not a little, by telling her, he hoped, with the blessing of God, very soon to be sent prisoner to the Tower (*this of course on account of his extremist political views, and also in emulation of Wilkes*) which would make his fortune. He would often look stedfastly in a person's face, without speaking, or seeming to see the person, for a quarter of an hour or more, till it was quite frightful; during all which time (she supposes, from what she has since heard), his thoughts were gone about something else. He frequently said he should settle the nation before he had done; but how could she think her poor cousin Tommy was so great a man as she now finds he was? His mother should have written word of his greatness, and then, to be sure, she would have humoured the gentleman accordingly.

Mr. Walmsley saw nothing of him, but that there was something manly and pleasing about him, and he did not dislike the wenches.

Mrs. Walmsley's account is:

that she never saw any harm of him—that he never *mislisted* her; but was always very civil, whenever they met in the house by accident—that he would never suffer the room, in which he used to read and write, to be swept, because, he said, poets hated brooms—that she told him she did not know anything *poet folks* were good for, but to sit in a dirty cap and gown in a garret, and at last to be starved—that during the nine weeks he was at her house, he never staid out after the family hours, except once, when he did not come home all night, and had been, she heard, *poetting* a song about the streets. This night, Mrs. Ballance says, she knows he lodged at a relation's, because Mr. W's house was shut up when he came home.

The niece says: for her part she always took him more for a mad boy than any thing else, he would have such flights and *vagaries*—that, but for his face and her knowledge of his age, she should never have thought him a boy, he was so manly, and *so much himself*—that no women came after him, nor did she know of any connexion; but, still, that he was a sad rake, and terribly fond of women, and would sometimes be saucy to her —that he ate what he chose with his relation (Mrs. B.) who lodged in the house, but he never touched meat, and drank only water, and seemed to live on the air—

The niece adds that he was good-tempered, and agreeable, and obliging, but sadly proud and haughty; nothing was too good for him, nor was anything to be too good for his grandmother, mother, and sister, hereafter—that he had *such a proud* spirit as to send the china, &c. (*to be mentioned in his next letter home*) to his grandmother, &c. at a time when she (the niece) knew he was almost in want—that he used to sit up almost all night, reading and writing; and that her brother said he was afraid to lie with him; for, to be sure he was a *spirit*, and never slept; for he never came to bed till it was morning, and then, for what he saw, never closed his eyes.

The nephew (C.'s bed-fellow, during the first five weeks he lodged there) says, that, notwithstanding his pride and haughtiness, it was impossible to help liking him—that he lived chiefly upon a bit of bread, or a tart, and some water; but he once or twice saw him take a sheep's tongue out of his pocket—that C. to his knowledge never slept while they lay together; that he never came to bed till very late, sometimes three or four o'clock, and was always awake when he (the nephew) waked; and got up at the same time, about five or six —that almost every morning the floor was covered with pieces of paper not so big as sixpences, into which he had torn what he had been writing before he came to bed.

In short, they all agree that no one would have taken him, from his behaviour, &c., to have been a poor boy of seventeen, and a sexton's son (*he was not a sexton's son, of course*)—they never saw such another person before nor since—he appeared to have something wonderful about him. They say he gave no reason for quitting their house. They found the floor of his room covered with little pieces of paper—the remains of his poettings, as they term it.

*   *   *

The date of his removal is not definitely known. The

first letter written to his mother from Brooke Street is dated the 8th of July; but, on the other hand, the third and last of the African Eclogues, *The Death of Nicou*, is explicitly dated: "Brooke Street, June 12;" yet against this we have Mrs. Ballance's evidence as to the trouble she had with him on his receiving the news of Beckford's death, which would seem to suggest that he was still in daily association with her until the 21st of June; and also Mrs. Walmsley's statement that he was nine weeks at her house, which would cover practically the whole of June. Dr. Gregory, who wrote the first full-length biography of Chatterton—it was published in 1798—says that the move was made early in July, and by the end of the first week of that month, it is quite certain that he was installed at his new address.

His reasons for leaving Shoreditch, though withheld from the Walmsleys, are not far to seek. He had never been entirely at his ease with Mrs. Ballance; he resented the proprietory airs she thought fit to adopt towards him, and was irritated by her counsellings and interferences, her regrettable lapses into a too rough-and-ready familiarity, her complete indifference and lack of understanding with respect to the importance of his work. When things had been going more or less smoothly, when he could impress her and reduce her to submission by concrete results, he had just been able to endure her company; but now, with Beckford dead, Wilkes as inaccessible as ever, the fate of the burletta in suspense, and his political writings a drug on the market, it does not require any great stretch of the imagination to perceive how harshly she must have grated on his nerves. Then the Walmsleys were an additional vexation. As a family they were altogether too intrusive. Not even the bedroom he paid for could he really call his own. He could not live as one of the household, indoors at all times of the day, and secure a decent amount of privacy for himself and his own concerns. The most desperate phase of his fight for existence was bearing down upon him. He knew this only too well. It was absolutely imperative that he should be alone.

*   *   *

The first thing he did with the five guineas from Luffman Atterbury was to lay out a portion of it on the long-delayed presents to his grandmother, mother, and sister. Over two months ago he had first spoken of them in the postscript of his second letter, but he had never had the money to buy them with until now:

DEAR MOTHER—
          I send you in the box—
Six cups and saucers, with two basons, for my sister. If a China tea-pot and cream-pot is, in your opinion, necessary, I will send them; but I am informed they are unfashionable, and that the red China, which you are provided with, is more in use.
          A cargo of patterns for yourself, with a snuff-box, right French, and very curious in my opinion.
          Two fans—the silver one is more grave than the other, which would suit my sister best. But that I leave to you both.
          Some British-herb snuff in the box; be careful how you open it. (This I omit, lest it injure the other matters.) Some British-herb tobacco for my grandmother, with a pipe. Some trifles for Thorne. Be assured whenever I have the power, my will won't be wanting to testify, that I remember you.
                              Yours,
                                   T. CHATTERTON.
July 8, 1770.
          N.B.—I shall forestal your intended journey, and pop down upon you at Christmas.
          I could have wished, you had sent my red pocket-book, as 'tis very material.
          I bought two very curious twisted pipes, for my grandmother

but, both breaking, I was afraid to buy others lest they should break in the box; and, being loose, injure the China. Have you heard any thing further of the clearance? Direct for me, at Mrs. Angel's, sackmaker, Brook-street, Holborn.

Three days later there is another letter on the same subject to his sister; and it is noticeable that just as he staves off his mother's projected visit to London, the prospect of which, in his present circumstances, must have added immeasurably to his other anxieties, so he tries to evade the equally embarrassing problem of the new silk dress he had promised to Mary Chatterton by pretending to disapprove of its colour scheme. And in neither of the two letters is there any reassuring forecast of successes still to come. His mother is dismissed with what is merely an inventory of the contents of the box, and his sister is told only of work that is already done. Faith in the future was second nature to him—or he strove his utmost to make himself and other people believe that this was so—but for the moment everything hangs in the balance, and one senses an atmosphere of decreasing energy, initiative, and hope.

DEAR SISTER,
    I have sent you some china, and a fan. You have your choice of two. I am surprised that you chose purple and gold; I went into the shop to buy it; but it is the most disagreeable colour I ever saw; dead, lifeless, and inelegant. Purple and pink, or lemon and pink, are more genteel and lively. Your answer in this affair will oblige me. Be assured, that I shall ever make your wants, my wants: and stretch to the utmost to serve you. Remember me to Miss Sanford, Miss Rumsey, Miss Singer, &c. &c. &c.

As to the songs, I have waited this week for them, and have not had time to copy one perfectly; when the season's over, you will have 'em all in print. I had pieces last month in the following Magazines:

Gospel Magazine,
Town and Country, viz.
                              Maria Friendless.
                              False Step.
                              Hunter of Oddities
                              To Miss Bush, &c.
        Court and City. London. Political Register, &c. &c.
The Christian Magazine, as they are not to be had perfect, are
not worth buying—I remain,

                              Yours,
July 11, 1770.   T. CHATTERTON.

On 4th July, two days before signing that receipt which
gave *The Revenge* into the uncertain keeping of Dr. Arnold
and Luffman Atterbury, he had written the last Rowley
Poem, *An Excelente Balade of Charitie, as wroten bie the gode
Prieste Thomas Rowley, 1464.* This was a version of the
Biblical story of the Good Samaritan, with a fifteenth
century setting, full of poignant allusions to his own
distresses, more deeply impregnated with his own saddened
and disillusioned personality than anything he had previously produced, and in itself a work which must for all
time rank as one of his finest accomplishments.

The poem tells how a pilgrim, sick, famished, and
penniless, finds himself in a desolate spot on the road to
the convent of Saint Godwin, without adequate covering
or protection, at the mercy of a violent autumnal thunder-
storm. Presently the Abbot of the convent, one of those
vainglorious, self-indulgent Princes of the Church, whom
Chatterton hated so vehemently, comes riding by on his
richly caparisoned palfrey. The pilgrim cries aloud for
alms, and is contemptuously rebuffed:

> *"Varlet!" replied the Abbot, "cease your din;*
> *This is no season alms and prayers to give,*
> *My porter never lets a beggar [1] in;*
> *None touch my ring who not in honour live."*

[1] C. has *faitour*; Bailey has "*Faitour*, a vagabond."

And now the sun with the black clouds did strive,
And shot upon the ground his glaring ray;
The Abbot spurred his steed, and eftsoons rode away.

So the pilgrim is left alone in his misery until, a little
while afterwards, there passes near to him on foot a second
priest; "Not dight full proud, nor buttoned up in gold,"
but a poor mendicant friar who, seeing the wretched
outcast from afar, turns from the highway and hastens
towards him. Once more the pilgrim asks for alms:

"An alms, sir priest!" the drooping pilgrim said,
"For sweet Saint Mary and your order's sake."
The Limitor [1] then looseened his pouch-thread,
And did thereout a groat of silver take:
The needy pilgrim did for gladness shake,
"Here, take this silver, it may ease thy care.
We are God's stewards all, naught of our own we bear.

But ah! unhappy pilgrim, learn of me.
Scarce any give a rentroll to their Lord;
Here, take my semicope, [2] thou'rt bare, I see,
'Tis thine; the saints will give me my reward."
He left the pilgrim, and his way aborde. [3]
Virgin, and holy Saints, who sit in gloure, [4]
Or give the mighty will, or give the good man power!

Mindful of the fact that Hamilton had published
Elinoure and Juga, the only one of the Rowley Poems which
had so far appeared in print, in *The Town and Country
Magazine,* Chatterton sent *An Excelente Balade of Charitie*

---

[1] A licensed begging friar, who begged within a particular limit or district.
[2] A half-cope; short cape or cloak.
[3] Went on his way; but there is no such word as *aborde* in any such sense.
[4] An unauthorised spelling of *glory.*

H*

to the same paper. But on this occasion luck was dead against him: the poem was rejected.

Once, in a fit of half-theatrical impetuosity, he had written to a Bristol friend: "Damn the Muses! I abominate them and their works: they are the Nurses of Poverty and Insanity!" Maybe those words, as is so often the way with dangerous phrases lightly uttered, came back to haunt him now.

*   *   *

Parliament had been prorogued on 15th May, but there was no slackening in the relentless vendetta waged by the King and his Ministers against those editors who were their avowed enemies. Hard on the heels of the City Remonstrance followed Junius's cold and merciless letter to *The Political Advertiser*, lashing the Government for its share in the Boston Massacre—the first blood wantonly shed in a war that was to last nearly eight years and end in the loss of the American Colonies—His Majesty's insult to the City; the continued exclusion of Wilkes from the House of Commons; and other recent misdemeanours. And this, in so far as it reacted on the Ministry, was the last straw.

Fell and Edmunds had already been made examples of, but the fiery cross still blazed forth from the strongholds of the Patriot Press. And so the Premier, Lord North, was goaded into yet more vigorous action. It became, potentially, a criminal offence to publish any letter written by Junius, that mysterious, untouchable political Jeremiah whose pen was as a two-edged sword, whose omniscient eye penetrated like some baleful supernatural ray into the farthest corners of Ministerial closets, whose courage and integrity were things to make corrupt officials turn pale and tremble in their red-heeled shoes.

On 1st July John Almon, the friend and biographer of

Wilkes, was arrested and tried before Lord Mansfield, at Westminster Hall, for having printed a Junius letter in his paper, *The London Museum*; Woodfall, of *The Public Advertiser*, erring in the same direction, suffered a similar fate; and on the 13th, Miller, of *The Evening Post*, was also seized and imprisoned. Something like panic swooped down on the newspaper quarter of the town. All the old freedoms, the right of criticising national policy, of voicing the opinions of an oppressed and insurgent populace, were arbitrarily wrenched away. An absolute Crown-and-Court Dictatorship seemingly held the whole of Fleet Street gagged and bound.

For Chatterton it was a speeding up of the end. Not vainly had he likened himself to a helpless pilgrim adrift in a hostile and unpitying world. It was but natural that the great ones of the earth should pass him by; he had nothing left that might secure their interest or their patronage; and even the lesser fry—those prototypes of the wandering friar, who themselves had known what poverty and desolation meant—could be of very little assistance to him in the straits to which he was now reduced.

And yet, in answer to a letter from his sister, he could still reel off his accustomed patter, go through his repertoire of threadbare tricks, keeping the colours flying at his masthead, feigning that all was well:

I am now about an Oratorio, which when finished will purchase you a gown. You may be certain of seeing me, before the 1st of January, 1771.—The clearance is immaterial. —My mother may expect more patterns.—Almost all the next Town and Country Magazine is mine. I have an universal acquaintance: my company is courted everywhere; and, could I humble myself, to go into a compter, could have had twenty places before now; but I must be among the great: State matters suit me better than commercial. The ladies are not out of my acquaintance. I have a deal of business now,

and must therefore bid you adieu. You will have a longer
letter from me soon—and more to the purpose.

Yours,

T. C.

20th July, 1770.

But the longer letter never came. The purpose—such
as it was—had been fulfilled.

CHAPTER XII

THE FINAL GESTURE

(1770)

Too late he saw that he had made a fatal mistake in coming to London when the spring was so far advanced. He should have set out much earlier or much later, so as to have avoided the summer lethargy and emptiness which had begun to settle down upon the town. But then he had imagined that London would be like Bristol, where people, intent only upon building up their businesses and amassing respectable fortunes, took no account of the seasons, and worked uninterruptedly all the year round.

July had been hard enough to get through, with its long succession of close, stagnant days, the world just stirring into sluggish activity at the imprisonment of the subversive editors, and again when, during the City Elections, Alderman Oliver was returned to the seat left vacant in the House of Commons by Beckford's death, and Alderman Trecothick was elected to carry on the Mayoral duties at Guildhall for the remainder of the term. But now, at the commencement of August, news was at a premium; the Ministers had retired to their country houses; middle-class families migrated in droves to Ramsgate, Brighthelmstone, and other South Coast watering-places; most of the principal theatres were closed; the coffee-houses and pleasure gardens were practically deserted; and the editorial offices were running at half-pressure and with depleted staffs.

Thus he was driven back upon himself. There was

nothing he could do—nowhere he could turn. He went on writing, mechanically, stuff that he didn't believe in, because he must fill in the dreary wastes of time somehow or other, because while writing he could for a space forget the hopelessness of his situation, and because writing was the main preoccupation of his life, as much a part of it as eating, sleeping, or breathing and, whatever happened, he must always write. Yet it was growing nearly impossible to place his work. In the daytime he trudged round from one newspaper office to another; but the editors who had treated him so graciously at first were far less genial as the weeks passed by. Perhaps he had outworn his welcome, had been a little too insistent of late in soliciting favours; perhaps he was less sure of himself, and consequently less amusing and attractive, than when success had seemed to be his for the mere asking. And then the dog-days weighed upon the editors, too; they all had worries of their own. Hamilton, his chief stand-by, was over-stocked with his material—which may have been the reason why *An Excelente Balade of Charitie* was thrown back upon his hands—and when Chatterton, driven by sheer necessity to do so, begged for an advance on those manuscripts which were already under acceptance, it may be taken for granted that the hardness of the times was referred to, and his demand refused.

Day by day his small reserves were dwindling. No one could have been more sparing, more thrifty, more self-denying than he. He wanted less to keep him alive than most people, but the Walmsley girl had been notably out in her reckoning when she had said that he seemed as if he could live upon the air—not on this stale, used-up London air could he live, so different was it from the invigorating tang of salt and freshness that blew across the wide waters of the Severn. Water and a loaf of bread he needed. With these he could shut himself up in his attic room that looked out towards the dome of St. Paul's, and be safe from the curiosity and still more burdensome pity of his house-mates, who could hardly refrain from staring at the changes that had taken place in his appearance; his hollow, sunken cheeks, the feverish brightness that haunted his eyes, and the nervous twitching of his facial muscles which he could no longer keep under control. But he must have that loaf of bread. Not only Bristol, but starvation itself, had now to be held at bay.

*   *   *

Wholly ignorant of the lamentable state to which his young friend had been reduced, George Catcott wrote to Chatterton on the 8th of the month.

BRISTOL. *August* 8, 1770.

SIR,
        I have your's of the 10 Ult. now before me, which shou'd have been answer'd sooner, cou'd I possibly have found a Leisure Hour to do it in.

As to the Gothic Dome which you so much commend, I must inform you I have seen one in the Possession of Mr Webb in Guiney Street, drawn by Hogarth, & is I suppose the same you mention. I must candidly own the Design is really elegant, & at first Sight struck me much, but when I view'd that of Mr Marshe's, the latter appear'd to me so lofty & bold, that I thought the other by no means worthy of being compar'd with it; it differs very much from the modern Steeples, is entirely Gothic, and agrees perfectly well with the present Edifice. I wish I had Time & Ingenuity enough to send you a drawing of it, but as that is Impossible, I will endeavor to the best of my small abilities, to describe it. That part of the Steeple already built, will be taken down, & a light 4 Square airy Building erected in its Room, rather higher than the present, & the disposition of the Lights so contriv'd, that the Clock Bell (the present Tenor), will be plainly visible from the Ground. Above this rises the Spire, in which are 12 Windows, so admirably contriv'd, as to enlighten every part of it. The exact height of it I have forgot, but I think including the

Tower its altitude from the Ground, will be 278 feet; & as I observ'd in the printed paper enclos'd will be by far the most elegant Structure of its kind in England. I am always open to Conviction, & ready to retract my Opinion, when convinc'd of my Error; But I really think there's no Impartial Person whatever who has the least Skill in Architecture, but must give it the preference to any of the preceding Designs laid before the Vestry, & I am persuaded you wou'd coincide with my Sentiments, cou'd you have a sight of it. I have promis'd in the Name of my Partner & Self, to subscribe (for that is the method by which they propose raising the Money) 10 Guineas, if I may be permitted to lay the top Stone, & put an Inscription there. I was once very sanguine in my Expectations of living to see it executed, but this like most other undertakings of a similar nature in Bristol, seems to be dying away, & I really believe it will never be executed.

You will undoubtedly be not a little pleasd when I inform you Mr Barratt has been lucky enough to rescue from Oblivion a large Box full of valuable Manuscripts relating to Bristol, which have been in a Gentleman's Family a few Miles from this City (whose Father intended publishing them ever since the year 1708). Mr Barratt wou'd be glad to hear from you, & desires to be inform'd what way you are in; I am told you're employ'd sometimes as a political, & at other Times as a poetical Writer, at a Salary of 2 Guineas a Week.

Since you are got under the Tuition of an Angel, shou'd be glad to be inform'd, whether he belongs to the Prince of Darkness, or the Regions of Light, I sincerely hope the latter.

I am inform'd the blundering Bridge Commissioners are going to take down the 2 new Houses lately built by Mr Gay, the end of Bridge Street, & make only one rank, if that is the Case, we may boast of having the best Row of Tradesmen's Houses in England. See the Bristol Gazett for Thursday July 26, 1770, where you will find a Plan laid down for them to pursue, of which I shou'd be glad to have your opinion.

I am Sir

Your obedient Servant

GEORGE CATCOTT.

If you send any more Letters, be sure don't omit sealing them as you did the first.

To this, for urgent reasons of his own, Chatterton made an immediate reply, sprinkling his pages with jaunty capitals, writing, as it were, fortissimo, with the loud pedal down (except in one highly significant instance) on any topic that might divert the attention of the inquisitive Catcott from himself.

LONDON. August 12, 1770.

SIR,

A Correspondent from Bristol had raised my Admiration to the highest Pitch, by informing me that an appearance of Spirit and generosity, had crept into the Niches of Avarice and Meanness: That the murderer of Newton, Ferguson, had met with every Encouragem^t Ignorance could bestow; that an Episcopal Pallace, was to be erected for the Enemy of the Whore of Babylon; and the present turned into a Stable for his (ten-)headed Beast. That a spire was to be patched to St Mary's; & the Streets kept cleaner, with many other Impossibilities: but when Mr Catcott the Champion of Bristol doubts it, It may be doubted. Your description of the intended Steeple struck me: I have seen it: but not as the invention of Mr Marsh; all that he can boast, is Gothicizing it: give yourself the trouble to send to Webley's, Holborn, for a View of the Church of St Mary de la Annunciada in Madrid; and you will see a spire almost the Parallel of what you describe. The Conduct of your Bishop is no more than what I expected: I had received information that he was absolutely engaged in the defence of the Ministry; and had a Pamphlet on the Stocks, which was to have been paid with a translation. In consequence of this information, I inserted the following in one of my Exhibitions.

Revelations Unravelled, by Dr Newton, Bishop of Bristol— The Ministry are indefatigable in establishing themselves; they spare no Expence, so long as that Expence does not lie upon them. This Piece represents the Tools of Administration offering the Doctor, a Pension or translation, to new-model his Treatise on Revelations & prove Mr Wilkes to be Antichrist.

The Editor of Boddely's Bath Journal has done me, the honor to murder most of my Hieroglyphics, that they might be abbreviated for his paper. Whatever may be the political Sentiments of your inferior Clergy, their Superiors are all flamingly ministerial. Should your scheme for a single row take place; Conscience must tell you, that Bristol will owe even that Beauty to Avarice; since the absolute impossibility of finding Tenants for a double row, is the only occasion of your having but one. The Gothic Dome I mentioned was not designed by Hogarth; I have no great opinion of him, out of his ludicrous Walk; there he was undoubtedly inimitable. It was designed by the great Cypriani. The following Description may give you a faint Idea of it. From a Sexagonal Spiral Tower (which I believe Redclift is) rose a similar Palisado of Gothic Pillars, three in a cluster on every Angle; but single and at an equal distance in the angular Spaces. The Pillars were trefoliated (as Rowley terms it) and supported a majestic oval Dome; not absolutely circular, that would not be Gothic; but terminating in a point; surmounted with a Cross: and on the top of the Cross a Globe. The two last Ornaments may throw you into a fit of religious reflection, and give rise to many pious meditations. Heaven send you the Comforts of Christianity; I request them not, for I am no Christian. Angels, according to the Orthodox Doctrine, are Creatures of the Epicene Gender, like the Temple Beaux: the Angel here, is of no such materials; for staggering home one Night from the Jellyhouse, I made bold to advance my hand under her covered way, and found her a very very Woman. She is not only an Angel, but an arch Angel; for finding I had Connection with one of her Assistants, she has advanced her Demands from 6ˢ to 8ˢ 6 per Week, assured that I should rather comply than leave my Dulcinea, & her soft Embraces. I intend going abroad as a Surgeon, Mʳ Barratt has it in his Power to assist me greatly by giving me a physical Character: I hope he will. I trouble you with a Copy of an Essay I intend publishing—

I remain

Yʳ much obliged Servant,

THOˢ CHATTERTON.

Direct at Mʳˢ Angel's.

*   *   *

And now we come to the last of the letters, one that is, in a sense, a digression, seeming to hold up such action as still remains, but which must have been written either just before, or just after, the above letter to George Catcott. Jacob Bryant, who first brought this curious document to light, expressly states that it was written within a fortnight of the poet's death. It is undated, and there is no clue to whom it was addressed. The general consensus of opinion is, however, that it was intended for William Smith, although Ingram (p. 113 of *The True Chatterton*) points out that the subject-matter closely resembles a letter which Mary Newton says her brother wrote to Baker, made up of "all the hard words in the English language"; and, to strengthen this theory, adds that the letter itself came from the collection of George Catcott, from whence also issued the Charlestown communication, already transcribed, with its references to Miss Rumsey, the verses to Miss Hoyland, and *The Tournament*. That this "Infallible Doctor" letter should have been composed at a time when Chatterton was at his wit's end as to how to keep himself from sinking under his distresses might appear incredible were it not for the recollection of that smooth and impassable *façade*, which he could always erect at a moment's notice between outsiders and himself; and, indeed, it may well be that he derived a certain sardonic satisfaction from indulging in mental acrobatics, and maintaining his equilibrium, when everything about him was in a state of upheaval and the very ground was slowly shelving away beneath his feet. All the "hard words" in the letter are to be found in Kersey's Dictionary—the Dictionarium Anglo-Britannicum—which shared with Bailey's similar work the honour of being the etymological fount and origin of *The Rowley Poems*.

INFALLIBLE DOCTOR,
    Let this apologize for long silence. Your request would have been long since granted, but I know not what is best to compose: a Hendecasyllabum carmen,[1] Hexastichon,[2]

---

[1] A Greek or Latin verse, consisting of eleven syllables.
[2] An epigram, consisting of six verses.

Ogdastich,[1] Tetrametrum,[2] or Septenarius.[3] You must know I have been long troubled with a poetical Cephalophonia,[4] for I no sooner begin an Acrostick,[5] but I wander into a Threnodia.[6] The poem ran thus; the first line, an Acatalectos;[7] the second, an Aetiologia[8] of the first; the third, an Acyrologia;[9] the fourth, an Epanalepsis[10] of the third; the fifth, a Diatyposis[11] of beauty; sixth, a Diaporesis[12] of success; seventh a Brachycatalecton;[13] eighth, an Ecphonesis[14] of Ecplexis.[15] In short, an Emporium[16] could not contain a greater Synchysis[17] of such accidents without Syzygia.[18] I am resolved to forsake the Parnassian Mount, and would advise you to do so too, and attain the mystery of composing Smegma.[19] Think not I make a mycterismus[20] in mentioning Smegma. No; my Mnemosyne[21] will let me see (unless I have an Amblyopia[22]) your great services, which shall always be remembered by

HASMOT ETCHAORNTT.

The signature, though it seems to have puzzled some of the learned antiquaries of the period, is, of course, simply Thomas Chatterton anagramatised. Apart from the conditions in which it was compiled, the whole performance, taking into consideration that Kersey was presumably within convenient reach, loses much of its lustre; yet as a piece of protective colouring, it no doubt achieved the end its author had in mind.

Infinitely more absorbing and to the main purpose

[1] An epigram, consisting of eight verses.
[2] A measure in verse of four metres, or eight feet.
[3] A verse of seven feet.   [4] A pain or heaviness in the head.
[5] A poem so ordered that the first letters of every verse may contain some name, title, sentence, or motto.
[6] A mournful or funeral song.   [7] A verse exactly perfect.
[8] A showing of a cause or reason.   [9] An improper way of speaking; a bull.
[10] Repetition of the same word for enforcement sake.
[11] An information, a description.   [12] A doubting.
[13] A verse that has a syllable wanting at the end.
[14] An exclamation.   [15] Astonishment.
[16] A mart-town.   [17] Confusion.
[18] A joining together.   [19] Soap, or anything that scours; a wash-ball.
[20] A disdainful gibe or scoff.   [21] Memory, or the art of memory.
[22] Dulness or dimness of sight.

is the answer to George Catcott which, when stripped of architectural superfluities and schoolboy vauntings of possibly non-existent love affairs, discloses the real motive that had gone to its writing only in the concluding sentences. Actuated by that passion for acquiring information and experience of all kinds which was so outstanding a trait in his character, Chatterton, while at Bristol, had prevailed upon Barrett to give him a serviceable groundwork of medical and surgical knowledge. And now, as a last desperate resort, he had determined to put what he had learnt to good account by doing his utmost to secure a post as surgeon, or surgeon's mate, on board a sailing-ship bound for Africa. True, not so long ago, he had declared to his sister: "I shall not take a step to the sea, whilst I can continue on land;" but it was manifestly impossible, as things were constituted at present, for him to continue on land. Moreover, there was at least one precedent in his favour; sixty years earlier, Smollett, finding himself unable to earn a living by his pen in London, had joined a King's ship as surgeon and remained at sea during the better part of his youug manhood, eventually returning to make a name and fame in literature that had been denied to him in his youth. Admittedly the circumstances were not quite the same, for Smollett had been trained as a medical student at Glasgow, and was afterwards apprenticed to a country apothecary; but, in the eighteenth century, expert qualifications were not unduly insisted upon in a calling, ill-paid and full of hardships and dangers; the ability to set a broken bone or to administer standard remedies for standard sicknesses being all that was nominally required.

The inference is that Chatterton had approached Barrett with a view to enlisting his help and recommendation before the answer to George Catcott was sent, and that he had trusted the latter, without being explicitly asked to do so, would use his influence towards the furtherance of the scheme. It was absolutely imperative that Barrett should be persuaded, since in him alone centred the poet's few remaining hopes. And those words: "Mʳ Barratt has it in his Power to assist me greatly . . . I hope he will," contain a cry from the heart which not even a jealous and inflexible pride was able to subdue.

But Barrett made no response—and the die was cast. He, far more than Walpole, was directly, or indirectly, responsible for Chatterton's death. Time, however, was to bring to Chatterton, if he had ever looked for or desired it, his just revenge. For the lives and deaths of these two one-time friends were destined to react upon each other in a very curious way. Nineteen years later, when the *History of Bristol* appeared in print, with all Chatterton's original archaeological improvisations preserved and published intact, such a howl of ridicule and execration went up on every side in academic circles that, a few months afterwards, Barrett, overwhelmed by disappointment at the failure of his life-work, died at Higham, in Somersetshire, of a broken heart, and the circle came full round. Writing from Strawberry Hill to Hannah More, on the 4th of November 1789, Walpole remarks:

I am sorry, very sorry, for what you tell me of poor Barrett's fate. Though he did write worse than Shakespeare, it is a great pity he was told so, as it killed him.

*   *   *

Already those iridescent curtains which Chatterton had hung between himself and reality were showing grievous signs of wear and tear, and through the rents that now appeared in them he caught desolating glimpses of the uglinesses, the cruelties, the hypocrisies, and the frustrations he had always, in his innermost consciousness known to be there. But then, primarily, anyway, since the days of

St. Mary Redcliff and Rowley, the curtains had been hung to deceive others rather than himself.

The last number of *The Town and Country Magazine*, instead of being filled with his writings as he had expected, was chiefly made up of other people's contributions. Hamilton had accepted more of his work than, at the present moment, he was able to use; so much of it, in fact, that for five years after Chatterton's death, articles and sketches of his, which were probably never paid for, went on appearing month after month. Elsewhere his manuscripts were treated in the same way; either they were rejected outright or held over indefinitely. Money was owing to him, but not a penny of it could he touch.

Older and more experienced hearts than his might well have quailed before the agonies that now beset him; the hot unsavoury streets, whose pavements scorched the soles of his tired feet; the strange light-headedness and detachment hunger often brought with it, making him feel as though his efforts to cut himself loose from life had been so successful that he could not find his way back into it again, but was doomed from now onwards to float everlastingly through a grey, dispassionate void which was neither of this world nor the next; and then his sudden more dreadful lucid intervals, when he was driven to knock at all the editorial doors afresh and, failing as usual to obtain the smallest crumb of comfort, dragged himself once more to Brooke Street, stumbled up the steep narrow staircase and, secure from prying eyes, locked himself into his room.

All his industry, all his resolution, all his amazing versatility and craftsmanship, had brought him nothing. In this vast, slippery, competitive London—without friends and without any capital to fall back upon—he had never had a ghost of a chance. Two courses remained open. Either very shortly he must take his leave of a world that had no use for him; or he must surrender in a manner still more injurious to his pride—go back home, even if he had to walk there, begging for bread on the road—throw himself on the none too tender mercies of his former Bristol patrons, confess that all his brave enterprises had miscarried, and submit, for a while at any rate, to be a burden to his family, on whom he had meant to heap happiness, riches, and distinction. This latter he could not bring himself to do. From every standpoint death seemed the lesser evil.

Of the hypothetical state of his mind at this juncture, David Masson, in his *Chatterton—A Biography* (pp. 256–257), writes most feelingly:

Physical causes were at work. Bereft of the amount of actual food and of other comforts necessary, even with his abstemious habits, to keep body and soul healthily together; wandering about London in a perpetual state of fever and excitement; returning home to write night after night without rest or sleep: little wonder if he had overstrained his physical capabilities, and if brain and nerve began to fail in their office. Whatever taint of hereditary insanity was in him—derived from the old line of sextons who had jangled in past generations the keys of St. Mary's Church in Bristol, and walked at midnight through its aisles, and dug the graves of its parishioners, or derived, more immediately, from that drunken, wild-eyed father whom he had never seen, but who used to tell his tavern-companions that he believed in Cornelius Agrippa the necromancer—it had at last come out in a way not to be mistaken. From his childhood there had been symptoms of it—his fits of weeping, his sudden paroxysms of passion, his long reveries when he gazed at people without seeming to see them, his frequent mutterings aloud. Not till now, however, had these traits passed the limits of what could be considered compatible with sanity. But now, almost certainly, these limits *were* passed.

All of which, save for the apparent implication that the "old sextons," generally the most robust and philosophical of men, were likely to spread the contagion of madness by virtue of their occupation alone, is plausible and convincing—so far as it goes. The legendary insanity might have been even more strongly stressed had Masson thought fit to mention the fact that, at one period of her life, Mary Newton temporarily lost her reason and it was found necessary to place her under restraint. Yet, if one measures the poet by his works, and surely there can be no fairer method of assessment, the impression left is one of a mind which, while occasionally capable of soaring to breathless, imaginative heights, was none the less forthright, evenly balanced, and perfectly controlled. There is, indeed, in his writing, a singular absence of morbidity, or even of that constitutional pessimism which was so marked an attribute of the writer himself. Again and again, one is arrested by a sustained and consistent objectivity that discovers itself to the reader in richness of colour and smoothness of texture, in concrete objects almost photographically visualised, and in the vigorous, healthy outlook of a man of action.

Undeniably he was the victim of certain temperamental inequalities; an ingrained melancholy, a native scepticism that made him sharply suspicious of all easy and ready-made beliefs; to which was added a curious faculty of intellectual recession, by whose means he could at will withdraw into himself and remain entirely oblivious of all that went on around him. But these peculiarities, in themselves, do not connote organic mental disease, and may commonly be found in many another creative artist whose sanity has never been called into question.

That the idea of suicide had always lain dormant at the back of his mind has already been clearly shown. Yet his attitude towards it was calm, logical, and self-possessed. It was a last weapon by which he could defend his pride and his independence and, if needs be, die, still undefeated by the hand of Fate. With average luck he might never be called upon to bring it into action; but, should the worst come to the worst, there was at least some solace to be gained from the feeling that he was not unarmed. Meanwhile, he would go on fighting to the end.

Not any of the precautions he took, however, his creeping softly in and out of the house, his lonely vigils in his attic room, his reluctance to talk about himself or to engage in conversation, could conceal from those he lived amongst how badly things were faring with him. In after years, Sir Herbert Croft sought out Mrs. Angel, who had since left Brooke Street, hoping to get from her some account of Chatterton's last days.

"Mrs. Angel, to whose house he removed," he writes, in *Love and Madness*, "I have in vain endeavoured repeatedly to find out. A person in distressed circumstances, as I understand her to be, is slow to believe that an inquiry after her hiding-place is only set on foot by the curiosity of honest enthusiasm. Mrs. Wolfe, a barber's wife, within a few doors of the house in which Mrs. Angel lived, remembered him, and recalls his death. She speaks also of his proud and haughty spirit; and adds that he appeared both to her and Mrs. A. as if he were born for something great. Mrs. A. told her, after his death, that, as she knew he had not eaten any thing for two or three days, she begged he would take some dinner with her on the 24th August; but he was offended at her expressions, which seemed to hint he was in want, and assured her he was not hungry."

Even in that mean and shabby street of tenement houses, where poverty, nearly as stark and pitiful as his own, was the daily lot of the inhabitants, most of whom were reduced to every ignoble kind of artifice in order to eke out an existence, there were those who knew and liked him, and who would have been ready enough to have shared with him their scanty provision, had he but given them an opportunity. But he was an impossible creature to help. There was about him a hardness, a sullenness, a lack of humility that checked intrusive sympathy, however kindly meant. Always he had fought shy of asking favours at the hands of others, or of incurring obligations which he was not in a position to repay. The thought of accepting the bread of charity was alike shameful and abhorrent to him, and roused in him a passion of resistance that even the fear of certain starvation was powerless to break down. He had at least given an equivalent for such benefits as had been doled out to him by Barrett, Catcott, and Burgum, had worked off all his debts to them—except the last subscription raised to send him to London—and now that would have to remain unpaid.

During that eventful month of August, Mrs. Angel was not the only person who was seriously concerned for her young lodger. Close by lived an apothecary named Cross, who was worried about him too. Cross and Chatterton had struck up an easy acquaintance, and the latter seldom passed by without looking in for a chat. The apothecary, as he afterwards told Thomas Warton, author of *The History of English Poetry*, found Chatterton's conversation—"a little infidelity apart"—most captivating. In the small dark shop, with its aromatic odours and gleaming array of bottles, it doubtless was that the scheme for his going to sea as a ship's surgeon had first originated; and out of one of the rows of shallow mahogany drawers, as likely as not, though we have no actual proof of it, came the fatal dose of arsenic—obtained maybe under some simple pretext, such as that of wishing to rid himself of the rats that overran his room—with which he eventually killed himself. Trained by his profession to be shrewdly observant of physical changes and deteriorations, Cross could hardly have helped noticing the poet's sadly altered appearance and rightly guessing its cause.

Time after time, he pressed Chatterton to dine or sup with him, but his offers of hospitality were either evaded or declined. Once only, towards the end, when he must have been fainting with hunger, did Chatterton allow himself to be prevailed upon to partake of a barrel of oysters, of which, as Cross puts it, "he ate voraciously." In all probability, it was the last solid meal he ever tasted.

So with almost superhuman courage he held out until the 24th of August. But by then the slow war of detrition was over. It was not to be expected that his body, strong though it might be, and never, so far as is known, subject to a day's illness, should keep pace with his still aspiring and unconquerable spirit. At last he had reached a point beyond which it was impossible to proceed further, and some time that night, or early the next morning, he mixed the arsenic with water, drank it off, lay down on his bed, and died, not with the bland and marbled resignation one may see in Wallis's *Death of Chatterton* in the Tate Gallery, but in dire and dreadful agony.

Footsteps had been heard in his room the night before by those who lodged beneath. Of late, instead of sitting quietly at his writing, he had taken to pacing restlessly like a caged animal, up and down the floor. The sounds continued for a long while, and therefore it was not surprising that on the morrow he should sleep late. But as the day advanced from morning to afternoon and he did not come downstairs, the rest of the household gradually became alarmed. Repeated callings and knockings on the landing outside meeting with no response, the attic door was forced open, and there he was discovered, according to Barrett, who must merely have been repeating what he had been told, "a horrid spectacle, with features distorted, as if from convulsions." And just as had happened every morning at Shoreditch, the floor was littered over with little pieces of paper, none of them larger than a sixpenny-piece.

* * *

He was seventeen and nine months old when he died, alone and a stranger in London. It had been hoped that some of his family might come to identify his body, to attend the coroner's inquest, and to give instructions about the funeral; but three days went by and no one appeared. In the Register of Burials at St. Andrew's, Holborn, his name was wrongly entered as *William* Chatterton, to which was subsequently added, in a different handwriting, "the poet." On Tuesday, 28th August, his body, enclosed in a shell, was taken to the burial-ground of Shoe Lane Workhouse, and laid—without any distinguishing mark or inscription—in a pauper's grave.

His disappearance from a world that had persistently rejected him caused no more dislocation than half an hour's shovelling of earth. Despite the scarcity of news not a line relating to his self-inflicted death appeared in any of the newspapers; for the trumpet of the angel with wings, invoked so long ago in his childhood, was to languish in silence yet another seven years.

But even now other faint stirrings and rustlings were abroad. At Oxford, for example, Dr. Thomas Fry, President of St. John's College, was presently to set out on a journey; this because stories had reached him of a boy called Chatterton and some mediaeval poems. His interest had at once been aroused, and himself a Bristol man, and an *alumnus* of its Grammar School, he had decided to revisit his native city, to seek out the youthful poet, whose home he imagined still to be there, and to lend him whatever counsel, encouragement, and kindly patronage it might be within his power to bestow.

BIBLIOGRAPHY

Cover His Face: A novel of the life and times of Thomas Chatterton, by Neil Bell. 1943.

The Life of Thomas Chatterton, by James R. Bennett. 1860.

New Lights on Chatterton, by Sir Ernest Clarke. 1916.

Chatterton and "Love and Madness," by Sir Herbert Croft. 1800.

Come of Age: a play in music and words, by Clemence Dane and Richard Addinsell. 1938.

The Life of Thomas Chatterton, by John Davis. 1806.

The Life of Thomas Chatterton (including his unpublished poems and correspondence), by John Dix. 1837.

Thomas Chatterton, by William M. Dixon. 1930.

Thomas Chatterton, The Marvelous Boy, by Esther P. Ellinger. 1930.

The Life of Thomas Chatterton, by George Gregory, D.D. 1789.

Chatterton and his Poetry, by John H. Ingram. 1916.

The True Chatterton, by John H. Ingram. 1910.

Chatterton: an Essay, by S. R. Maitland. 1857.

Chatterton: A Story of the Year 1770, by David Masson. 1874.

Chatterton: a Biography, by David Masson. (A revised version of the above). 1899.

A Life of Thomas Chatterton, by E. H. W. Meyerstein. 1930.

Thomas Chatterton, by Helene Richter. 1900.

Thomas Chatterton, The Marvelous Boy, by Charles Edward Russell. 1908.

Chatterton: A Biographical Study, by Sir Daniel Wilson. 1869.

Chatterton: A Play in Three Acts, by Alfred de Vigny. Paris, 1835.

INDEX

A

Advice, The, 106
Ælla, Song to, 130, 131, 132, 133
Ælla, Tragedy of, 71, 77, 114, 140, 147–158, 177, 195, 196
Agrippa, Cornelius, 12, 187, 248
Allen, John (Bristol organist), 220
Almon, John (Editor of *London Museum*), 234, 235
Amelia, Princess, 95
Amphitryon : A Burletta, 221, 222
Andersen, Hans, 109
Anecdotes of Painting (by Horace Walpole), 79, 82, 85, 94 *n*, 98, 104
Angel, Mrs. (of Brooke St.), 226, 231, 240, 242, 250
Annual Register, The, 195
Apostate, The, 146
Apostate Will, 26–28
Arnold, Dr. Samuel, 222, 225, 232
"Asaphides" (Pseudonym of C.), 157
Astrology (Ebenezer Sibly's work on), 9
Atterbury, Luffman, 225, 232

B

Bailey, Nâthaniel (*Dictionary*), 41; Notes to *Rowley Poems,* 128, 133, 136, 138, 139, 140, 141, 142–146, 149, 153, 156
Baker, John (of Charles-Town, South Carolina), C.'s letter to, dated March 6, 1768, 43–44; 53, 106, 117, 243
Balade of Charitie, An Excelente, 71, 232, 238
Ballance, Mrs., 194, 198, 216, 226, 227, 229
Barrett, William, 16; Buys Redcliff parchments from Morgan, 47; 54; C.'s confession to, 55–59; 60, 62; Share in de Bergham Pedigree, 66; 69, 71; Alleged

malign influence on C., 90–91; Helps C. to write to Walpole, 93–95; 96, 110, 113, 121, 159, 161; Tempts C. to drink, 165; 174; Cross-examines C. on intended suicide, 179, 180; C.'s poetical reference to in Will, 182; 185, 192, 203, 218; Buys box of MSS. relating to Bristol, 240; 242, 245; Death at Higham, 246; 251; Description of the manner of C.'s death, 252
Barton, Dr. Cutts, 184
Battle of Hastings, 55–57, 113, 121–123
Beckford, William (Lord Mayor of London), 210, 216, 219, 229
Benson, Thomas (*Vocabularium Anglo-Saxonicum*), 71
Bingley, William (Editor of *North Briton* and *Bingley's Journal*), 215, 216
Boddley's Bath Journal, 241
Bourton, Simon de, 109, 118, 119, 120
Bridges across the Avon, Old and New, 49
Bridge, Mayor's First Crossing Over the Old, 50–51
Bristol Cathedral, 12, 25, 37
Bristol, Charters of, 41
Bristol in Eighteenth Century, 35
Bristowe Tragedie, 113, 123–126
Britton, John, 75
Broderip, Robert (Bristol organist), 220
Broughton, Rev. Thomas (Vicar of St. Mary Redcliff), 165, 178, 184
Bryant, Jacob, 70, 102, 243
Burgum, Henry, 33; First meeting with C., 58; 59, 62; C. makes pedigree for, 64–66; 69, 71, 140, 178; poetical reference to in Will, 181; 184, 192, 203, 218, 251
Bush, To Miss, 232
Bute, Lord, 178, 201

255